TOO GOOD TO GO DOWN

THE INSIDE STORY OF MANCHESTER UNITED'S RELEGATION

WAYNE BARTON

EMPIRE PUBLICATIONS

First published in 2018

EMPIRE PUBLICATIONS
1 Newton Street, Manchester M1 1HW
© Wayne Barton 2018

ISBN: 978-1-909360-62-4

CONTENTS

ACKNOWLEDGEMENTS

IN MY 2015 BOOK '74/75, I told the story of Manchester United's only post-war season in Division Two through the accounts of the players and manager, Tommy Docherty. Although there are fantastic accounts of United's history that include this period, I felt that there was perhaps room for a book which looked more intensively about the passage of time which included the Doc's 'restoration' of the club and the derivation of how they had 'lost' their identity. The idea was part of a larger project which would take in the 26 year wait for Manchester United to win a league title.

I had done most of the research — enough to start writing — when I was contacted in May 2018 by Tom Boswell, a filmmaker at BT Sports, who was reading '74/75. Tom is a Chelsea fan, although he assured me that his interest extended far beyond the daydreams of Jose Mourinho taking Manchester United into a lower division. We talked about that period of history, how it could be that an institution like United were relegated and how realistic a story it was that they were so swiftly restored in their position as one of the top clubs in the country. We both agreed that the story should be more prominently known and when it became clear that Tom was honestly passionate about the story then we agreed to work together.

It has been a great thrill working alongside Tom, who is a keen football historian with a track record in making football films and documentaries which, in my opinion, is second to none. His previous work is outstanding and I consider it an honour that we have worked together on this project. I have not quite convinced him to follow Red instead of Blue but I can assure every Manchester United fan reading this who has not yet seen it that the film is in capable hands.

Just as with writing, telling the story on screen becomes a

challenge. Partly because of Tommy Docherty's controversial career at the club, partly because of the complexity and high profile nature of the stories which preceded his arrival and dominated his early days. It is a significant part of the club's history which has previously been overlooked by today's generation and largely swept under the carpet by the club. I wanted to ensure there is, on record, a heartfelt thanks and pat on the back from me to Tom.

Before thanking the roll call of players and notable personnel I also wanted to take the time to thank Brian Greenhoff, to whom the film and this book are dedicated.

Tom was able to enlist a stellar cast who contributed to both film and book and I want to thank them all. So that's a big thank you, in chronological order, to Tommy Docherty, Alex Stepney, Stuart Pearson, Sammy McIlroy, Lou Macari, Gordon Hill, Pat Crerand, Willie Morgan and Jim McCalliog. Thanks to Paddy Barclay, Cliff Butler and Martin Edwards and finally a thank you to a hero of mine, John Cooper Clarke.

Sincere thanks and gratitude to Kim Blackman, Damian Bradshaw and David Corfield and a huge thank you to Cal Gildart and my editor Ashley Shaw at Empire Publications.

There are a few friends and family I have to thank deeply for their support. Dave Murphy, who kept me on the right track in a difficult time; Pete Yorn, for the same; a big thanks to Dan and Kim Burdett for always being there. To Hayley and Elfyn Roberts (and Gruff); to Gemma and Steve, Oyvind Enger, Matt Galea, Nipun Chopra, Luke Smalley, Tyler Dunne and Eifion Evans; also to Mikiel and Phil Gatt. To my Uncle Stuart and Aunt Carole; to all of my family who have shown support. Thanks mum for your constant believing in these adventures and thanks to my wonderful wife for coming on them with me.

Wayne Barton

For Freddy and Noah

"THE BEST THING THAT COULD HAVE HAPPENED"

A S THE MANCHESTER UNITED team flew to Spain ahead of their European Cup semi-final second leg against Real Madrid, their favourite son tried to lift the spirits of his colleagues. The previous weekend United had relinquished their hold on the Division One title, to Manchester City no less, and despite a narrow victory in the first leg against Madrid, expectations of progress to the final among the wider press and public were not high. Real had a formidable record at the Bernabeu having only lost once (to Juventus in 1962) in 36 previous home games.

"Don't worry about losing the league title," Bobby Charlton reassured his peers on the flight, in earshot of the travelling journalists, "it's the best thing that could have happened. Now we have got to beat Real to get into Europe next season."

In its contemporary context the statement was completely reasonable and even inspiring. Charlton, the experienced talisman, had duelled with Los Merengues before. A decade earlier he and his United team-mates looked set to wrestle the Spaniards' European crown from them before the tragedy of Munich ended those dreams. Now only Charlton and team-mate Bill Foulkes remained on the playing staff from that trip, following a path they should have walked with their peers ten years earlier.

Charlton's remark was calculated to banish all thoughts of disappointment and concentrate minds on the task at hand and he had a point; domestic disappointment would be beneficial in refining the focus, particularly to veterans like Charlton and Foulkes, for whom this probably represented a last tilt at the title the club yearned for above all others. If they had won the league, then their trip to the intimidating Santiago Bernabeu would have been buffered by more than the single goal lead they carried from the first leg; the players may have felt the consolation of a return to the tournament in 1968-69. Back in the days when only the domestic champions and European Cup holders qualified for the following year's competition, the opportunity to test yourself among Europe's elite did not come around every season. Charlton, more than anyone, was aware that such chances were not to be taken for granted.

Bobby, blissfully unaware of subsequent failures to win the First Division, would have been stunned had you told him that it would take twenty-six years and five managers before the club would regain that particular Holy Grail, reshaping his off-hand comment from a positive call to arms into what might be regarded, when taken out of context, as arrogance.

★

The mood in the dressing room at half-time against Real Madrid was far less relaxed. United were on the brink of yet another failure in this their fourth European Cup semi-final. It needed a remarkable second half revival, that saw the team throw everything at their illustrious opponents, and an inspired piece of finishing from centre-half Foulkes, to squeak into the final.

A fortnight later, at approximately 9.40pm on the evening of Wednesday, 29th May, 1968, the whole of Wembley Stadium took a sharp intake of breath. For a brief second there was the opportunity to appreciate the anticipation of something wonderful; a pause between the hope and the glory, and the opportunity to experience both rolled into one. George Best had tracked the path of goalkeeper Alex Stepney's long kick. He anticipated the subtle change in direction as his team-mate Brian Kidd rose to flick the ball with his head and, reacting quicker than his marker Benfica defender Jacinto Santos, seized control of destiny. Jacinto was not the first defender, nor would he be the last, to suffer at the nimble feet of the Northern Irishman. George Best's brilliance and speed had a tendency of making even the best defenders in the world look leaden-footed. He was here one minute and, as Jacinto had just learned, gone the next.

It was Best's next movement which provoked such a hush over

football's most famous stadium. With the ball under his command he drew Benfica goalkeeper José Henrique from goal. The 'keeper followed the natural direction of Best's run; the momentum of the forward was taking him across goal on his right hand side, so the goalkeeper aimed to narrow the angle and make it impossible for Best to get his shot away. Yet impossible, for George Best, was simply a challenge. In an instant he dropped his shoulder and changed direction, shifting the ball to his left foot, opening up the goal. It was a remarkable piece of football wizardry; a demonstration of intuitive brilliance triumphing over physical tiredness, the kind of movement which should not be expected after 90 minutes physical on lush turf.

And so arrived a moment in time where Best had destiny at his feet; his own magnificence had created an opportunity for the hundreds of thousands watching and listening around the world to appreciate the gravity of what was to follow. George Best had a relatively simple task from this point onwards; a task he would fulfil with ease. That one swing of his left foot, straightforward as it was, brought with it a sizeable reward. It was a blow from which Benfica would never recover.

The Portuguese had given their all. United assistant manager Jimmy Murphy had cajoled his boys as they sat on the pitch after the ninety minute whistle saying "They're shattered, they're shot!" and brimming with an unusually high degree of self-confidence after watching a closely contested 1-1 draw. "This is going to be our day!"

The emotional poignancy of the moment between Best's left foot connecting with the ball and the sphere crossing the line would have been felt no more keenly than by Murphy. It was a moment of fulfilment, perhaps of vindication. The leather footballs of the 1960s were far heavier than those of the modern age; consider the added weight of the grief, hopes and dreams of the young footballers who had perished in the Munich Air Disaster of February 6th, 1958, the added weight of ten years labour alongside manager Matt Busby during which they had to rebuild a footballing institution for a second time. They had tried to stay as true to their original vision as possible even if this time around the odd corner was cut in the transfer market with the likes of Denis Law and Pat Crerand bought to supplement the home grown lads, Jimmy's 'apples'. Now, as Willo the Wisp Best rolled the ball over the line, a dream had been realised with the entertaining swagger Busby and Murphy appreciated.

The following twenty-eight minutes of extra-time were United's playground, an opportunity for their stars to enjoy themselves on the pitch, a blurry half-hour for those on the bench as all of their collective ambitions were realised. Manchester United were Champions of Europe — the culmination of one of football's most famous stories. "This is not the end!" Busby said at a civic reception in Manchester the following day.

★

Yet time has proven that this was indeed the end for the soon to be knighted Matt Busby. Yet at that moment, on the evening of 29th May 1968, there was evidence to suggest that United had enough to continue at the top of English football. That the club failed so spectacularly is the subject of this book.

One of the most commonly stated reasons for the subsequent collapse is that the squad was over the hill. Yet Alex Stepney was 25, a spring chicken in goalkeeping terms; David Sadler was just 22; Tony Dunne was 26, approaching his peak years; Pat Crerand 29. World Cup winner Nobby Stiles had just turned 26, George Best had just turned 22, Brian Kidd had marked his nineteenth birthday by scoring one of the goals at Wembley as he took his place in the side due to the injured Denis Law (himself at his physical peak at 28), meanwhile man-of-the-match John Aston was a month away from his 21st birthday. The only players who could be said to be nearing the end of their careers were Bobby Charlton (31), Shay Brennan (31) and Bill Foulkes (36).

If it can reasonably be said that United needed to replace Foulkes and start to make plans for a new defence built around the intelligent David Sadler, then there were at least three reasons why supporters could have confidence that such a transition would be handled efficiently. The first was the identity of the men tasked with that transition. Sir Matt Busby and Jimmy Murphy had overseen change much more drastic than this. The second was the club's youth reserve. There were no obvious names that stood out in the way they had before but Bobby Noble's emergence, as well as the club's great tradition, suggested that it wouldn't be long until another gem would emerge. And if they didn't, there was the third reason, and that was Manchester United's affluence. Matt Busby was not a manager known for spending frivolously but he would spend to strengthen his side when necessary.

Yet even if, with all these cards stacked in their favour, it was a stretch to have predicted a period of dominance for Manchester United from May 1968 onwards, certainly nobody could have forecast how quickly and devastatingly things fell apart. For the club which stands alone as English football's most successful and most popular, Manchester United's lean periods are almost newsworthy as the glory days are at other clubs. One only needs to observe the focus that has been trained on the club in the post-Sir Alex Ferguson era. Their league finishes in the four seasons since have been 7th, 4th, 5th, 6th and 2nd and yet they remain the most newsworthy team. As journalist Martin Samuel put it on Sky Sports' Sunday Supplement show, "you will never go poor writing about Manchester United." There was just as much attention on the club in the period between May 1968 and April 1974 when the unthinkable occurred and Manchester United were relegated to Division Two.

How could a team who had three Ballon D'or winners, another World Cup winner and a legendary management team go from winning the European Cup to suffering relegation in the space of just six years?

Perhaps United's ageing management duo had been caught out by the pace of change in English football. Tactics and training methods developed at a remarkable pace between 1965 and 1975. United, still reliant on selecting the best XI and letting them get on with it, were caught and then surpassed. A glance at the league championship winners during the period covered in this book highlights an unheard of freedom at the top of the First Division; Manchester City, Leeds, Everton, Arsenal, Derby County, Liverpool and Leeds (again) would win the league as United declined. What they had in common were modern, forward-thinking coaches and squads filled largely with players famed more for their stamina and team ethic rather than their individual skill.

As successive managers came in with a remit to modernise the club, established players were resistant to change and still had the ear of their former boss, Sir Matt Busby, now installed as General Manager.

It is perhaps for these reasons that it would take six years and three managers for United to resemble a team who could reasonably be described as a Manchester United side. And, just as Tommy Docherty seemed to have finally figured out how to get his team playing, they were demoted. The story of how football's greatest institution got to that point is one of the most compelling in the history of the sport.

CONTROL

I N SIR ALEX FERGUSON'S 2015 BOOK 'Leading' there is a full sub-section on 'Control' and how important it is for any manager, let alone the manager of Manchester United. There was never any suggestion that in 1968 the newly knighted Sir Matt Busby had lost the respect and command of his dressing room to the point where it might explain the subsequent fall from grace.

Indeed, the news of his knighthood was accompanied by the following report from Frank McGhee of the *Daily Mirror*: "The basic reason his players have faith in Matt Busby is that he has confidence in himself. He could not and would not have rebuilt a team after the horror of Munich had he not been certain of his own ability to do it. But you don't break up teams, sell players, call players into the office and rip scars in their egos without hurting. Matt Busby has done all that — and the fact that he has never enjoyed it will not prevent him from doing it again. Perhaps the greatest tribute to him is that so many he has hurt still trust and like him."

And yet the headline in the *Daily Express* which accompanied the story which shook the footballing world just 8 months after his Wembley triumph explained Sir Matt's impending retirement in just four big, bold words: I'VE LOST MY GRIP.

By Tuesday 14th January 1969 after a turbulent start to the season during which United had lost 12 of their 32 games and won just 11, Sir Matt found his club in the sorry and deeply concerning position of 16th in the league, 19 points behind leaders Liverpool (a chasm in the days of two points for a win). Despite the attacking riches they boasted, United had scored just 27 times in 25 league games. Given that the season before the same squad had scored 110 goals across 54 games in all competitions, the swift decline seems mystifying.

There were many theories as to why this had happened. Some

believed that, having realising the ultimate ambition of winning the European Cup, Busby's fire had waned. Others recognised that he had ignored, or put aside, his growing disillusion of how the game was evolving, with a growing emphasis on stamina, defensive team-work and a 'win at all costs' approach which meant his skill players were often the target for violent assault, in order to take United to the pinnacle of Wembley, but he had no plan for how success would follow. As club statistician Cliff Butler recalls, "There was almost a sigh of relief, I think when they won the European cup in '68 — 'We've done it, we've reached the goal we always wanted' — and I think after that you're always gonna get something of a dip unless you go back and win it again, you're striving once more. It was not an anti-climax, but certainly, things were never quite the same for a few seasons until the memory of finally claiming the European Cup had passed."

In November 1967 United travelled to Sarajevo for a European Cup second round, first leg tie. United earned a 0-0 draw in testing circumstances. Busby's post-match comments however underlined the brutality of the Yugoslavs. "It was one of the most disgraceful exhibitions I have seen. I am very pleased with the way the boys kept their heads under extreme provocation. We were lucky to get away with bruises." Bill Foulkes described it as 'diabolical' while Bobby Charlton quipped, "It was a bit on the rough side, wasn't it!" This was not the first time United had been faced with physically intimidating opponents and it should be said that it was never an excuse that any United player would use, let alone the manager. But Busby's approach was always the same; a player who was representing Manchester United had to conduct themselves in a certain way and that way directly opposed these rough-house tactics. If a United player found themselves in disciplinary trouble, their manager would be the first to condemn them for letting the club and themselves down.

So one can't help but think that the Intercontinental Cup tie — United's 'reward' for defeating Benfica at Wembley — went some way to persuading Matt Busby that his values were somewhat at odds within a sport which, in all actuality, desperately needed them. His team faced Estudiantes of Argentina, and, perhaps naively, Busby expected a fair and sporting game. "I have had a personal assurance from Estudiantes that they wish to play this game without any fury," Busby told the *Express* on 21st September 1968. "They did the kindness to write and say how honoured they were to receive such a great team and expressed the hope that this contest would be a credit to international football. My players have been around the world sufficiently to know that they are only inviting trouble if they step out of line. We have had a series of talks and the players have agreed that they must be prepared for anything. The only menace can come from the crowd. I know that Estudiantes are not one of the Argentinian millionaire teams who can be pretty ruthless in these prestige games. Their captain is a dentist, two are fully qualified doctors and there are lawyers and law students among the team. We expect a hard game. It should be a great test of courage and skill. I have repeatedly told my players that the only provocation can come from the fans who can get a bit het up. Luckily, we are accustomed to this terrace menace. But just to make sure that we do not let British football down I have given a stern warning to every player that if they step out of line they will face a sentence from me they will never forget."

An official reception had been arranged prior to the first leg in Buenos Aires but at the last minute the host team pulled out leaving Busby annoyed. He was further irritated by pre-match comments made by Benfica coach Otto Glória who described Nobby Stiles as 'an assassin' and 'brutal, badly intentioned and a bad sportsman'. Some of the home contingent would have remembered Stiles from the World Cup game between England and Argentina in 1966 which was particularly physical. The reminder only stoked up the fires and Stiles was singled out for some dreadful treatment at the hand of the Estudiantes players being kicked, punched and even head-butted by future national team coach Carlos Bilardo.

Stiles later remarked in his autobiography that the contest had become so violent that when the players went into the dressing room at half-time, they wouldn't have been surprised if Busby had told them to get dressed and leave. However, they were left surprised by Busby's alternate plan — to not only play the second half, but to try and beat the host's offside trap. That plan seemed painfully naive only minutes into the second period when it became clear that the Paraguayan officials were not concerned with United's clever timing and consistently declared them to be offside. On one such occasion, and after such intense provocation, Stiles eventually broke, swearing at the referee and getting himself sent off. United came away from the game with a 1-0 defeat but paid a much higher physical cost.

As United returned to Manchester, Busby told reporters at the airport: "We shall continue to play in this competition because we want to be the best in the world. You cannot stop playing these games because of certain incidents. What better exponents of football have there been in the last 10 years than the Brazilians and they are from South America. I was of course very upset at some of the things that happened in the first leg. But there is no question of us calling off the return match at Old Trafford. We can take tough play but we are not used to what went on in Buenos Aires. I think my players were wonderful under the conditions. I am hoping that the second leg will be more of a football match. We certainly have got to play football to win it."

Bobby Charlton, who had suffered a head injury that needed stitches, told the press: "I expect the Argentinians to be just as bad in the second leg. They have a goal lead and will hang on to it for all they're worth. But we will behave—we've got to. We want to beat them more than ever now. They have some good players but you had to keep looking behind all the time. If there was any sign of danger to their defence they just brought you down."

However, if United were essentially blameless for what had occurred in Argentina, they were far from angels on domestic soil and so there was a diminishing sympathy for them as far as the press were concerned. The week before the return leg, United faced Arsenal at Old Trafford and the 0-0 draw saw controversy on and off the pitch. "Manchester United appeared in their goalless draw against Arsenal to be in need of some stern discipline," reported John Morgan of the *Express*, "none more than Denis Law and George Best. If Sir Matt could persuade them to behave a little more sportingly on the field it might go a long way towards reducing the violent crowd reaction to which he, and everyone else, objects."

Arsenal goalkeeper Bob Wilson claimed to have been hit by missiles thrown by United fans. "I can't imagine what will happen to the Argentinian goalkeeper Poletti if the United crowd gets frustrated in the match against Estudiantes. I have never had so many things thrown at me. They don't like it if United don't score."

Perhaps United were so prepared for aggression that they needed to be reminded they were also in a sporting contest — that reminder came from Juan Veron (father, of course, of future United midfielder Juan Sebastian Veron) in the 6th minute when he headed in to the United net. And, ironically, it was the visitors' heavy-handed approach which actually reduced United, and not themselves, to ten men, when Denis Law had to be stretchered off near the end of the first half after suffering a wound in his leg which required four stitches. The cynical tactics undoubtedly worked, but even so United's supporters would have left Old Trafford wondering just how they were not watching their own team celebrate. First of all, though, things got much worse. With just five minutes left, George Best finally had enough of the vicious provocation and retaliated, swinging a foot and a punch back at defender Hugo Medina after being fouled. Best was sent off for his reaction, despite United actually having been awarded the free-kick. Willie Morgan scored from the set-piece and equalised. In the dying seconds of the game, Brian Kidd had the ball in the net for what seemed like a winning goal on the night to take the game to a play-off. The home support was bemused to see the Estudiantes players celebrating; it transpired that referee Konstantin Zevicic had bizarrely blown the whistle for full-time just as Kidd readied his strike.

"George Best was ordered off five minutes from the end of a game in which Estudiantes of Argentina became Club Champions of the world last night," reported Norman Giller. "The game ended in crazy confusion with United's fans screaming their delight at what they thought was a second goal by Brian Kidd that would have forced a play-off. But Yugoslav referee Konstantin Zecivic had blown the final whistle a split second before Kidd fired the ball into the net. As the Estudiantes players ran triumphantly around the pitch with their hands raised in the air, the misery of the moment suddenly hit hard at the capacity crowd whose cheers switched to loud jeers. Oscar Pachame, Estudiantes' half-back, stood on the touchline applauding United players and shaking their hands as they trudged dejectedly off. All he got in return from goalkeeper Alex Stepney was a backhanded slap round the face. It was an ungentlemanly gesture that aptly summed up the feelings that had been simmering between the two teams right through the game. It was all a hangover of the bad-tempered clash in Buenos Aires. This should have been one of the greatest nights in United's glittering history. It turned into one of the saddest."

"I was proud of them (the supporters) tonight," Busby said afterwards. "I only wish we could have given them a victory to cheer."

The manager was far from proud of the antics of his goalkeeper. Stepney was called into Busby's office the following morning and fined £50 after being told "You have brought disgrace to this club." Stepney protested and said Busby's 'wise old eyes' were 'heavy with understanding'; his manager said even though he himself had felt that way many a time, you had to control yourself in those situations.

United were deflated but might have considered they got off lightly considering events in the same competition the following year. There Estudiantes faced Milan, travelling to Italy for the first leg where they were defeated 3-0. The comprehensive victory rendered the second leg a procession but the Italians — hardly shrinking violets themselves — must have known that their opponents would not go down without a fight. Yet even they would have been stunned by the events which unfolded as the game went down in infamy. As the Italian side emerged from the tunnel to take to the field, home fans poured hot coffee on them from the fences. Milan striker Pierino Praity was knocked unconscious and despite suffering from concussion, continued to play for 20 minutes. Estudiantes' Goalkeeper Poletti, who Bob Wilson had previously expressed concern for, punched Milan forward Gianna Rivera. That was nothing compared to what laid in wait for French international Nestor Combin, who was born in Argentina and faced particularly hostile treatment from the 'hosts' both on and off the pitch. The whistles and jeers were nothing compared to the kick in the face he received from Poletti and then the elbow from Ramón Suárez which broke his nose and cheekbone, leaving his shirt and shorts covered with blood. Despite his injuries, the referee insisted the player should continue. He fainted on the pitch, and was then arrested by police on account of alleged 'draft dodging' for avoiding military service for the country! Poletti was given a life ban from the sport (which was subsequently overturned), Suàrez was suspended for 30 international games, and Eduardo Manera suspended for 20. Poletti and Manera also served a month in jail so serious were their offences (and so brightly were the spotlights shining on the Argentinian authorities to treat the matter with severity due to concerns about their hosting the 1978 World Cup). Stepney's indiscretion, which Busby deemed to have brought shame on the club, seemed quite minor in comparison! The Intercontinental Cup abandoned the two-legged format in 1980 and all subsequent games were one-off 'finals' which took place in Japan until it was incorporated into, and replaced by, the World Club Cup in 2005. In 1999 United won against Palmeiras of Brazil. The South American side were coached by Luiz Felipe Scolari and the build-up to the tie included the suggestion that there might well be physical altercations on the touchline as well as the pitch, such was Scolari's combustible reputation. The event passed without controversy; Gary Neville later remarked in his autobiography that he lamented the missed opportunity to play in front of a partizan Palmeiras crowd. He would have only needed to speak to legends of the club to hastily revise his romantic perception.

Back in early 1970 United's league problems were so pronounced that Busby realised the prospect of continuing their European exploits the following season would not be straightforward. "We have to win the FA Cup or the European Cup to stay in Europe next season," he admitted. "We hope to win one or both — we can rise to the occasion." There was nothing strange in those comments, just that they were reported on 14th January, so must have been said the previous day. And it was, of course, that day that Busby stunned football by announcing he would retire at the end of the season.

"It will come as a great surprise to a great many people that I have relinquished control of Manchester United," he said. "But it will come probably as a greater shock — and I'm not sure I have fully accepted my own reasons — to everybody to know why I have done it. I don't mind admitting here and now that the reason is: I am losing my grip! That is the honest reason after months of heart searching. I have not had enough time with the players, and yet, in Soccer, players are the all-essential beings. Therefore a manager must be with them and must live with them and know them. As things have happened over the last few months this has not been possible. Therefore it is time for me to go. The decision — which is my decision and my decision only — was inevitable. Manchester United need new blood, a new supply of ideas from which they will progress and do better if it is possible. The big thing now is for Manchester United, which I believe to be the greatest club in the world, to appoint my successor. I shall have some say in whom my successor shall be and I have very definite ideas on the subject.

He must be:

1: Young, in is early 30's, up to the absolute age of 45.

2: He must have experience because Manchester United are not in a position to experiment.

3: He must be a manager who has proved himself to be a leader, who commands respect, and the players must know what he's talking about.

4: He must have the human touch. The advice he gives will have to be the best for the players, but, more important, the best for the club.

5: He must NEVER, EVER, make a promise without ever being able to fulfil his words.

"There is a sixth quality which Manchester United now expect… the man chosen will have to be right in his decisions and though he will be given time to prove that he is right this is a final condition… until he is dreadfully wrong. And I hope my man will NEVER be dreadfully wrong. The man who takes on Manchester United has a difficult job. He must — and I repeat must with all possible emphasis — have success in terms of Championships or Cups, otherwise he is going to be deemed a failure. Frankly, it is not the sort of job that I might have taken on 30 years ago. So, we need a new face, we need new life in the club, we need new blood… And though in my opinion I'm not old, we need this complete transfusion to take the club even further. I knew the minute I offered my resignation from team managerial duties that I would be offered either a place on the board or that a post of general manager would be created. But I did not want to become a director. After 23 years of waking and living the life of Manchester United a directorship seemed to me to be a sort of vacuum. That I didn't want. Eventually, if it is the wish of the present board, then I shall join the board because Manchester United is my life. But between now and then I will work for United.

"My successor will have heartbreak, heartache, headache, success, and happiness in some order or other. But I promise him this — he will never have any interference from me. As this season ends, Matt Busby, who was knighted on behalf of some great boys past and present, is bowing out of football team management. From there on I shall be on the administrative side… and who knows? Maybe I will start being able to enjoy a game of Soccer again."

Busby's confession and explanation was almost as stunning as his decision. This was a man who, after all, had been a trailblazer not just for Manchester United but for the sport itself. His ambitions for the club had been in tune with the evolution of the game. But if Busby was seen as a pioneer in the 1950's, there was just a suggestion that by 1969 his approach to the game was outdated.

The young and innovative coaches in football were inevitably linked with the Old Trafford job in the newspapers as news of his retirement broke. Those names included Don Revie, Jock Stein and Dave Sexton. It seemed most likely that United would appoint a successor from within. Wilf McGuinness, first team coach at the club, was installed as the favourite. Assistant Jimmy Murphy was only a year or so younger than Busby and, as reported by Frank McGhee of the *Daily Mirror*, was ruled out of contention for the top job for that reason.

McGhee showed prescient thinking when observing that inheriting such a talented squad might not necessarily prove to be the incredible opportunity it seemed it might be. "Players of the calibre of George Best and Denis Law, for instance, can be notoriously tricky to handle," McGhee wrote. "Their responses to new ideas on training, tactics and discipline are not bound to be as receptive to a young man in a tracksuit — a man who could hardly have been their equal on the field — as they have always been to a man of Sir Matt's stature."

In that respect, then, perhaps only Jock Stein was a suitable candidate. At Celtic, Stein was on his way to his fourth consecutive League title and had of course won the European Cup with them in 1967. Don Revie, whose Leeds United team were set to win the First Division, was perhaps the only other manager with a track record comparable enough to have commanded respect from United's star players.

Norman Giller reported, "Noel Cantwell is favourite to take over from Sir Matt Busby as manager of Manchester United. Cantwell, former United club captain, is still highly rated at Old Trafford despite his slender success as Coventry City's manager… But as United skipper Bobby Charlton stressed last night: 'Nobody could possibly replace Matt. They can succeed him, but they can't replace him. I was stunned when he told me the news of his resignation. It was a real blow even though it has often been suggested that he would 'move upstairs' after our European Cup victory in May.' Charlton himself could be the surprise choice of the United board, but he will probably prefer to carry on playing for a few more seasons."

"There will be no interference from me," Busby told Frank McGhee. "I will be there to give advice and help if it is asked for, but he will have full control of team matters, buying and selling. He will have what I insisted on having 25 years ago when I took over. Making the decision at this time will give the opportunity for a new man to be appointed and get to know the whole get-up before the start of the new season. The demands are just beyond one human being. I felt I had got to the stage where I was not spending enough time with the players and to the age when I couldn't run around with the team. Team manager has always been a job for a man in a track suit. I lived in one myself for twenty years. I once remember Harry Catterick saying that people didn't realise the tension and strain for a manager of just one League match. Imagine what it is like for twenty-three years of it. Years ago there was never the same strain. Teams sometimes won and sometimes lost, and that was accepted as the way things were. Nowadays winning has become all-important and of course, the financial rewards have become far greater. But I think the game has lost nothing. It has become greater. Great players of any age would be great players today but there is more specialised training, greater tactical knowledge and, as a result, the ability of players today is unsurpassed. It has been a wonderful life. It has been a demanding one, but wonderful. Not only that, it's a wonderful game."

"Now the guessing games have started — before even the shock of Sir Matt Busby's decision to step back into the background as general manager subsides," reported McGhee. "Who takes over as Manchester United's new team boss? Will McGuinness, the early favourite, Don Revie, Jimmy Adamson, Jock Stein, Dave Sexton — almost everyone except Uncle Tom Cobbleigh — has been linked with the job. I do not know who will get it. And neither, incidentally, do Manchester United… Sir Matt's right hand, Jimmy Murphy, assistant manager throughout the Busby regime, was not considered for the new job because he is only a year younger than 'the boss'. But his wisdom, experience and inspiration are still readily available freely offered."

Don Revie ruled himself out. "I would like to emphasise that

I am very happy at Elland Road and my big ambition is to finish as team manager at Leeds in the same proud manner Sir Matt has done," he said.

It was suggested that the decision to retire at 59 was because of the physical toll of the job. Busby had famously been given the last rites in Munich and, with the benefit of hindsight was seen to have cut a tired figure in more recent months. His wife snapped back at the rumours, telling the press, "He certainly hasn't given the job up through ill-health, or on the doctor's advice. It is simply that he is getting too old, frankly, to go running around in a tracksuit on a cold and wet morning."

From Munich, Dr. Peter Maurer, son of the chief surgeon who helped to save Busby's life after the disaster, sent the message: "All of us at the hospital have admired the way in which he has led Manchester United to success after success. We are sorry that he has decided to resign."

The tributes came closer to home too. From across town at Manchester City, manager Joe Mercer said: "Matt Busby climbed on to a pedestal long before he took up management. There was something about him as a player, something different. He was filled with that Scottish desire to play pure football even if the bloody stand was burning down." From Liverpool, Busby's good friend Bill Shankly said, "Matt's record is unparalleled. He began with a good team that grew old. Then concentrated on a youth policy that was wrecked by tragedy but he built them up again."

There were still a few months left of Busby's reign, however, with his retirement set to take effect at the end of the season. United were clearly not going to win the First Division as a leaving present — their game prior to the announcement had been a 2-1 defeat at eventual champions Leeds. The game following the announcement was a 4-1 win over Sunderland, with United seemingly reinvigorated to end their legendary coach's career on a high. Even though Busby was on the wind-down, he wasn't afraid of making big calls. United's poor form had been attributed in most quarters to their ageing defence and the manager's first attempt at fixing that was to start from the very back. Alex Stepney was dropped, a regular theme in forthcoming years, with 20 year-old Jimmy Rimmer given a chance in goal. "He (Stepney) has hit a wee bad patch," Busby said. "A rest will do him good."

Next up was Watford in the FA Cup. In one of the more bizarre links, the manager of the Third Division Hornets, Ken Furphy, was named as 2-1 favourite to succeed Busby with a London bookmaker. Furphy did his chances no harm by taking United to a replay with a draw at Old Trafford. United won 2-0 at Vicarage Road. The *Express* reported of the replay on 4th February: "Even the normally demonstrative Law had the decency to realise that Watford did not deserve to be so completely beaten, and that United had done nothing to add to their football fame... United are through, but they go through with faint glory." By the time of the replay, Stepney had already ended his brief exile. After a 6-2 triumph at Birmingham City in the next round, United's FA Cup hopes were ended in the sixth round by Everton.

And so all hopes of a glorious exit were pinned on the European Cup. After taking care of Waterford, Anderlecht and Rapid Vienna, United faced AC Milan in the semi-final. With a couple of weeks to go until that tie was played, however, there was renewed speculation about who United's new manager might be, as the club had been very quiet in the months since the announcement.

Alan Thompson of the *Express* played investigator by reading between the lines of Busby's statement that the club would not be advertising for his successor. "They have not advertised the job, so I am led to the conclusion that it is unnecessary... because they have the man for the job within the club," Thompson surmised. After again dismissing Murphy — and this time also Jack Crompton — on grounds of age, Thompson declared it was an 'inescapable conclusion' that the job would be handed to Wilf McGuinness, who was still a 20-1 outsider with many bookmakers.

The day after Thompson's report — perhaps sensing that speculation would only intensify from that point — United announced that it would indeed be McGuinness who would take charge from the end of the season, with confirmation of Busby's sidestep into a general manager role.

What should have been the start of the Scot's move out of the limelight, however, began with him taking centre stage to discuss the club's future under his successor. "To all practical purposes he is team manager," Busby told the press. "The managership will automatically follow. Everybody is on trial. You, me, him… we are always on trial. If he wants to buy a player then that's all right. If he wants advice he can have it, and Wilf will have all the support in the club. But this will be his team and these are his players. All the great names in the game began as coach or chief coach, and Wilf is in need of a bit of experience before he goes into the turmoil of it all. He is in charge of team selection, coaching, players, training. But for the time being I shall be club spokesman. When he becomes team boss this will also be his responsibility. We had about 30 serious applications for the job, even though we did not advertise. We delayed asking for applications to give ourselves time — myself and the directors. We felt that we wanted someone from the club, and needed time to look at all the possibilities. We have been watching Wilf and seen his reaction to certain situations. This led to the ultimate decision… Old Trafford has become a very big place. This is not a normal football club."

In other reports, the outgoing manager was quoted as saying: "From the moment I was given the Manchester United managership more than 23 years ago I have been conscious of the absolute necessity of having a youth policy. So it is that, from time to time, during that long and successful period, when we have needed a youngster to step in to fill a gap in the team we have found one within our own ranks. In the training staff, too, we have been and still are wonderfully served by former United players. Jack Crompton came back from Luton after Munich to take over as trainer. Johnny Aston plays a sterling role with young players, among whom his son, John, became one of our European Cup winning team. Now our youth policy has paid yet again by producing the man who is to take over, as chief coach, all things to do with the playing side of the club. Of course, Wilf's being United man and boy was not the only criterion. He has other assets in plenty. We have watched Wilf carefully for years, since he first became assistant trainer in 1961. He deals well with players. He respects them and they respect him. We are convinced that the potential Wilf has had for some years is rapidly ripening and that all he needs is the experience that only the big, hard life in charge of the team can give him."

The headlines had their own sense of foreboding, concentrating on Matt rather than the successor. McGuinness' quote was sandwiched in one of the columns of the *Express*: "Born Collyhurst, October 1937, almost underneath the viaduct in Twyford Street. Now I am right-hand man to the greatest man in football. Greatest man in the world, next to my Dad. And all because I broke my leg. Otherwise I would still be a working type of player, not a backroom boy at the age of 23. I can't pretend I hadn't hoped there would be new opportunities ahead for me when the boss revealed he was to become general manager. It was a personal and secret thought. You don't rush into things at Old Trafford. That was the first lesson I learned from the boss. I have never stopped watching him and learning from the day I went to United at 15, knock-kneed, flat-footed and not all that talented. I have seen him handle difficult situations and difficult men smoothly and brilliantly. To all the many people who have helped me I say, 'thank you'. If I have not learned enough for the future from the boss and Jimmy Murphy, it will be my fault alone."

"I feel very, very fortunate," he told the *Mirror*. "I'm quite sure I shall get along with the players. They know me, I know them. When I first became assistant-trainer I had to face a similar situation, only some of the players then were a lot older than me. I felt overwhelmed when the boss gave me the news this morning. It was the first time I became really aware that I had got the job."

Speaking today, former chairman Martin Edwards admits that the decision to appointment McGuinness was taken by one person. "I think everybody was nervous because, you know, Matt had been in the position for 24 years and been such a great manager and won so much and I think he decided to step down. He wasn't pushed by the board in any way but I think he felt he had done a long stint and of course he'd been through Munich and all the rest of it and won the European Cup the year before. He reached his holy grail in winning the European Cup and was probably a little bit tired but obviously the feeling was that he was going to be hugely difficult to replace and so it proved of course…

"Matt wanted to retire, Wilf was very much Matt's choice, Wilf had broken his leg at quite a young age, he played for England, broke his leg, 22 years old or whatever it was and went into coaching… Wilf was part of Alf Ramsey's coaching staff that won the 1966 World Cup, people forget that, so he had a bit of experience in coaching and I think Matt just felt it was… he would rather promote from within. So it was very much Matt that led. He (Matt) became general manager so in a way Wilf was more like a coach and Matt had the title of general manager so he was still there in a supervisory role but obviously you know, Wilf was managing the team and deciding the tactics by the players with some assistance by Matt."

With that in mind, all attention could now be focussed on the tie with AC Milan. The Italians were famed for their miserly defence and won 2-0 in the San Siro to give themselves a huge advantage. For most of the return at Old Trafford, the Italians seemed in complete control. Then, in the 70th minute, Bobby Charlton's goal gave the Manchester crowd hope of an improbable comeback. The hopes turned to reality in the 78th minute when Denis Law appeared to have grabbed an equaliser. However, French referee Roger Machin judged that the ball hadn't crossed the line. United were unable to get another in a frantic end to the game and were eliminated.

Predictably, Law was incensed. "I know a goal when I've scored one and it was certainly in," the striker snapped. "Pictures and the television play-back only confirm something I was convinced of at the time. The ball was six inches over the line when it was cleared."

If that sounded like the expected sour grapes of a wronged man — for Law, who had missed the previous year's final, it would have been doubly aggravating — then there was some sympathy from the unlikeliest of sources. Italian journalist Gino Palumbo wrote for *Corriere Della Sera*, "The English now maintain they scored a second goal in the second half and that the referee did not notice the ball had crossed the white line of Cudicini's goal. The impression from the Press seats is that the English were right. It was a goal and the referee was mistaken in not giving it."

United might have expected to have got short shrift from the officials. Their involvement in the Intercontinental Cup was still fresh in the mind of continental observers and even their Quarter Final tie with Rapid Vienna had seen some controversy. "Nobby Stiles, Manchester United's ferocious fragment of football trouble, is once again in the middle of a squabble on the eve of the second leg of the European Cup quarter-finals against Rapid Vienna tomorrow," Desmond Hackett of the *Express* reported. "United's perpetual villain is the target of a pretty tough Press campaign because of his inhospitable treatment of certain members of the Vienna team when United splendidly established a three-goal lead last week."

John Fitzpatrick's red card in the first leg of the semi-final barely helped matters, even if his dismissal was for retaliation. Before his disallowed goal in the return, Law had sought to level the score in a more controversial fashion, swinging an arm at defender Roberto Rosato — a former team-mate of his from the pair's days at Torino — and knocking two of his teeth out. Law stayed on the pitch despite his own indiscretion but years later he revealed he still harboured a cynical view about Machin's neutrality. "There seemed to be question-marks," Law told the *Telegraph* ahead of a Milan/United tie in 2010. "There always seemed to be a bit of a problem with Italian teams. We would have beaten Milan and met Ajax in the final. Years later, they (Ajax) became a fantastic team but at that particular time they were very ordinary (albeit with a young Johan Cruyff). There was only going to be one winner. Milan. It was frustrating. When I missed the European Cup final the year before, I didn't worry because I thought: 'We'll go on and win it again because we have such a good team.' The referee spoiled that."

Whichever way you look at it, and regardless of the validity of United's complaints about dodgy referees and decisions, it could also be fairly suggested that they did not help themselves. And, though he never said so directly, there was also enough evidence to tie together the theory that Busby's decision to call it a day was influenced by the indiscipline of his own team as much as the sport in general; that stepping back was a concession that he had neither the ability or inclination to deal with what felt like a major change in the game. Busby was perceived, with justification, as a great gentleman of the game. His response to Stepney's early-season indiscretion revealed his exasperation; it mattered not that the goalkeeper could rightly claim to have acted in frustration on behalf of the aggression handed out to his team-mates. Compared to Stiles, Law and Best, Stepney's act had almost been that of a shrinking violet.

Two days after that European anti-climax, 45,860 supporters turned out to see United defeat Leicester City 3-2 in what was scheduled to be Busby's last match in charge of the club. In his programme notes for the game, Busby focussed on the fortunes of the present team rather than reflecting on his legacy. "One appreciates that at home at any rate we have suffered some disappointment in both the League and the Cup, but it has been extremely encouraging to see that the sort of support we have always enjoyed has been maintained," he said. "This season has also seen the appointment of Wilf McGuinness as chief coach, and I am sure that this young man will do extremely well when he officially takes up his duties next month and begins preparations for next winter. Certainly, he can look ahead to wholehearted co-operation from everyone within the club, and I feel sure he has the best wishes of all our patrons as he makes his plans for the future."

Journalist David Meek also spoke positively of the appointment in his own column. "Next season Wilf McGuinness will be in charge of team affairs as Chief Coach while Sir Matt Busby concentrates on the administrative side of an organisation which, as Sir Matt says, has become more of an institution than a football club," he wrote. "The demands on Sir Matt personally have also grown enormously and he feels it is now time to make room for a younger man to work with the team, which of course is exactly what he and Jimmy Murphy did for so many years... Now to the

31-year-old McGuinness goes the supreme distinction of following in the famous footsteps of Sir Matt himself. It is a tremendous undertaking and challenge; following a man like Matt Busby could never be easy. At the same time there are resources at Old Trafford which many managers must envy. There is for instance a highly talented playing staff, a youth set-up ensuring a supply of promising players and, as Jimmy Murphy points out, a wealth of advice and hard experience freely available for the new man. Wilf McGuinness also has the character and personality to take his big job in his stride. He was a leader even as a youngster. He captained Manchester Boys so well that he skippered his way right through to the full England schoolboy side. It also tends to be overlooked that he has been United's assistant trainer now for the last six years and that in this time all but the most senior players have been through his hands. The bulk of the staff will find him no stranger and all the time he has been broadening his experience. He was so successful as trainer with the England youth team that last year he was made their manager and he was also called up by Sir Alf Ramsey as an assistant trainer with the World Cup squad in 1966. Wilf McGuinness is a logical, extremely capable choice to lead the team into the next era."

There was no suggestion that Busby's retirement was an act of self-preservation with regards to his own legacy. Perhaps, disciplinary issues aside, he observed the prospect of the necessary forthcoming transition and decided he was too long in the tooth to commit to another three or four years of rebuilding. This was understandable. Regardless of those red cards and fiery individuals, even a man with such a grand reputation for foresight could not have predicted how quickly his life's work would turn to ruin.

GETTING TO GRIPS WITH BEST

THERE IS A POINT in United's decline when George Best becomes more of a handful for his own club than for opposing defenders. The start of the 1968 Ballon D'or winners slide into ill discipline was most probably the Estudiantes game in which he was dismissed in the last minute but by then the violent attention devoted to the mercurial Irishman had started to fray Best's nerves. Back in the sixties, protection of star players was limited and every team seemed to have a hatchet man designated to shut down the opposition's star man.

With his dark hair and stylish swagger, George Best was to sports fans what the Beatles were to music lovers. Beatlemania was at its peak when Best first made his way in English football, and the two were closely linked. What wasn't natural, and what took some getting used to, was the fervent attention usually preserved for those in the arts, suddenly being focussed on one individual in a team game. Best, still in modest Manchester digs, was the first young footballer left to deal with this unprecedented spotlight. Previously, promising young footballers had been youthful versions of their more experienced team mates. Duncan Edwards, for example, was a humble lad from the Black Country who adjusted well to army life during his period of National Service. On the pitch he looked no different to the likes of Roger Byrne and Tommy Taylor. Yet Best soon became a pop star in shorts; a boy who not only did not play like any other footballer before him, but also looked like no other footballer before him.

Football in the sixties was on the rise. Domestically there was an unprecedented sharing of the spoils as a different team won the First Division in every season between 1959 and 1976. Following the abolition of the maximum wage in 1961 footballers moved from being regarded as talented tradesmen to artistes. The media promoted individual talents and Best's artistry was proof that the game's individuals were on a par with pop stars and matinee idols. Following the success of the English national team in winning the World Cup in 1966, Irishman Best still stood out as the most gifted player in the British game, the boy with the world at his feet who finally delivered on that promise with that sumptuous winning goal in 1968.

In football, opponents will often go to nefarious lengths in order to stifle more talented opponents. Clearly, it had been noted that United could become ruffled and distracted by underhand tactics. They would respond to provocation and it would impact upon their performance. Having seen team-mates Nobby Stiles and Denis Law in trouble with referees, it was no surprise that the impressionable Best, who stood out as much as anyone, followed suit. After all, he was at an age when men were men, and so it should only be expected that there was only so far you could push someone before they would retaliate.

George Best was still only 22 when Sir Matt Busby announced his retirement. He was as good as anyone in world football and by any application of the word 'peak', the expectation was that it should be years before the football public would see him at his very best. Yet there was no blueprint for how someone in Best's unique position should handle his fame or how he should be handled. From the outside at least, it seemed that Busby was the best possible mentor for Best in many ways. In his own squad, Best had the shining example of Bobby Charlton when it came to conduct. But even then, with Best's 1968 European Player of the Year award fresh in the memory, there were seeds of discontent.

Firstly, no football manager had had to handle a player with the sort of attention Best was receiving. Player and manager were learning together. There was no suggestion whatsoever that Busby was unable to deal with Best's stardom — after all, look at what the pair had achieved together. Old Father Time was the reason used by Busby for his retirement, and perhaps this is the most logical and straightforward answer for the beginning of the downward spiral for Manchester United Football Club and its players. If Busby had been five years younger, or had Munich not aged him so much in other ways, he could have maintained his enthusiasm for the game, dealt with and protected Best, and built United's next great team around him. The complications which would follow with regards to Busby and Best were probably more to do with the idea of perceived interference from the former manager at crucial times in the near future.

Moreover, if Busby believed he could rely on Charlton's example as a model professional to provide guidance to the Irishman in his absence, then he had made a rare error in judgement. In his autobiography 'Blessed', Best later described his fractured relationship with his team-mate. "Bobby and I had never been the greatest of mates, on or off the field," he said. "I think he thought I was a greedy little so-and-so who wouldn't give him the ball, but then I thought he was a bit of a glory hunter as well, looking for the chance to unleash one of those long-range shots rather than giving the ball to me. He was a bit dour as well and a real moaner on the pitch, but a United man through and through. So while I didn't think it was worth giving my all in such a poor team, Bobby didn't see it like that. He felt that it was up to the senior players — and I was now one of them — to work even harder to pull the club up. He was such an establishment man that Denis began calling him Sir Bobby long before he was knighted."

The attitude of two of United's biggest names gives an insight into just how they may have perceived the appointment of Wilf McGuinness, who took over as team manager in the summer of 1969. McGuinness's playing career had been cruelly curtailed by injury problems; a fine wing-half, while not as talented as Duncan Edwards or even Eddie Colman, Wilf's own reputation was boosted by the fact he had captained his city, county and country at schoolboy level. He had retired after suffering a broken leg in 1960 at the age of 22, at which point he started a new career as a coach, learning from Busby and Jimmy Murphy. His appointment at the age of 31 was a risk but he knew the club as well as anyone. He had not, however, enjoyed the stellar playing career of a Bobby Charlton or a George Best.

Around the same time as McGuinness' unveiling as team

manager, Captain James Thain, the pilot who had received the blame for the Munich Air Disaster, was finally cleared by a British inquiry. Thain stated he intended to continue his fight for justice. "At present, the official German report — which is the one on record — still blames me," he said. "I want the Board of Trade now to put that right. I am after justice."

McGuinness had to deal with political rather than practical matters as his first action. The club were under scrutiny for irregular payments to players, and there was pressure to see them face a heavy sanction. Peterborough had been relegated from the Third Division in 1968 after being deducted 19 points for irregular payments and bonuses to players. United were fined £7,000 and were banned from playing friendly matches against European teams for a season (being out of Europe meant that participating in games against the continental elite would have been a lucrative pursuit). The *Daily Mirror*'s Ken Jones suggested that although the offences were relatively minor (and conceded that the friendlies expulsion could cost the club an estimated £30,000), "Down in the Fourth Division, however, they are still entitled to ask whether there is one law for the rich and another for the strugglers... If there is to be any consistency should not United be starting next season in the Second Division?"

United were punished on five counts by a joint League and FA commission. Shay Brennan had been given a loan of £1,000 to be paid back at £10 a week, but permission had not been previously granted by the League management committee. They paid lodging money to landladies for apprentices and amateurs in excess of the League maximum of £4 (United had paid around £7.40), amounting to two separate charges. Senior players were paid £250 in lieu of a club tour that was cancelled due to fixture congestion caused by the 'big freeze' the previous winter. Eleven senior players were also paid £250 in appearance money for the World Club Championship games against Estudiantes which had not been specified in their contracts.

McGuinness's first days in charge were met with much publicity. Staged photographs at the Cliff training ground showed him remonstrating with players with Matt Busby stood behind him. It was an attempt to show the public that there had been a natural succession in Manchester United's management. Yet that isn't quite how it was behind the scenes. In the early months of 1969, when United were uncomfortably quiet on the matter of Busby's successor, goalkeeper Alex Stepney recalled that some at the club had grown concerned about newspaper rumours. "I did hear, from an impeccable source, that there was a minor crisis among the club staff when Noel Cantwell's name was first mentioned in connection with the job," Stepney wrote in his self-titled 1978 biography. "A delegation was formed and its members presented themselves in front of Sir Matt, who must have been getting distressed by the whole tiresome business. It consisted of chief scout Johnny Aston senior, first team trainer Jack Crompton, and McGuinness who was then reserve and youth team coach. They told the United doyen that if Noel returned they would all be leaving. Sir Matt listened to them and decided that, in the interests of club spirit and as some recognition of their feelings and loyalty, he could not bring Noel back to the club. The old man probably thought that, at the age of fifty-eight, he had fought enough battles without having to fight his own men. Perhaps it was a pity that he seemed to be taking an easy way out. Noel shared Sir Matt's belief about the way the game should be played, and he had won the respect of all the players during his days as club captain and chairman of the Professional Footballers Association before Derek Dougan."

If Stepney was disappointed with the decision not to hire Cantwell, he was quick to put on record his contemporary reservations about the appointment of McGuinness. He said: "The job was Wilf's. I felt I did not know him as well as I might. In view of Noel Cantwell's remarks when I first joined the club in 1966 ('be very, very wary of Wilf McGuinness') I had kept him at arm's length. In his jobs with the youth team and the reserves our paths did not cross too often... When he was given the job I decided to throw everything in behind him, as indeed I would with any new manager. He had my full support, but there were certain doubts about him that I could not erase from my mind.

"I had caught him out once. It was the morning after the first team had returned from a European jaunt and Wilf was still a rather junior member of the hierarchy. The lads were in the dressing-room talking about the match and the night out afterwards. I had slipped away to the club offices for something and as I returned to the dressing-room corridor I could see Wilf crouched at the door with his ear to the key-hole. 'Gotcha!' I shouted. He was caught, red-handed. He was desperately sheepish when he looked up and saw me approaching. What could he say? His face coloured up, he mumbled something, tried a false smile and walked away."

However, the goalkeeper insisted that the new man — new in some respects — should be given a fair shake at the start, while acknowledging there could have been potential difficulties. "It was not an easy time for all the senior players who had been a part of Manchester United's greatest triumphs while Wilf had with the reserves," Stepney said. "If some of the established international players found his appointment difficult to accept it would have been understandable. But at the outset none of them showed any open resentment."

Best's sentiment was similar. "Sir Matt and United had been looking everywhere for a new manager, which you would have thought would have been an easy task," Best said, "but the big-name managers were probably frightened off by the thought of Sir Matt looking over their shoulder and just before the end of the 1968/69 season, it was announced that reserve team coach Wilf McGuinness would take over in the summer. I don't know who was more surprised, the players or Wilf… taking over the first team was a task he was never going to win and one of his first problems was that, at the age of 32, he was younger than some of the players he would be picking. That would make it hard for him to win the players' respect, although I, for one, was willing to give him a chance."

George Best would provide the biggest challenge for the new boss. His petulance was shown when he knocked the ball from the referee's hands following United's League Cup exit in December earning him a six week suspension. In April this was compounded by outright disobedience when he became romantically involved with a married woman on the afternoon before an FA Cup semi-final against Leeds in April and then missed a sitter in the game.

Like the Fab Four themselves, George had matured to a point where cynicism had replaced joyful exuberance. No longer was he the shy and retiring Belfast lad, rather an increasingly wayward force frustrated at the direction of a team that was clearly on a downward spiral and there was nothing the new manager could do about it. As a result George would soon find solace in nocturnal pursuits, the beginning of a vicious circle which would play out until the player's inevitable retirement from the first class game in 1974.

RESPONSIBILITY WITHOUT POWER

G EORGE WAS FAR FROM McGuinness's only problem. The first indication of what to expect came before the first home game of the season. United faced Everton at Old Trafford and as supporters waited to see what the managerial change would bring, they would have had the opportunity to scan through their programme. Perhaps the manager's notes would give some kind of idea. Hopefully it would be something familiar. It was — but instead of their new manager, the newly-retired one maintained his own column.

"We are now at the start of another new season and I am very glad to welcome you all back to Old Trafford," were the authoritative words of Sir Matt. "As you know Wilf McGuinness has taken over the responsibility of team matters and team selection and he will have the full support of the Directors, players and staff. I feel sure he will do a very good job and that the standard of football will continue to be of a high quality. I know I can count upon the continuation of the wonderful support you have given to us for so long and this is the best way you can assist the players to achieve further success... In welcoming you all back to Old Trafford I know you will want to join me in wishing Everton and their supporters the very best of good fortune in 1969/70 as we look forward to a highly entertaining game tonight and one in keeping with standards set by our two clubs in previous meetings over so many years."

There was also a message from Chairman Louis Edwards. "We believe the changes will help to steer Manchester United towards further honours. With your continued support I am confident this will happen,"

Conspicuous by its absence was any comment from McGuinness himself. The closest we got was a column from Arthur Walmsley, sports reporter of *The Sun*. "Wilf McGuinness's first pronouncement regarding his immediate plan for the United team will have found a warm response in the minds of all serious Old Trafford supporters. When the Reds reported back for training new team coach Wilf said his aim was to harness the great individual talent in the side to a more integrated team plan. So right from the start I believe Wilf has gone to the heart of the matter of what accounted for United's inconsistency last season. There were, of course, the aggravations last season of serious injury to key players — few clubs in the First Division can have suffered so badly in that respect as United. But underlying all the misfortunes was a basic lack of team rhythm with success all too often dependent on the extempore brilliance of a dazzling solo run.

"The last thing one would wish is to see United degenerate into one of those well-drilled sides in which individual expression is totally suppressed into a team plan requiring almost robot obedience. It has been the essence of United's magic and magnetic attraction that their players of high individual skills have been given free rein of expression. It is unthinkable, for instance, that George Best should be brainwashed into playing a set piece role in the manner of less talented players. The same could be said of other United players. Thus the task that Wilf McGuinness has set himself is a much more subtle and difficult one than it would be with most other clubs. Indeed, if there were not a precedent for it one might seriously doubt if he could achieve it.

"Yet those of us who can remember the birth and maturing of the pre-Munich side know beyond doubt that it is possible. That side was abundant in individual ability — I have only to name Billy Whelan, Dennis Viollet, Eddie Colman, Duncan Edwards and Tommy Taylor to prove the point. Yet the great strength of that all-conquering team was its collective unity. Here was individual genius not suppressing itself into a colourless, mechanical whole, but imposing a self-discipline to employ individual ability not merely as a means of self-expression but to the greater cause and effect of the team.

"In short, the keynote was economy. Economy of solo dribbling, economy in passing — was there anything to surpass

Duncan Edwards bullet-like cross-field pass which switched play from one side of the field to the other in a flash? And coincidentally, an economy of effort which frequently left the side still fresh as daisies in the last half hour when the opposition was wilting. But because attack was always the motivating force there was nothing dull about the pre-Munich side. Indeed, its superlative efficiency at times was breathtaking and did not preclude exhibitions of dazzling ball artistry from such as Whelan and Colman. Thus we had the best of all worlds. I am sure the style of the pre-Munich team was not far from Wilf McGuinness's mind when he set himself his first objective with the present team."

Suggesting that McGuinness could have a United team playing the sort of football of the 1956/57 side was surely setting him up for a fall. Perhaps the most significant handicap in this regard was the instant marginalisation of Busby's assistant, Jimmy Murphy. After all, if anyone was responsible for the development of that magnificent side it was Murphy. The Welshman's control of the youth and reserve side had created a conveyor belt of talent that seemed as if it might never end before Munich's cruel intervention. The list of qualities Walmsley purred about were instilled by Murphy — economy and simplicity. Like Murphy, McGuinness had coached the reserves, but the similarities ended there. This is not a disservice to McGuinness; the events of February 1958 had a devastating effect on the infrastructure of the club. One of the biggest impacts was that United had to compromise their ideals in order to maintain their level of competitiveness. They could not afford another ten years of patience if they wanted to continue to succeed. It meant more big name signings, less autonomy, less control for the likes of Busby and Murphy. Yes, they bossed everything, but for Busby, he had to be eased in after convalescence, and for Murphy, he was almost exclusively with the first team while the reserves and youth sides were left to McGuinness and John Aston Sr. After Murphy had made good on his post-Munich promise to deliver another FA Youth Cup winning side, his work there was effectively done. Unlike Busby, Murphy was no less enthusiastic about the sport or the evolution of it. His greatest joy remained simply being on the training pitch with his players. Retirement for Busby meant the end of the line for Murphy as far as coaching was concerned. Though still contracted to the club, the Welshman was unsure of his obligations, instead retreating into a lesser role of scouting opposition teams and prospective new signings. The loss of Murphy's experience and knowledge on a day-to-day basis was perhaps even more crucial to United than Busby's retirement. McGuinness later wrote in defence of his decision to sideline his mentor "How could I be Jimmy's boss when he taught me everything I knew?"

The idea of an in-house appointment leading to a smooth transition was not borne out by logic. It would be unfair to compare McGuinness and Murphy but on face value, McGuinness had been reserve coach for a long enough time to command respect from the second string. And yet the form of the reserve side after news of Busby's retirement was made public left a lot to be desired. In the fourteen Central League games which followed the announcement, United failed to score on seven occasions.

Of course, the first team was blessed with extravagant attacking riches, and in McGuinness' first informal matches in charge of the club — the previously arranged (so beating the forthcoming ban) friendlies against a Welsh XI, a Copenhagen select team in Denmark, and FZ Zurich of Switzerland produced 2-0, 6-2 and 9-1 wins suggesting cause for optimism.

McGuinness' first official game in charge was a 2-2 draw at Crystal Palace. The most significant selection was that of Jimmy Rimmer, immediately getting the new boy off on the wrong foot with Alex Stepney. Rimmer was blameless as McGuinness lost his home bow against Everton (0-2) but there was some comfort in the knowledge that it was a defeat to a strong Everton side who would finish the season as champions. Less forgiveable was a 4-1 humbling to Southampton in front of 46,328 at Old Trafford three days later. The execution of the defeat revealed some painful naivety on behalf of the hosts; three times the Saints exposed Shay Brennan and three times their forward Ron Davies (who would also get the fourth goal) was able to outfox veteran Bill Foulkes to head home. Both defenders were in their thirties and if their errors were indicative of the need for replacement then the repetitive nature in which they were exposed suggested that McGuinness did not react quickly enough to resolve the issue during the 90 minutes.

He certainly reacted after the game. Rimmer, Brennan and Foulkes were all dropped. For the latter, it would prove to be his 688th and final appearance for the club. If these were bold yet understandable changes, the other casualties from the Southampton game made headline news. When Manchester United named their team to play Everton in the early return at Goodison Park, the names Bobby Charlton and Denis Law were absent. Unsurprisingly, United lost 3-0.

"Wilf's manner of telling players that they were dropped often rubbed them up the wrong way," Charlton said later, "the way he did it meant that he lost their confidence."

Others were more straightforward. As far as Willie Morgan was concerned, Charlton should have been the man picking the team! "You're following arguably the greatest manager of all time so that makes it difficult to start with," says Morgan. "Wilf was the wrong choice, I mean what Matt did at the time was revolutionary to appoint within a club, it was just Wilf was the wrong man, it should have been Bobby. Bobby Charlton would have been great I think... Wilf was antagonistic to everyone, he just wasn't the right person and that was the start of the downfall, I mean Wilf tried to change it drastically, he'd drop Bobby, he'd drop me, he dropped George, he dropped Denis and started bringing in a lot of the youth players who just weren't good enough at the time and that's how we got into so much trouble."

As if to underline the issues, United didn't score a goal for the rest of August, seeing the month out with consecutive goalless draws at Wolves and at home to Newcastle. Three points from six games represented a disastrous start. After the Everton game McGuinness had reacted quickly; this time to bolster the defence, making Ian Ure of Arsenal his first signing for £80,000. Ure is commonly used as an example of United's underwhelming recruitment in this period but the truth is that he was a player Busby had previously scouted and wanted to bring to the club. "This is no panic buy," Wilf told Nigel Clarke of the *Mirror*. "We have been after Ure for some time. It was a question of when he became available. We have not been influenced by our poor start to the season. This boy is a good player, he will do well for us."

Ure said, "I couldn't have gone to a better club if I had been able to take my pick. I am very flattered they have come for me." He later admitted that he couldn't believe they'd even approached Arsenal. At 31 the Scot had a questionable injury record and his arrival coincided with clean sheets against Wolves and Newcastle but United were hardly convincing. Then there were rumours circulating Manchester that McGuinness and Murphy actually wanted Spurs Welsh centre-half Mike England as Foulkes replacement but had been countermanded by Busby.

On November 15th United were beaten heavily in the Manchester derby 4-0. Their form had generally stabilised (that was only their third defeat since the Goodison Park drubbing) but the problems were already obvious. McGuinness seemed to have endless issues with his forward players and some of them of his own making. He and Charlton had been good friends for years and it seemed to some as if he had tried to show him who was boss by dropping him. Though he later admitted it was a mistake, the relationship further deteriorated following an incident between the pair on the training pitch when McGuinness ordered Charlton to do twenty press-ups for having his hands in his pockets as he listened to a team talk. Given that Bobby had already changed after training to go to a prior engagement in London; the club captain felt embarrassed by the order, although he did as McGuinness requested. In years gone by the story has reflected more embarrassingly on the new manager.

"It showed an appalling lack of judgement on McGuinness's part," recalled Alex Stepney. "Of course no one at a football club likes to see fit young men lounging around with their hands in their pockets. But Bobby was wearing a suit, it was raining and he was entitled to feel particularly angry at being ridiculed in this way… But Bobby, new suit and all, got down and compounded the farce by doing his twenty press-ups. He finished with his shoes and hands covered in mud. I felt that Wilf was completely in the wrong even to ask Bobby, and that Bobby was equally foolish to carry out the instruction. Wilf should have ignored this particular situation. He was very fortunate indeed that it was Bobby and not one of the less docile members of the team he chose to pick on."

Willie Morgan recalls the event, "We were down at the Cliff, in the pouring rain and thick mud, and Bobby had done some training and gone back in, got a bath, got dressed with his suit on and Wilf asked Bobby if he could come back out in the middle of the pitch in the rain and of course it was freezing, Bobby put his hands in his pocket and we used to do this stupid thing, where if we were caught with your hands in your tracksuit, you had to do ten press ups and he made Bobby do ten press ups."

Another forward seeing his playing time cut was Brian Kidd. He was dropped as United secured a morale-boosting 4-1 win at Anfield and when he was only named as a substitute for the League Cup semi-final second leg against Manchester City, he dropped a pre-Christmas bombshell in the press. "I have had as much as I can take, and a letter to the club asking for a move has gone in the post tonight," Kidd told the *Daily Mirror*. "I was on the verge of a transfer request after the way I was dropped last month and then I decided to wait and give it a bit more time. But things haven't really improved and I knew before Wednesday's match that this was going to be my decision. My mind was made up when I was told I wouldn't be needed for the team's most important game so far this season. I was terribly disappointed. It was my worst moment in football. I was fit and I wasn't needed. It wasn't the first time I had sensed it, but suddenly it all welled up and I realised I would have to start looking for my footballing future away from Old Trafford."

It was a further headache to compound McGuinness' woes. United drew 0-0, which meant they were eliminated due to their first leg 2-1 defeat. At the end of the game George Best approached referee Jack Taylor to complain about his booking in the match. Taylor was carrying the match ball and Best knocked it out of his hands. The forward was subsequently fined £100 and banned for four weeks.

At least the Kidd situation was resolved quickly. Four days after his transfer request, all was well. 'The magic touch of Sir Matt Busby made it a happier Christmas for Manchester United star Brian Kidd yesterday," reported Bob Russell of the *Mirror*. "Kidd, who asked for a transfer last week, emerged from a half-hour talk with United general manager Sir Matt and team boss Wilf McGuinness to say: 'I'll be staying at Old Trafford. Sir Matt and Wilf have made me see things in a different light, and for that I am very grateful to them.'"

Later that season, Kidd was at the heart of the selection debate as United tackled their second semi final of the season; they got to that stage of the FA Cup, where they faced Leeds United. The first game at Hillsborough ended goalless on 14th March. Denis Law had been absent with a knee injury but returned to play against Burnley and Chelsea in the league, declaring himself fit for the replay at Villa Park. "It is a long time since I felt so happy with my fitness. The knee isn't giving me any trouble and I am enjoying playing," Law said.

A 'First Division scout' told the *Daily Mirror*'s Ken Jones: "The main thing about Law today is that he looked interested." Jones reported: "The scout might have found the key to a situation which will give Manchester United area for thought when they sit down to sort out their line up. Is Law interested enough to play an influential part in a semi-final that will be won and lost by lightning reaction to a half or quarter chance? His contribution at Chelsea was sporadic, but there was an air of commitment about him that has rarely shown itself over the past two seasons. If there is any value in statistical evidence then it is worth pointing out that Law challenged for the ball twenty times and only just came out second best in a personal duel with Chelsea centre half John Dempsey."

Law was a substitute as Kidd was preferred (he would be substitute again in the second replay, which was finally settled in Leeds' favour four days afterwards). It was a blow for the Scot who wasted little time in airing his grievances. McGuinness had his hands full, though, and his main headache on the day of the game at Villa Park was George Best. Having returned from suspension with that famous six goal haul in United's 8-2 win at Northampton Town, on the afternoon of the game at Burnden Park Best was found in the room of a girl in the team's hotel and McGuinness was livid; Best protested his innocence, saying nothing had happened — the girl was married, and he was getting her phone number, was his explanation — but he was so frustrated with his manager's attitude that he went back and slept with the girl anyway. When he went down to join the team, McGuinness threatened to send him home, but Matt Busby intervened and said they would sort it out back in Manchester. Best, by his own admission, had a stinker in the game, and word had clearly got out about the incident as he was taunted by the Leeds players and fans. Stepney was among the United players who felt Best should have been dropped, saying McGuinness would "have had everybody's respect and understanding, but he behaved like an ostrich, and that was diabolical."

Manchester United's first full season post-Busby had been bumpy to say the least. Perhaps the footballing climate was a little more generous in those days but two semi-finals in the domestic cups suggested that there was hope of progress despite the eighth place finish in the league. Even that represented an improvement on Busby's last season, where United finished eleventh. The rocky start and the travails with certain big names were thought an expected part of the transition.

Yet McGuinness was not being helped as much as he might have liked. Before transfer deadline day, he made an enquiry for Southampton's Ron Davies but when he was given a quote of £200,000 (the price paid by Tottenham Hotspur the previous month to break the British transfer record when they signed Martin Peters from West Ham), the United board put an end to negotiations. Davies would later sign for United but by that point many clubs had learned how to deal with his aerial prowess and his spell at Old Trafford was decidedly poor.

It was a similar story for names who would go on to have

successful careers. United desperately needed a new full back and centre half and McGuinness wanted Mick Mills and Colin Todd of Ipswich and Sunderland respectively. He also admired Malcolm Macdonald of Luton Town. Not for the first time, a United manager succeeding Matt Busby would claim they were not backed in the transfer market. Beyond the process of acclimatisation one only has to look at the record of those three names to conclude that they would have given United a boost in crucial areas.

In public McGuinness couldn't complain about the support he was given. In the summer of 1970 he was officially given the title of team manager (having been appointed with the sketchy moniker of chief coach and future manager) which would have given him the security of future planning, even if he was frustrated in his attempts to bring in reinforcements. That said, even the announcement of McGuinness' transition was handled badly by Busby. Nigel Clarke of *The Mirror* reported: "Busby hinted at a shift in backroom power when he said he might well be going back into the dressing room from time to time to handle the team. He added: 'There could be occasions when I will be helping in the handling of the team during the match. I shall see how things go. For the moment Wilf will continue as coach.'" It had been expected that McGuinness would be given sole charge, swapping the title of coach for title of team manager.

It may not have been his intention — it almost certainly wasn't — but reading Busby's comments it is inescapable to conclude anything other than that McGuinness was being undermined. The subtext in there was that so long as the major players weren't upset, McGuinness was free to select who he wanted. Which was all well and good, but there was never any respite for the chief coach/ future manager/team manager from the issues he had with the senior players. As McGuinness prepared his failed bid for Davies at the end of the 1969/70 season, it was hoped that the move would be partly funded by the outgoing transfer of Denis Law, who was put on the transfer list on April 7, 1970. "I will go anywhere," was the headline Frank Taylor reported for *The Mirror*, with the headline given the lead of "Sir Matt Busby puts his 'Great player' up for sale at £60,000".

"I wouldn't hesitate to come South if the right offer came along," Law said. "Naturally, I'm a bit upset to be leaving United after so many wonderful seasons. But I was half-prepped for this move last Friday after I'd had a chat with the boss, Sir Matt Busby. I had an inkling then something was in the wind."

Law rubbished rumours of retirement. "I believe I've got a few years of this class of football left in me. I have many friends in Manchester but in football you've got to go where the job is. If and when I sign for anyone, they will know that they are getting a player who will give his utmost and who has no injury snags."

Busby added "We feel it will be in his best interests to move on. He has had a lot of injury worries in the last two seasons — we think it will be better for him to have a fresh start elsewhere. He is still a great player."

Forthcoming events would only serve to further undermine McGuinness's position but it is easy to see that the players were losing respect for the man who was ostensibly in charge, as noted by Law's reference to Busby as 'boss'.

United's semi-final defeat to Leeds meant they qualified for an end of season game against Watford in an FA Cup third place play-off game to be played at Arsenal's Highbury Stadium on the eve of the final. A few days before the game, Alex Stepney asked if he could travel down to London on Thursday, instead of on Friday with the rest of the team. McGuinness refused without discussion and Stepney then went to see Matt Busby and ask for his permission instead (something Stepney admitted was a mistake on reflection). Busby said he would sort it out; McGuinness then later approached Stepney and said "You can go to London on Thursday. But don't you ever do that again. Don't you ever go behind my back like that." Stepney said 'things were never the same' between he and McGuinness after this incident.

He was, however, named as first choice goalkeeper going into the 1970-71 season. Yet the club endured just as poor a start as the previous campaign losing at home to Leeds on the first day, drawing 0-0 at home to Chelsea and then losing 4-0 at Arsenal, a game in which Stepney injured his shoulder. On 19th September 1970 Stepney played against Coventry City in the reserves as he came back from injury. The following Saturday he believed he was being recalled to the first team as he had been told to report to Old Trafford on the morning of the first team's game against Blackpool. When he arrived McGuinness asked Stepney to go with the reserve team to Sheffield United. In an attempt to placate the Londoner, McGuinness reassured him that he was still his 'first team goalkeeper'. Stepney asked if that was the case, why was he not in the first team. "You are my first-team goalkeeper playing in the reserves today," McGuinness told him. In reply, Stepney told his manager that he could expect a transfer request to be submitted on the Monday morning. For the remainder of this managerial reign, Stepney played reserve team football.

Looking back at the events in 2018, Stepney recalls that a request to leave the club at the time was turned down, leaving him feeling the writing was on the wall. "I knew the situation with Wilf and at that time I asked for a transfer, I was out for six weeks, and of course you know that was the opportune time for Wilf to bring in his goalkeeper that he'd brought up through the ranks in Jimmy Rimmer," Stepney says. "I still wanted to be playing in top class football, I didn't wanna be playing in the reserves and knowing the situation between me and the manager, I thought it was best to put in a transfer request — straight away the club turned it down, so then you realise, deep down you're still wanted."

At least McGuinness, having failed to buy a striker, could count on Denis Law, who made his own return from injury in the Arsenal game after being taken off the transfer list. That announcement had been made — by Busby, of course — on the same day of McGuinness' 'promotion' confirmation. "Denis has trained throughout the summer, and there is no doubt that at long last he is back to peak fitness," said Busby. "As things stand now he is wanted at Old Trafford and will be needed for the start of the season to play a major role."

Law was back in the team for a month before having another month out with injury. Meanwhile United, whose own expectations had been tempered to accept mid-table football while the turbulence of transition cleared, were now facing the full consequence of failing to strengthen their side. McGuinness picked reserve players he trusted but who were simply not good enough to make the grade for long term careers at the club. Most of these had to play in defence due to United's failure to recruit there. Although the great Bobby Charlton was still trying at 33, George Best by his own admission had lost interest when the team weren't playing well. With an uncertain goalkeeping situation, a substandard defence, and a forward line that was inconsistent in terms of availability and application, playing against opposition who knew how to press the buttons of these players who were so easily triggered, McGuinness had a multitude of issues.

"The United players of the time had become used to Matt Busby," recalls journalist and author Paddy Barclay. "One of the greatest managers in the history of football and one of the most charismatic characters. He then sort of kicked himself upstairs and brought in Wilf McGuinness. And people have said with Matt, 'well everyone knows his great things, rebuilding the club after the Munich Air crash and so on, the great things that he did'. Everybody knows the great things he did, but everyone says the worst thing he did was arrange his own succession, in that he brought in Wilf McGuinness. The problem was that there was a group of great players, and Wilf was a good player but he wasn't Denis Law, he wasn't Bobby Charlton, he wasn't George Best... the idea was they would be coached by Wilf McGuinness while Matt had a general administrative role. But Matt was still the boss, those players weren't going to stop calling Matt the boss. When they were dropped — as they rightly were, they had to be phased out — there was a rebellion against Wilf. And he actually did reasonably well to get to three semi-finals. But it was never going to work, the players, they hung Wilf McGuinness out to dry. He was very badly treated by the senior players. There's no worse enemy in senior football than a senior player who can see the end and doesn't want to face it."

Pat Crerand agrees. "I think Wilf's problem when he became manager of Manchester United, Wilf had known all the players since he was a player and I think he found that very difficult. I mean he played with Bobby Charlton for a few years… it must be a problem if you're managing and you've got players that grew up as your best pals, and a great friend of yours, and you've got to have a go, you've got to speak to him to get a link between them. I think that was an impossible job for Wilf, he would have been better probably going somewhere else and then coming back."

After a 1-0 defeat to Southampton on 21st November United slipped to fourteen in the table. However McGuinness had led United to another League Cup semi-final, due to be played against Aston Villa a few weeks later. Before the first leg United lost the Manchester derby 4-1. It was another demoralising display at Old Trafford which became headline news because George Best broke the leg of City player Glyn Pardoe. United drew the first leg with Villa 1-1 and then played Arsenal at Old Trafford in the league. In the programme for the game it was notable that Busby was still writing his programme notes in which he focussed on stressing Best wasn't that sort of person and condemning the press's overreaction.

Best himself felt that there was now some persecution against him from the newspapers, and had felt that way for the better part of the year. He said of his return against Northampton in the early part of 1970: "It was interesting that the press, who'd always been gushing about my feats before, now put a negative slant even on my outstanding football feats. One paper carried the headline 'SIX OF THE BEST ON BAD BOY'S RETURN'."

Some criticism, however, was fair. With the entire world knowing what Best could do when he fancied it, a return of just seven goals by mid-December was hardly representative of the player at his physical peak. The Arsenal game was not one of his better afternoons, with United's 3-1 home defeat plunging them to an embarrassing eighteenth going into Christmas.

Two days before Christmas 1970 United visited Birmingham for the return leg of the League Cup semi-final against Third Division Villa, having drawn the first leg 1-1. Brian Kidd scored to give United a one goal lead on the night and on aggregate but Villa levelled before half-time before Pat McMahon scored in the

78th minute for the hosts and United — despite having recalled Pat Crerand and Willie Morgan, and boasting Best, Law, Kidd and Charlton in their line-up, were eliminated at the semi-final stage for a third successive time in domestic cups.

All in all it suggested an unlucky run for McGuinness. He would have felt heartened by the continued support for the team, as United — normally — continued to get great attendances. In January 1970 sports reporter Ken Jones wrote about a sell-out game at Upton Park: "It would seem that Leeds, with a clear nomination as favourites in three major competitions, have no reason for envy. And yet, on the day when they returned to lead the First Division, they found themselves coveting the appeal of Manchester United. West Ham's gates were closed on Saturday on a post-war record crowd of 41,643. Even allowing for the attraction of a home debut by £90,000 Peter Eustace, it was still a remarkable tribute to United's reputation."

The game against Arsenal was played on the last Saturday before Christmas and perhaps that accounted for the crowd being a miserable 33,183 which was 12,000 or so below the average for the season. United's Jekyll and Hyde form reappeared on Boxing Day at Derby County's Baseball Ground. United recovered from conceding in the third minute to lead 3-1 by the fourteenth; Derby turned it around again to lead 4-3, before Brian Kidd's late equaliser earned a thrilling draw.

Yet if anything, it gave a worrying insight into how distant United were from their best under McGuinness. Even with Best and Law turning on the style, there were still unresolved issues in defence. This was the fourth time in 1970-71 that United had conceded four goals. If McGuinness could fairly argue that the defenders simply weren't up to the job, there was also enough evidence to suggest that the manager hadn't really shown any capability so far in improving the players he had.

There never came a time when his relationship with the star names settled; even right at the last, Best failed to turn up for training on Christmas Day as he was hungover. He reported for the game the following day and McGuinness was intent on sending him home, but once more Busby stepped in saying Best would play but would be fined £50. It may well have been the case that McGuinness had done the best he could with the cards he had been dealt. It could be said that this was one undermining in front of the players too far. How could they respect him?

Outside of the club, it was clear that others were well aware of difficult days ahead. Derby manager Brian Clough was asked if he thought United's fantastic football, particularly in the first half, was a sign that they were on the road to better times.

"Anyone who believes that Manchester United's revival is on because of this result sees more into the game than I do," Old Big 'Ead pronounced, "I think that anyone who feels a revival is due just because of this draw is talking a load of rubbish. Let's face it, we both have our problems. But most of Derby's problems are eased by the fact that we have more players under the age of 25. Two or three new players could make a big difference for Derby, but I wouldn't like to say how many new players United need."

Representing United to the press afterwards was Busby. "There is no easy game for United, and we wouldn't have it any other way," he said. Alan Williams of the *Daily Express* said of that statement: "It is equally true that there is never a dull game with United. And Soccer is all the richer for it."

On 29th December 1970 Wilf McGuinness was relieved of his duties as Manchester United Team Manager. He was demoted to reserve team manager rather than sacked which could perhaps be seen as one final act of killing with kindness. For in truth McGuinness had never been manager of Manchester United, he had merely been the unwilling participant in an experiment by Sir Matt Busby to retain control of footballing affairs without doing all the hard graft, such as taking training, deciding tactics and giving team talks, that was the bread and butter of the job.

It was a flawed plan that ended with Busby regaining the official title of team manager which he had never, in truth, actually relinquished.

CATCHING LIGHTNING

" I SEE MY TASK THIS MORNING very simply, very clearly," Sir Matt Busby told the *Daily Express*. "I have to make Manchester United look like Manchester United again, a team who play football not only because they get paid for it but because they love it and their personalities demand that they play it a certain way. This is no reflection on Wilf McGuinness. I feel for him deeply this morning. I can understand the bitter disappointment he feels, and he can be assured that the directors and myself believe his contribution to the club is far from over. I know also that the football world has its eyes on Manchester United and Matt Busby now. There will be questions like: 'What will Busby do now?' 'How can he win?' I have some clear answers to these questions. I know I cannot win personally, and I can say this no longer concerns me. There is only one issue now, and that is Manchester United. For myself the limit of ambition now is that in the next few months the players begin to play again. That the mood of the club is changed and is bright again when a new man comes in this summer.

"There must be a minimum requirement for this new man. He will have to bring into the club a certain level of experience, certain personal success. It may be that he will not be a man who has won a great list of trophies, but he must have had some years in command. He must bring from outside his own aura, his own strength. When I say that I cannot win, I mean that I can no longer think in terms of building new teams, of seeing myself involved for more than a caretaker period. But this does not disturb me. I do not want any more medals. I've had more than 23 years in the mad, mad world of football. I've won, I've lost, I've suffered, and I've celebrated. I've drunk my fill of that wine. If I have built my managerial career on anything it may be an ability to make players feel food, feel important. And I'm hoping that this gift has not left me. It will be needed so much now. Obviously the confidence of the lads is down. My "come-back" leads me straight into this key problem, and it will be one I will be attacking this morning. It is going to be one of the great challenges of my career. I have to be honest and say that it is a formidable, worrying one. But I am going into it with one great conviction - I still believe in Manchester United."

An *Express* report on the same day said that the new manager of Manchester United would have a salary of £10,000 and 'the freedom to spend heavily in the transfer market'. Three names were apparently on the short list — Frank O'Farrell, Huddersfield boss (and former United defender) Ian Greaves, and Brian Clough. Don Revie, Bill McGarry, Noel Cantwell, Jimmy Adamson and Dave Sexton were linked, while Jock Stein and Tommy Docherty were also mentioned.

Once again Revie was first to rule himself out of the running writing in the *Yorkshire Evening Post,* "I expect loyalty from the Leeds United playing and administrative staff — and they expect loyalty from me in return. That is why I am not interested in becoming manager of Manchester United."

United were not to be rushed into making a new appointment, just as they hadn't been two years prior. Indeed, they were still uncertain just who would take the hot seat as late as April 28th 1970. That was the date of Leeds United's Fairs Cup game with Liverpool at Elland Road. Busby was in attendance but not to convince Revie; instead he was with Jock Stein. Tempted by a move to England, negotiations with the Celtic boss stalled on Busby's request that several club staff be retained, while Stein was insistent that he should bring in his own men, and after returning to Scotland and consulting his family, he decided to remain at Parkhead.

Busby's loyalty to the current staff at the club may seem surprising considering how McGuinness must have felt, but Wilf himself admitted, "I think it hurt him to tell me" about the sacking.

"I think you could draw parallels with Sir Alex Ferguson, it's after the Lord Mayor's parade isn't it, you cannot follow somebody like that, it's almost impossible," says club statistician Cliff Butler. "David Moyes proved that; it's the worst job to take when you're following somebody who is so huge. Ferguson and Busby are Gods in Manchester so I think Wilf was on a hiding to nothing and one of the problems I think was that he was a contemporary for some of the players so I think it would have been hard for to give them orders, to tell one of them you're not playing on Saturday and as much as you're all mates you know, it can affect things."

Back at United, the mood among the players who had caused McGuinness so many headaches was generally that the right decision had been taken. "If Wilf had come to the club as a complete outsider things might have been different, but he was always on a collision course with the many powerful personalities in the first-team dressing-room," Alex Stepney admits now. "He was too well known by people in and out of the club. All his little frailties were exposed and multiplied… it seemed that he wanted to hide. In the end he was even hiding from the Press, which is something no Manchester United manager is allowed to do. United is a vast organisation, constantly in the news, and managers are under fiendish pressure. They need to be football coaches, philosophers, diplomats, public relations men and entertainers all at the same time, in a job that consumes its incumbents twenty-four hours a day, seven days a week. Wilf, in my opinion, was not up to it. I am satisfied that the senior players gave him their full support, certainly at the outset, although I know that my own feelings towards him were never quite the same after that incident over the London trip."

Busby's first games back in charge were the FA Cup 3rd round tie against Middlesbrough and the replay after a 0-0 draw at Old Trafford. Boro won 2-1 at Ayresome Park ending United's last chance of silverware for the season. Nobody thought it was a realistic proposition that this side could put together a run of form that would secure European football for the next season, even with Busby back. Too much had changed, or perhaps too little…

"With no immediate replacement for Wilf, Sir Matt returned as manager, but none of us believed that it could ever be the same as before," George Best said. "The team was too much in decline and we all just hoped that the club could get a big-name man in before too long. I never thought of leaving because I'd had such great times at United and couldn't imagine playing for anyone else. But when Jimmy Murphy was pushed into a scouting role in 1971, it really did seem like the end of an era."

Compare that to Stepney's recollection of Busby's first league game back in charge, against Chelsea at Stamford Bridge, and you might well notice the difference in mood of a player happy to be recalled to the first eleven. "When he (Busby) strode back into the dressing-room at Stamford Bridge for his first game back, having restored me to the team as one of his first moves, the atmosphere changed," the goalkeeper said. "The lads wanted to go out and die for him and the club once more. We played with all the old fervour and won 2-1. It seemed that the vintage Manchester United show had hit the road again."

That familiarity would have been reassuring after the more problematic recurring issue of Best's unpredictability in the lead up to the game at Stamford Bridge. Best had been given a suspended six-week ban for the Pardoe incident in the Manchester City game before Christmas and had taken it badly. He had attended the hearing with Busby and was hungover. In the elevator afterwards he threw up. Best said he felt like a 'baby with his dad' and admitted his diminished interest in playing. He didn't turn up for training the rest of the week and missed the train to London for the game with Chelsea with the team; however he caught a later one and instead went to spend the weekend with Irish actress Sinead Cusack.

Busby told reporters Best was dropped as he made his way to London. "Obviously, serious disciplinary action will now have to be taken against Best," he told Steve Curry of *The Express*. "Naturally I'm very upset about this. It is something we don't want at a time when the club needs all shoulders to the wheel. This is not the first time this has happened. When we played Tottenham in December he missed the train, though he was at the barrier as it pulled out. That time we gave him the benefit of the doubt. It could happen to any of us. But then he missed the train on Monday and again today. He has not been doing it on the field for us lately. I don't know what's wrong with him. We encourage him to discuss any problems with us. Perhaps he is bottling everything up inside. It may be that his life outside football has got something to do with it. Whatever it is he is being a very silly boy. The unfathomable thing is that when he does train he is as eager and enthusiastic as anybody in the club. He's a good trainer. On Thursday he was full of himself. But obviously the directors will want to know the full story on Monday and disciplinary action will be taken."

The manager was asked if the matter was serious enough to threaten the forward's career at the club. "I can't comment on that at this stage," Busby said, before elaborating, "I think it best that I save what I have to say for George. The sooner we get to the bottom of this affair the better. My office door will be open to him tomorrow morning. We have plenty to talk about."

Manchester City boss Joe Mercer told the press that he felt United were culpable. "The events of the last few days do not do credit to George Best," he said, "but it shouldn't be ignored that the club must also carry a share of responsibility. It is within their powers of control that… the train (was) missed."

"It's hard for me even to explain what state of mind I was in to do such a thing," Best admitted in his autobiography 'Blessed'. "I just felt that the whole world was on top of me and when I woke up that mid-morning and realised I'd missed the train, I didn't think that it was worth bothering. If I'd been thinking clearly, I might have been able to catch a later train to get me there in time but I convinced myself I wouldn't make it and told myself that even if I got down there, I'd only get a rollocking from the Boss, who probably wouldn't play me anyway. I had phoned Sinead earlier in the week to arrange to see her after the match so I saw no reason not to go through with that part of my plans. I didn't think it would be such a big deal. But once the press found out I wasn't playing and realised that I was with Sinead, a quiet weekend in North London became more like the Siege of Sydney Street."

Such was Best's fame by now that the press pack surrounded the actress's Islington flat on Saturday evening. George took his time to return to Manchester, knowing an exasperated Busby would be waiting but not pressing. "To most people Matt was portrayed as the great father figure, but to me he was more like a headmaster," Best said. "Yes, he'd given me the odd pep talk and tried to keep me on the straight and narrow but that was more in the interests of the club and how he perceived its image. He certainly would have thought it undignified to make any direct contact with me or to appeal to me through TV. He would no doubt have seen that as a sign of weakness, both on a personal level and as the head of a club like Manchester United. Sir Matt just let the situation blow over and waited for me to return in my own good time, as I always had. And when I got back to Manchester, he didn't sit me down for a chat and ask why I was behaving the way I was. He just called me in and told me he was suspending me for two weeks. I don't know whether he had given up on me or just couldn't understand me... United had never had to deal with a star football player before and Sir Matt had little idea of how to handle me or what was happening around me. Willingly or not, I represented a generation that was alien to him. In that sense, he would have been more like a grandfather figure than a parental one." On the football, Busby was at least pleased with how United played in their star man's absence. "This victory against Chelsea was our best performance for some months," he said.

Reporting on the match for *The Express*, Norman Giller said he had been approached by some of Best's teammates anonymously who made the following comments:

"We won because George wasn't there to hog the ball. He has been handicapping us this season by holding it too long."

"I can't see the Boss changing this winning team. Best has mucked the Boss about too much. Now he has got to take his punishment."

"George has my sympathy because of the tremendous pressure he has been under. He has sickened everybody by the way he has treated the Boss this week."

"We played this one for Matt. I think we were all a bit shocked at the way George has treated the Boss in a week that was so vital for him."

On January 13th, Best told the press "I was wrong… It is a private and personal problem. The only person I could tell about it was the boss. I won't tell anyone else." Busby emerged from a board meeting insisting there would be a clean slate. "We have settled it amicably," he told journalists. "We are starting from scratch."

On January 22nd, Busby was speaking at a Dublin lunch and the incident had done nothing to influence his praise for the winger. "Best is endowed with greater talent than any player I have ever seen," he said.

The winger would be missing for United's first home league game in Busby's second reign. Although he had never really given up his role of addressing supporters in the match programme, this time around he did at least talk about the events of the last few weeks.

"I knew it was not going to be easy taking over team command again, and this is certainly the way it worked out," he wrote, "we seem to have run into one crisis after another. One thing I would like to make clear at the start is that my motives for agreeing to take over control of the playing side again must not be interpreted as a reflection on the coaching abilities of Wilf McGuinness. It was a simply a matter of how best to meet a number of difficult situations that were building up and it was felt that for the good of Manchester United, my experience would stand us in better stead… It came as a pleasant surprise to find that the trip to Chelsea brought us not only a very good result but a most encouraging performance. I say it was a surprise because I had been prepared for the worst after a period when everything seemed to be going wrong. But I must say I was not greatly surprised to see Manchester United playing again, for despite all the people who seem to be writing us off as completely finished, we have not reached the end of the road by a long chalk. We have some good players at Old Trafford, and some good youngsters on the way up. It's true the team have been suffering from a lack of confidence, but the win at Chelsea may go a long way towards taking care of that problem. When I saw Alan Hudson score the first goal completely against the run of play I thought the pattern of things going wrong was about to continue and that it might prove a crushing blow. But in fact the lads tried all the harder and eventually got the goals their play deserved. Their spirit impressed me… and while the spirit is right we need not fear the future. It was a win in the real United manner, a win through football. The boys all wanted the ball and it was our best performance in a long while. Now we must aim to keep that football flowing against Burnley our visitors to Old Trafford this afternoon."

When Best did come back into the side there were a few familiar faces, victims from the McGuinness axe; Stepney, of course, and also Willie Morgan, Pat Crerand and Alan Gowling. The latter scored four in a 5-1 thrashing of Southampton at Old Trafford but a gate of just over 36,000 suggested not even the return of a legendary manager could get the interest back into a season that was going nowhere. That disinterest seemed to get through to the players — their run of form following that Southampton win included six defeats in eleven games.

Best was cleared at an inquest to determine if he had deliberately broken Pardoe's leg and for a short while there seemed to be the hint that he might have found the inspiration to improve this indifferent team in the way only he could, hitting a run of five goals in four consecutive games. In fact, with 22 goals in all competitions — his fourth consecutive tally above twenty — one would think his contribution couldn't be questioned at all, although that idea would quickly be countered by the poser of what he might be able to achieve both personally and for the team if he truly applied himself.

One player who wasn't willing to wait was Brian Kidd, who, on 17th April, declared once more that he wanted to leave the club. "My face doesn't fit with Sir Matt Busby and I will again ask for a transfer," he told the press. "The club can expect my written request to arrive on Monday. I want to leave Manchester United as quickly as possible so that I can get all the travel and moving to a new place over with and be settled with a new club before the start of next season. I've been completely slung out after one and a half games. I don't know whether this was supposed to make me feel sick to the teeth and sorry for myself, but I just want to move."

He clearly had no interest in who United were going to name as Busby's second successor. In March Noel Cantwell was named as favourite with the bookmakers. Although it was never implicitly stated, with the club's staff largely the same, one could imagine that the opposition to hiring Cantwell, and the reasons for it, remained. United didn't comment, and as the weeks passed it was presumed that this rumour was wide of the mark.

It took until 27th April for the press to strongly link Frank O'Farrell to the job. Having just led Leicester City to promotion, *The Express* said the achievement "could very well have clinched the job" for the Cork man.

By that point United had just concluded their home league programme, wrapping up with a 3-2 win over Ipswich Town. For the final time in his role as manager, Busby used his programme notes to speak to supporters. "I know I was very conscious of the fact that our game at Crystal Palace last weekend was my last visit to London as team manager, and not unnaturally I wanted to finish on a high note, perhaps even a game to remember," he said. "When we were two goals down after only 25 minutes play I began to think it would be a game to remember all right... for all the wrong reasons! Happily we pulled round and on the way towards finishing 5-3 winners showed the flair that I have always tried to make a special part of Manchester United. I have aimed for this because I believe this is not only the kind of football that in the long run achieves success but is the way the spectators want to see the game played. The team did not disappoint me against Palace; in fact they managed to cram into one game just about all the emotions of football ranging from despair to elation. It was an accurate reflection of my four months back in charge of team affairs. First, we had that extremely encouraging run of good League results which lifted us to a respectable place in the First Division and gave us thoughts of Europe again in the Fairs Cup, then came a disappointing Easter which set us back and was a blow to our ambitions. But that of course is what football is all about and I have had 25 years of the emotional stress that this way of life involves. It is the reason why I am ready to make way for a younger man to come and take charge of the team this summer and I wish him well. But as I step aside once more, I shall always cherish the memory of the outstanding flair that I like to associate with Manchester United and which the players showed me so convincingly on my last trip to London as team manager."

Busby's was ever the calming voice, betraying the truth that United were struggling to name a replacement. O'Farrell may have emerged as flavour of the month but, as noted, just days later, United's 'godfather' was sitting in an East Lancashire motorway petrol station trying his best to convince Jock Stein to take the job. Perhaps that suggests that Stein had been first choice for months. The only choice, perhaps. But weeks later after the curtain finally fell on the Busby reign with an entertaining 4-3 win at Manchester City, United's supporters were no closer to knowing the identity of their next coach.

On 19th May, the Leicester City manager made public his intention to remain at Filbert Street. "I feel it necessary to avoid further speculation about my future," he declared. "It is only fair to people both inside and outside the club that my intentions should be known. There are still some details to be settled regarding the new contract but I have told the chairman that my intentions are to stay. We have done a lot of hard work in the last two years and there is still a lot more to be done."

Over the following week a new favourite emerged, Chelsea's Dave Sexton. But as the Blues prepared for their post-season tour, their chairman Brian Mears said, "I shall be making a statement about Dave Sexton's position at Chelsea tomorrow before we leave for America."

The *Daily Mirror* interpreted that statement as confirmation that Sexton would remain in London. "If Dave had been definitely going to Old Trafford, then surely the Chelsea chairman would have said so and ended all conjecture," stated their report. "The fact that he is waiting until the moment the team leaves indicates he first wants United to know the news. What better time could there be for announcing that Sexton is staying than when his team is boarding an airplane for the USA. Certainly Sexton must have been on the brink of moving for some days. I can now reveal that Mr. Edwards missed United's tour of Germany in the hope that he could clinch a Sexton move to Manchester."

Having failed in their private pursuit of Jock Stein and their more public chase for Sexton, it was time for United to test Frank O'Farrell's resolve when it came to honouring his words. It would be third time lucky in early June as the situation was finally resolved; but O'Farrell would quickly discover that luck was only one factor he would need to count on in order to succeed.

A FALSE DAWN

STOP ME IF YOU'VE HEARD THIS ONE BEFORE... a manager with a fine record at a smaller club is given the task of succeeding one of the greatest managers in football history at Manchester United. For David Moyes read Frank O'Farrell.

On June 9th, 1971, it was announced that the Irishman would become Manchester United manager and Sir Matt Busby would move 'upstairs' to become a club director. Again, Martin Edwards, by then a director at the club, says the decision was taken by Busby himself. "Frank had been at Leicester City, he had been in the final of the FA Cup against Manchester City and he was doing a good job at Leicester, he was a young manager, part of the West Ham fold. A lot of managers had come out from the 'West Ham academy' and I think Matt just felt Frank O'Farrell was a young ambitious manager who was going to be successful in the future, hence the appointment."

"I'm taking over at Old Trafford on July 1," O'Farrell told the *Daily Mirror*. "I've been given the assurance that I shall be in complete control as manager there. I shall be manager in every sense of the word. Sir Matt Busby will be a director but that will make no difference to my job. My contract with Leicester ends this month and I was determined that I should see that contract out. The experience at Leicester has been a tremendous help. After all, taking a club through to the FA Cup Final in the first season and then being relegated immediately afterwards is something for a manager to face. Now Leicester are back in the First Division. I'm delighted about that and naturally am sorry to be leaving. But to get the opportunity of taking over a famous club like Manchester United is something I simply couldn't turn down."

This time Busby's comments to the press were the sub-plot rather than the main event. "I'm very glad the position has been resolved, and I'm very happy with the appointment," he stated. "I feel Mr. O'Farrell will do a first class job and given time will bring future honours to the club."

In fact, in the summer of 1971 you could barely stop O'Farrell from talking which, considering the reputation which would follow, was something of an irony. It all seemed positive when he said he was intimidated by the Busby shaped shadow that loomed over the Old Trafford hot seat. Far from it, he intended to embrace the challenge. The issue with talking the talk is that people expect you to walk the walk. O'Farrell was very talkative before his official work at the club had begun, helped by his good relationship with the *Daily Mirror*.

On 10th June he told them "I want to carry on in the Busby style. I aim to continue Manchester United's tradition as one of the brightest and most entertaining teams in football. The Old Trafford fans will obviously be wanting to know if there will be dramatic changes and instant success. In football, I have long since learned that it is not like instant coffee — you can't have success as quickly as that. I am going to Old Trafford as the new man without any pre-conceived ideas. I think it would be quite wrong to have any. I shall meet the players for the first time when they report for training on July 16. From that point on Manchester United are MY TEAM. It is some challenge for a humble Irish boy who once worked as a fireman on a railway train. But if I didn't think I could do the job I wouldn't have taken it. Some months ago, I wrote that George Best was possibly the most complete footballer in Britain. He is certainly the most complete player since Tom Finney. I have also had the distinction of playing against Bobby Charlton and Denis Law so I know all about their capabilities as players. Even so, I cannot pre-judge at this stage whether or not there will be any changes at Old Trafford. One thing is certain, however — no one will be leaving United until I have had a good look at the playing strength. Neither is there any reason for any player or anyone in an official capacity to be shivering in their shoes simply because I have been appointed the new manager.

"The one thing that will help me to sort out the strengths and weaknesses at Old Trafford is the fact that we have competitive matches in the Watney Cup, starting with an away game against Halifax Town. It would be quite wrong of me to come in and try to change things overnight — but these matches will help me to get a true picture of just what I must do to bring back the old glory to United. It has been said that the presence of Sir Matt Busby could be a hindrance to a new manager because of his immense prestige. I don't see it that way. I've never forgotten the comforting words he spoke to me when Leicester lost 3-2 at Old Trafford in the last match of the 1969 season and were relegated. I felt very sick at heart. I had been with Leicester five months then and we had also been beaten in the Cup Final. Sir Matt told me: 'The strength of a man is how he recovers from adversity.' This bucked me up to face the players and start the rebuilding job which took Leicester back into the First Division after two seasons. As I see it, Sir Matt has given his life to Manchester United. His aim has always been to make them the greatest club in the world. From July 1 that will be my aim, too… I knew Manchester United was the only club I would ever leave Filbert Street for, and I told my directors so. For managers, the opportunity of a lifetime knocks only once — as it did for me on Monday."

If there was one key element missing from his plans, O'Farrell was quick to address it, telling reporters on 24th June: "I have already made it clear that going to Old Trafford with a completely open mind and without any preconceived ideas — bar one. That exception is a youth policy. Sir Matt Busby was perhaps the first to realise that the real strength of a club is finding and developing their own players… I shall certainly make it one of the cornerstones of my policy at Old Trafford."

United did have talent in their youth team, and O'Farrell was probably right on the money with his comments about expecting instant success. Saying anything other than the things he had would surely have put a few noses out of joint in the dressing room. Wilf McGuinness had hardly been a victim of player power, it was more that he simply couldn't deal with the egos and personalities who were deliberately testing him. Nobody expected miracles but they expected improvement. O'Farrell had a good track record in that regard but what was there left to get out of the likes of Shay Brennan, Bobby Charlton, Pat Crerand and even Ian Ure who, at 32, was an injury prone veteran? Nobby Stiles wasn't even thirty and he had decided to not wait for the new manager to be named, moving to Middlesbrough for a modest £20,000, showing how badly injuries had affected him. The idea that United could expect the necessary improvement, so that they were serious trophy contenders once more, with an ageing squad was fanciful and unrealistic.

Though his contract was officially in effect from July 1st, it would be a couple of weeks before O'Farrell met his players, and on the 9th he took to his column in *The Mirror* to reassure supporters that he had high hopes. "This is a big club with big ideas," he said. "There is a new stand nearing completion, and although it is simpler to predict how long it will take to build a stand than build a football team, I believe that when that stand is finished we will have a clearer picture of Manchester United's prospects. Success WILL come. Of that I am sure. But, obviously, I have to see the players in competitive action before I can see what course I think we should take... On Monday, Malcolm Musgrove joins me from Leicester City. The following Thursday I meet the United players officially for the first time. Then we get down to the real business."

Musgrove was a highly-rated trainer and although most of the spotlight was on the manager, it was clear that United's players would benefit from some fresh ideas. As George Best had previously said, the atmosphere around the squad had probably been affected more by Jimmy Murphy's reduced role than Busby's retirement. O'Farrell could certainly not fault his new squad's willingness to welcome their new leader.

On 16th July he told *The Mirror* "This is it! The moment of truth for Manchester United and me. For today United begin their assault on the Watney Cup, the League championship, the Football League Cup and the FA Cup — on the playing fields of Heaton Park! I would be a mug to forecast what we might do, but this I know: I have taken over a team of triers. I wrote to all the United lads when I was appointed manager, to introduce myself and invite them to return for training — holidays permitting — before the scheduled time for reporting back this morning. I have been staggered by the response. Denis Law, Bobby Charlton, George Best, Pat Crerand, Alex Stepney, Tony Dunne, David Sadler, Willie Morgan, Francis Burns — indeed, most of last season's first-team players are already back in action. I wanted them back early, if at all possible, because I didn't want a crash course to get them fit before we play in the Watney Cup at Halifax a fortnight tomorrow. They sill looked sharp. In fact Malcolm Musgrove had to stop them yesterday from trying too hard. We shall start this afternoon with a five-mile jog — I hope to do two-and-a-half miles and then I shall start looking for a place to rest. I shall tell the players when I meet them officially for the first time this morning: 'We want to do well. And there is no time like the present to win something. If we get into the winning mood right away, anything is possible. That is why I believe this Watney Cup is so important.' It all depends on our application NOW and whether we get the right sort of breaks. The fact that a man like Bobby Charlton comes straight back from holiday and gets into training within twenty-four hours is a sure sign of the professionalism in this club.

"I was naturally sorry that Jack Crompton, who has been such a good servant to the club both as player and trainer since 1944 — apart from a brief spell at Luton — has decided to leave Old Trafford. No one likes to see a man of Jack's calibre leave the club, but the parting was without acrimony, because Jack didn't feel he could stay on in the job I offered to him as second-team trainer-coach. It has been astonishing to read in recent weeks that some club directors seem amazed, when a manager moves, that he tends to take his right-hand man with him. I believe Jack Crompton understands this, because there is nothing subversive or revolutionary about this step. The important thing is that it is done in the right way. The thinking is perfectly logical: a new manager likes a man who understands his methods and tactics to stay with him so that he can help pass them on to the players. I have worked very closely and with some success with Malcolm Musgrove at Leicester, and that is why I wanted him with me at Old Trafford, without in any way denigrating the work that Jack Crompton has done over the years with United."

A clean slate for everyone then? Not quite. United may have wanted to forget the last two years existed but there were reminders for the new boss to deal with. Crowd trouble in the previous season's home game with Newcastle, when a knife was thrown by a supporter on to the pitch, led to a sanction being imposed on the club. United were punished with the Football League commission ordering that Old Trafford must be closed for the period 'August 14 to August 28 inclusive' which effectively meant the first two home games of the season had to be played at a ground more than twelve miles away from Old Trafford. Further, it was ordered that they must pay compensation to both Arsenal and West Brom — the clubs they would be playing — if the receipts 'did not match up to the average at Old Trafford last season'.

O'Farrell addressed the issue in the press. "MANCHESTER UNITED have overcome terrible misfortune in the past and I'm quite sure we will rise above this blow of having Old Trafford closed for the first two home matches. Naturally I was disappointed when the decision went against the club. And I certainly could have done without this at the start of a new job. But what I want to make quite clear is this: I don't want people feeling sorry for me or the players. I think it is bad when you get with this sort of mood. This is now a challenge for the players and I'm sure they are ready to gear themselves up and try even harder to overcome this stupendous challenge. Challenge it most certainly is. We didn't have a bright fixture list to start the season, and now we face Derby County and Chelsea away from home, the re-arranged "home" matches with Arsenal and West Bromwich, and then we play Wolves and Everton away from home. Any team that could pull six points out of that little lot would be doing extremely well. You may take it from me this setback will make us all try harder than ever, so that when we do get back to Old Trafford the fans will be eager to see us.

"All I will say is that I hope the man who threw that knife — if, indeed, he was a United supporter, which I cannot believe — will now realise the bitter disappointment he has inflicted on 50,000 staunch United fans, true sportsmen and as good as gold, who now have to wait or travel to see their team play. This is the sad part, and yet I hope with all my heart that out of this good will come. That the fan who steps out of line — and this applies to all clubs — will realise that thousands of innocent people are punished for one stupid act. Furthermore, I hope that the good fans — and they far out-number the bad ones — will take immediate action should they see any wrongdoer trying to give the club a bad name. By that, I mean they should report incidents and give names, so that firm official action can be taken without the need of the club facing a disciplinary commission as United had to do yesterday. All of this means that I will probably have to miss Leicester City's promotion dinner next Monday and I expect to be busy arranging a suitable ground or grounds where we can play Arsenal and West Bromwich. It looks as though our matches might go on at Blackburn, Burnley or Preston — or some club with their sort of facilities."

O'Farrell initially persuaded West Brom to reschedule the game until September 29th before unsuccessfully attempting to have the Arsenal game moved to Wembley. Bill Shankly offered Anfield as an alternative saying, "I shall be happy that this great Stretford End crowd can come on to the Kop at Anfield. I know just how eager Manchester United were to help Liverpool in the past," O'Farrell claimed Shankly told him, before concluding his *Mirror* column by saying: "It is the wonderful spirit which exists between clubs like Liverpool and Manchester United which has made this worrying week well worth while. It has made me realise just how many friends United have in football."

O'Farrell's first games as Manchester United manager came in the Watney Cup, which was a reminder of just how far United had fallen from grace; this was a competition between the two highest-scoring teams from each English division who hadn't been promoted or qualified for Europe. Having lost 4-1 to Derby in the 'final' of 1970, United's involvement was even more embarrassing in 1971. O'Farrell's first game was a 2-1 defeat at Halifax. Conceding two goals to Third Division opposition would be embarrassing enough for the defence but the first was a header from a corner which neither Crerand nor Charlton, both midfielders, picked up.

In the second game of the tournament United defeated Luton 2-0, but faced further embarrassment losing 2-1 to Second Division Fulham in a bad-tempered game in which George Best was lucky not to have been sent from the field. However, that was far from O'Farrell's biggest pre-season concern. Having committed to giving his squad a chance, it seemed that some in the squad — namely, Brian Kidd — did not reciprocate the patience. And, despite it only being a friendly game, Kidd took being named as a substitute at Halifax very badly indeed.

"I am very disappointed because I've worked damn hard in training," he said. "I was really looking forward to the start, and now this. It's a body blow. I was so angry when I saw the team that I just didn't say a thing, in case I might come out with something I would later regret. I fully expected to play, that's why I feel so sick. Why shouldn't I be? I'm a professional... I suppose some people will automatically assume that I'll hand in another transfer request. This is nonsense. Of course I'm fed up, but this is the start of the season, not the end of the world."

His manager was sympathetic. "Kidd's reaction is natural but, in view of my decision to take things from how we finished last season, some players had to be disappointed," he said. Kidd could relax; he would be first choice when it came to the real action.

United's start to the campaign was uncompromising; with the Arsenal game moved to Anfield, and the West Brom game now moved to Stoke City's Victoria Ground just three days later, it meant United faced six consecutive games away from home. Three of the 'normal' away games were at Derby County, Chelsea and Everton; it was not quite so drastic as to say United's hopes of winning the league might be over before September but it was, surely, true to say O'Farrell should get a more definite and clear assessment of the capabilities, or otherwise, of his squad.

Or was it?

With the benefit of hindsight we can look at the circumstances and suggest the idea that Manchester United were in a false environment as the 1971/72 season got underway. Firstly, this was a new manager with no close-hand familiarity with the behaviour of his players. It was in their best interest to put in the maximum effort. One of the major questions that had been asked about United's disappointing mid-table finishes was how could that be possible with three of the best players in the world in their team? They certainly had the ability and in Best, Law and Charlton they had players who, if the mood took them, could probably have dragged Accrington Stanley to a halfway decent position in the First Division. United could score goals and they could hammer teams. And, in such an environment, you would get the best out of Best, who would feel as if it was all worth it.

O'Farrell gave an upbeat spin on the start to the season. "Even though we face this harrowing start of away games, we shall still go forward in search of attacking football," he said. "It is the only way United can play."

United stormed into a 2-0 lead in their opener at Derby, only for the hosts to stage a second half fight-back and earn a draw. It was, nonetheless, a positive start, and the Red Devils did not drop their heads when trailing at half-time to Chelsea four days later. Kidd, Willie Morgan and Bobby Charlton scored in a frantic ten minute spell midway through the second half. Peter Osgood pulled one back for the Blues and George Best, complaining to referee Norman Burtenshaw in protest, was sent off.

United won 3-2 but Best hogged the headlines again as the *Daily Mirror* front page spread read 'SOCCER'S VIOLENT NIGHT'. In addition to George's dismissal, there had been ten arrests and a pitch invasion in Leicester City's home game with Nottingham Forest, twenty-four arrests at Exeter and in total three players sent off and thirty-eight players booked. Upon being sent off the United winger couldn't believe it, "He sat down on the pitch in disbelief and held his head in his hands," reported *The Mirror*. "Then he broke into tears as United's coach, Malcolm Musgrove, led him off."

O'Farrell defended his forward: "One of George Best's biggest assets — and problems — is that he is such a fiercely determined competitor. I would have quite understood if he had pulled out of the team to play Chelsea at Stamford Bridge on Wednesday night.

I'd seen the bruises and swellings on his ankles and feet! So far as I am aware, the fellows who had given George those bumps and bruises were not booked. But it seems that under Soccer's current code of conduct the spoken word is considered a bigger "crime" than a kick on the leg."

Ahead of United's first 'home game' of the season just two days later, Louis Edwards wrote a welcoming note to O'Farrell in the programme, pledging his support. "It is not possible to guarantee results on the field, the game would be much the poorer attraction if that were the case, but we are conscious of the magnificent support you gave to us last season and I can assure you that Mr. O'Farrell and his staff will be doing everything possible to achieve success and to provide the exciting football which has been the hallmark of Manchester United's play of the past."

It was certainly exciting; United recovered from an early setback and defeated Arsenal 3-1 with two late goals from Charlton and Gowling. Despite a Friday night crowd of just 28,000, which meant United would have to compensate Arsenal, O'Farrell was delighted. "It was tremendous wasn't it?" he said of his side's performance. "It's the best start United have had for years, I believe. We're top of the League. That's confounded some of you people."

On the following Monday they maintained the promising start with a 3-1 win over West Brom at Stoke's Victoria Ground and O'Farrell's *Mirror* column was understandably positive. "We are all well pleased at Manchester United at the splendid start we have made this season," he said. "But our joy and enthusiasm is tempered by a sobering thought. That knife, which was thrown on to the pitch causing Old Trafford to be closed, has so far cost the club not less than £20,000. This includes the payments we have to make to Liverpool and Stoke for the use of their grounds. It also includes about £1,600 we must pay Everton, because their gate for last Saturday's match with Sheffield United fell below the 46,000 they stipulated before our match with Arsenal was allowed to go on at Anfield last Friday... The smart manager can soon tell when his team are doing well by the number of phone calls he gets. Mine has scarcely been off the hook all week. I'm pleased about that. United are news again, but let us not kid ourselves. Seven points from four "away" fixtures is the brightest start United have made for eight years. But no one at Old Trafford is getting the flags out... yet!"

That run of away games concluded with a 1-1 draw at Molineux and a 1-0 defeat at Everton but nobody was particularly downbeat about the situation. Their response to that setback at Goodison Park was a fantastic run of nine wins in eleven games. United were on a roll, although according to goalkeeper Alex Stepney, all was not exactly as it seemed.

"He (O'Farrell) was respected throughout football as a man of integrity and honesty, and now he was taking on the most demanding club job of them all... there was a clerical manner about him, but he seemed to have acquired the right kind of assistant in Malcolm Musgrove who came with him from Leicester," Stepney said. "Malcolm was a former winger, an earnest chap with an eager voice and a determination to have things done right. I liked him. Everything worked marvellously for them in the opening months. We were playing exciting football and carved ourselves out a five-point lead at the top of the First Division. It was almost time to stop, think and take stock of the position. My own findings were not all that comforting.

"I had to admit to myself that the situation did appear slightly false. We were conceding too many goals and there was a definite case for strengthening the defence. I knew that; I was playing behind the existing one. Perhaps Frank and Malcolm could not believe their good fortune. At any rate, they took little action. Frank would come down and stand in the middle of the training ground while Malcolm got along with the coaching. Why worry? As Christmas came, Manchester United were top of the table."

It was true that United had conceded thirteen goals in their first fourteen games but against the backdrop of the First Division in general it didn't seem as if that record should ring any alarm bells. By that stage, every single team had conceded more than ten goals, and only six teams had conceded fewer than United. Perhaps that should have given them an inkling that cracks were being papered over. So long as Frank O'Farrell could keep his team attacking and entertaining, it wouldn't be an issue.

Of course, a large part of that attacking flair depended on George Best. He was due for a hearing on 13th September which would determine his punishment for the incident at Chelsea. Best had picked up a knock after scoring twice in a League Cup win at Ipswich Town on the 7th of the month and, with United due to travel to London to play Crystal Palace on the 11th, he was told not to travel to the Rothman's Golden Boots team awards in London on 9th September. However, Ken Jones of *The Mirror* was not impressed with Best's no-show saying, "The word from Georgie is that he is injured. He said last night: 'I had to stay behind at the ground for treatment to my injured ankle. But the organisers were told about it, and I'm sure that they knew I couldn't be there.' If that's the case, then someone let Georgie down. But he has been absent too often for his own good. He can't blame us if we draw our own conclusions. So he had to come from Manchester. But then so did Francis Lee and Joe Mercer and Malcolm Allison. Billy Bremner and Don Revie came from Leeds. And Ferenc Puskas had to come all the way from Athens to make the presentations. Maybe it is a long way to limp. But George should really have made a better job of explaining that."

Best played at Selhurst Park and was down in London again two days later to find out if his suspended six-week sentence from the Pardoe broken leg incident would be imposed. This time Ken Jones seemed more sympathetic. "Dare they rob us of Best?" he asked. "GEORGE BEST is established beyond all reasonable doubt as one of the great entertainers in the world of football. What football must decide today is whether it can afford to cut Best off from an adoring public. The outlook for him is undoubtedly bleak. Sent off for dissent at Chelsea last month, he appears before an FA disciplinary committee in London today under the cloud of a suspended six-week sentence imposed last season. It is ironic that he should be one of the first players to suffer from a clean-up campaign which was essentially designed to protect forwards of his calibre. Best gained his universal reputation for appealing football during an era of butchering tackles and cynical defensive play."

Best was given a reprieve at the hearing as it was found that the phrase "you're a disgrace" had actually been said towards Willie Morgan, his teammate, rather than referee Norman Burtenshaw. The case was argued by Cliff Lloyd, secretary of the PFA.

O'Farrell was relieved. "I'm very pleased," he admitted. "It was a very fair hearing. No one was fairer than Norman Burtenshaw. He deserves a lot of credit for the way he put his side of the case."

Best said: "It's a very happy verdict for me, and it was a very fair hearing. Now I can concentrate on playing my football." In his autobiography published years later, Best admitted he had sworn at the ref!

These footballing issues were part and parcel of being a manager, so wouldn't necessarily have been alien to O'Farrell. After twelve goals in the first sixteen games, he might have been wondering what all the fuss was about when it came to keeping a handling George Best. The problem was, though, that Best *was* a phenomenon. That early season run of form included a bewitching hat-trick against West Ham United at Old Trafford. It was perfect in every sense of the word; the first, a header, the second, a predatory left foot effort, and the third, a trademark solo dribble which made a fool out of the legendary Bobby Moore before being powered in with Best's right foot. He was unplayable and United were reaping the benefits.

Best had gone on record as referring to Busby as someone who didn't understand him. If Matt Busby couldn't, and Jimmy Murphy was nowhere to be found, then what chance a manager who had mostly coached in the lower divisions? More to the point; how could anyone be expected to know how to handle George's specific level of stardom when even the man himself couldn't? This was uncharted territory, and for all of the theories and debates about how Best let himself down after 1968, there is a deeper and sadder suggestion that he never stood a chance. After all, it is all well and good discussing the issues of petulance and retaliation, or perceived persecution by the press and authorities, and whether or not Best might have controlled himself better at times but there is an altogether more troubling aspect to this story that went unreported at the time but is well known today... George was only a few months away from effectively being out of top level football for good and he was still only 25.

Yet in the autumn of 1971 the new boss could have been forgiven for thinking that the so-called 'hot seat' was actually an easy chair. After that West Ham game, O'Farrell explained: "This is the crunch period for Manchester United. By the end of October, I shall know whether United are going to be up there challenging for League and League Cup honours... At the moment United are second in the First Division, which is higher than I dared hope for when I took over this job."

He then reacted to a 3-0 win at Huddersfield, another game in which Best scored, by insisting: "We cannot blow any trumpets yet. It's too early. We have got to look for consistency if we are to achieve anything. What we have achieved so far has been down to rather a lot of hard work by everyone."

United won their next two games by a single goal — Best scoring against Derby County, and Charlton scoring at Burnley — before a trip to Newcastle on the 23rd October 1971. In the week before the game, police received a tip-off from someone claiming to be from the IRA saying George Best would be shot if he played. His family were understandably concerned and Frank O'Farrell gave him the choice. George thought that if he decided not to play, they might be able to threaten him every week and force him to never play again, and made calls to his father to reassure him he would be fine.

At the time St. James Park was surrounded by high-rise tower blocks so police were deployed there to keep an eye out from the rooftops. On the morning of the game the team coach had been broken into so had to be checked for explosive devices; Best travelled on the coach with two police chaperones who would not allow him to sit by the window. United's players were terrified by the experience. Paddy Crerand was so spooked he refused to sit next to his pal.

"I remember arriving at the stadium in Newcastle... we didn't have the security like they have today," Alex Stepney recalls. "You pulled up outside, you had to walk from the coach into the actual stadium itself, and the amount of police that were around, from the coach, they actually lined it into the stadium. That's the kind of thing we had to deal with in those days and George coped brilliantly with it."

If Stepney's recollection seems flippant then one youngster taking it very seriously indeed was Belfast-native Sammy McIlroy. "When George did get that death threat, you had to take it very, very seriously because there were bad times back home, my parents were there at the time. I was very worried about them, because there were a lot of people getting killed, there were shootings every day and when the IRA gave you a threat in those days, you had to take it seriously… it was going to take something worse, if you can say worse than that, to stop George from playing football, but at the end of the day we were a little bit concerned, because the IRA were a major threat to the world in those days and you know, how do you protect George on a football field? It was very difficult but he wanted to play and he did play, and he actually scored that day as well."

Despite what must have been a very anxious and trying time for all, United won the game 1-0, with Best, typically, as McIlroy rightly recalls, scoring the goal. Newcastle boss Joe Harvey showed some gallows humour afterwards when he said, "I wish they had shot the little bugger!"

With growing concerns about Best's safety and speculation that an incident may occur during Northern Ireland's Nations Cup game with Spain — it had been dubbed "The Fixture Of Fear" — O'Farrell withdrew his player from consideration for selection. "George has been extremely worried since I told him of the first threat to his life at Newcastle last Saturday week," said the United boss on November 2nd. "Now the police have been informed by a person living close to George's home that there has been another threat to 'get him'… The value of human life is the thing that matters… It's something you cannot ignore, especially as he comes from Belfast and his family could be involved. It is very unfortunate that a brilliant footballer like Best should be involved in this sort of thing. If you study his performance closely in the last couple of games, you must accept that it has affected his play."

He may have had a point. United had to rely on a late equaliser from Alan Gowling to get a draw at home against Stoke and had no response to a goal in the fourth minute at Old Trafford against Leeds. Seeking distraction from his problems, Best headed out. "Football used to be my escape from all my fame problems but now drink and women replaced it," he said, which, considering the threats that now seemed present at football, seems much more understandable than it might have done at the time. "It became a crazy game," he said, "like being a naughty boy wanting to prove how much I could get away with. And as I got away with more and more things, I pushed the stakes even higher." Best's behaviour became more erratic after his sister was shot in the leg in Belfast; he had to feel the threat was real.

In the short term it was difficult to tell; Best recovered from that shaky moment by hitting another mesmeric hat-trick at Southampton to help United on their way to a thrilling 5-2 win. The victory delighted the United boss. "When I took over at Old Trafford, I knew that, in addition to make Manchester United successful, I had to preserve their reputation of being the top attraction in English football," said O'Farrell. "That is why the sight of a packed Southampton ground last week made me nearly as happy as the result. For the moment, at least, I am realising every manager's dream of having a winning and entertaining team... I realised my good luck in having players at Old Trafford with outstanding ability. I also knew that to be successful I would have to get them playing as a team — without stifling individual ability. The public never know what they will get from Manchester United. But they know what they expect."

There seemed to be a fine harmony within the club which had kept the Northern Irishman on the straight and narrow. It was a mood which was apparent in the public attitude of the previously want-away Brian Kidd, who gushed to the press about life at the club after scoring in a win against Leicester in November.

"I was brought up in a part of the city, not far from Old Trafford, where football meant just one thing… United. After I had signed associated schoolboy forms, I wanted my release because I didn't think I would make it. Sir Matt Busby made me change my mind," Kidd said. "The club was going through a funny stage. I try not to think about it, and I certainly don't like to talk about it. That's all behind me now. Frank O'Farrell and Mal Musgrove have made a hell of a difference."

The *Daily Mirror*, who had been used by O'Farrell as a mouthpiece, posted a large feature on 14th December celebrating Manchester United's triumphant return to the summit of English football, with the following questions to, and answers from, the United boss.

Can United last the pace in the Championship?
I think we can. A certain person has said that we are not good enough, but I think that we are proving ourselves. There are a lot of games to go, and anything can happen in the middle of the winter when there might be snow and ice around. We shall need a bit of luck, but then who doesn't?

What could upset United's challenge?
Nothing, I hope. But you are always hoping in this game. We have been fairly lucky with injuries. But you never know when you are going to get them. Fortunately John Fitzpatrick is now getting over a knee injury and young Sammy McIlroy has shown that he can come in to the attack at any time.

Have you made United more defensively-minded?
More defensively-minded, yes. More defensive, no. A lot of fuss was made when Sir Alf Ramsey chose three attack-minded players in midfield against Greece. We have been doing that all season.

Was it difficult to introduce more deliberate tactics at Old Trafford?
Not at all. All the players felt that there was a need to do this. We stress certain points when they crop up, and the response has been tremendous. They have learned to help each other.

Most clubs liked to play United because they got an open contest. Has this changed?

Most definitely. That particular point irritated me. We have altered that. Like West Ham, we are more difficult to play against now because we contest the centre of the field more successfully.

How long can Bobby Charlton and Denis Law go on?

I don't know, but I sincerely believe they should both be playing international football.

It has been said that your team would be exposed if people set out to attack you.

Anyone is welcome to try. Our defenders are doing a good job for us, and they are now working better together. Every team has problems. Managers are never satisfied, or at least they shouldn't be.

You have yet to buy a player for United. Will it bother you when the time comes?

Why should it? You always have to be careful when spending other people's money. But I think I have learned the hard way... I know the spotlight will be on when I buy for United. But I can call on a lot of sound advice if I need it.

The feature, written by Ken Jones, also included a lengthy explanation of United's tactical revolution. An infographic was provided with a systematic breakdown of a flexible 4-3-3/4-2-4 formation that showed Alan Gowling's repositioning into midfield in place of Paddy Crerand.

"Manchester United were once known as a team you couldn't trust," Jones began. "Brilliantly successful one week, desperately disorganised the next. Frank O'Farrell set out to introduce more consistency and better organisation. Instead of asking two players to contest the middle of the field, he elected to use three. Bobby Charlton was already there. Willie Morgan came in from the right touchline to join him, and the trio was completed by Alan Gowling. All three are encouraged to go forward, and Gowling, although making a great contribution in defence, has scored critical goals. There is more solidity in defence because full backs are no longer drawn forward into positions where Steve James and David Sadler would be left without support and cover. But United's strength is the fear which opponent have of great attackers. George Best is nominally a winger, but plays as a second striker with Denis Law. Width is a fundamental principle in attack, and it is Denis Law and Brian Kidd who provide that width. Law will often operate from the right touchline, where he is happiest, and Kidd has the skill and inclination to make decisive breaks from the other flank. With the midfield men encouraged to come forward, United manage to retain their flair while establishing a more secure system of play."

Jones may well have been putting everything on United winning the League but outside of Old Trafford, rivals were beginning to have their own jabs. One of those rivals was just across the city at Maine Road, and Malcolm Allison was not amused with the talk that United were the best side in the division. The teams had met in a famous 3-3 draw in early November, a game in which Sammy McIlroy had made his debut and scored.

"For most of the match we outclassed them," insisted Allison. "This match has convinced me we will win the championship this season."

And the City manager was talking again, despite seeing his own team go down 3-1 to Derby in early December. In his eponymous autobiography, Alex Stepney recalled that Brian Clough and Malcolm Allison 'chorused in unison' to declare 'Manchester United will win nothing. They will blow up. They haven't the players.'

Stepney felt that remark got under O'Farrell's skin: "It seemed to me that almost from that day Frank O'Farrell went into retreat. Suddenly, from being the cheerful Irishman at the top of the heap, he stopped communicating. He started ignoring his players. He would sit behind his desk for days at a time so that we rarely saw him. He was no longer the nice guy because, when we did see him, there would be times when he would walk straight past without even saying 'Good morning'."

Certainly, you could feel O'Farrell's irritation in his comments made before the December 27th game with Coventry City. Coventry had signed 19 year-old Ron Healey on loan — Healey was a reserve goalkeeper at Maine Road, and was brought in as an emergency recruit to play in the festive game. "What a start—at Old Trafford," said Healey. "It should be a thriller. I just want to try and stop United."

O'Farrell 'angrily condemned' the loan. "I think this is very unfair," he said, clearly under the impression that Healey, an employee of a title and local rival, would try that little bit harder. The game finished 2-2.

If there were the inklings of the pressure getting to the United boss you might attribute that to his surprise at the caustic approach from opposition managers; perhaps, at Leicester, he had been used to more friendly and good-natured competition.

It shouldn't have mattered. As 1971 turned into 1972 Manchester United had a three point lead at the top of Division One, with their most consistent spell of form for a good few years behind them. O'Farrell had more than proven himself capable of getting good performances out of a squad of players he inherited. The three consecutive draws at the end of 1971 needn't have been a cause for concern.

Like another who would inherit the hot seat 43 years later, Frank O'Farrell was about to learn that this was no ordinary job.

CRACKS

AS KEN JONES' TRIBUTE REVEALED, there seemed to be few concerns about Manchester United's squad and first team composition as 1972 began. And, should concerns creep in, then at least the club had the man that some members of the press were describing as 'Britain's top manager' to put them right.

Even this early, though, those inside the Cliff training ground were beginning to have their concerns, as Alex Stepney's comments suggested. Things had gone well, but there had yet to be a spell of adversity in which O'Farrell would be tested. If recent history was enough evidence to go on, this was a squad who would need a strong leader in those times.

So, just how much of United's squad really needed replacing? Stepney himself had found himself victim of the axe but at 29 was at his goalkeeping peak. O'Farrell had kept faith with him despite Busby and McGuinness both giving the record signing spells in the reserves. It meant that as good as Stepney was, there was possible room for improvement in that area. Of course, it is entirely possible that Stepney's form, like that of David Sadler — who was still only 25 — was affected by the poor defence around him. Ian Ure was already a permanent member of the reserve side and alongside Sadler in front of Stepney was Tony Dunne (30), Francis Burns (22) and Steve James (22). This would be James' strongest season, where he looked as if he might be a decent squad member at United in the long term, and his form in the team prior to Christmas 1971 had suggested his star might shine even brighter than that. Dunne was just thirty but like those of a similar age — Stiles, who had already left, Crerand, and Law — the nature of the game in the 60s meant you could add a theoretical five years on compared to today. These issues were exacerbated by United's poor facilities and poor medical department, if it could even be classed as that. Ian

Ure's description of his medical in Paddy Barclay's biography of Sir Matt Busby is a real eye-opener. Ure described his knee problem as 'chronic' and that he'd been having operations for five years at Arsenal, as well as taking painkillers that were normally given to racehorses in America.

"I certainly wouldn't have signed myself," Ure admitted. "I don't blame Arsenal for getting rid of me. I blame United for signing me. They must have been bloody blind. The medical was a farce. An absolute farce. In fact it wasn't a medical at all. I never saw a doctor. There was just Jack Crompton. He told me to bend each knee 90 degrees and that was no problem for me because I'd taken four or five of the pills that week!" Ure claimed that from his observations, Law's knee was just as bad and Stiles hadn't been in much better shape.

Alan Gowling's form as a midfielder was earning rave reviews. His conversion from being a centre-forward helped United at defensive corners in a way that the shorter Crerand hadn't been able to. However, what was advantageous at set plays was less so in open play, due to Crerand's greater experience in that role. Gowling was just 22 and even O'Farrell would privately admit that this was only a temporary solution. His midfield partner, Bobby Charlton, was now 34 — and, like his veteran teammates, an old 34 — and in order for his career to have any longevity eked out of it he needed runners around him. He didn't have it behind him in Tony Dunne and neither Gowling or Willie Morgan possessed the defensive discipline needed to help Charlton influence the side as he once had.

At 27, Morgan was another who should have been at his peak, and although he drew comparisons to Best due to his flamboyant style, he lacked the goal-scoring touch of the Irishman. Never mind, Morgan was there to load the gun while the strikers fired the bullets and at this point, Best was still scoring goals and if he had an off-day, there was always 22-year-old Brian Kidd or the wily Denis Law (now 31) to get the ball in the net.

As admirable as their contribution had been so far, Burns, James and Gowling were destined for careers away from Old Trafford and for Burns and Gowling that time was approaching more quickly than they may have anticipated. Clearly Dunne, Charlton and Law were nearing the end. In Stepney and Sadler, United could boast two European Cup winners at a good age, and yet neither player seemed to convince. That left Morgan, Best and Kidd; all of them unpredictable and not all for reasons that would have pleased the man in charge.

So when United were brought back down to earth with a bump in January 1972, losing all four of their league games; 3-0 at West Ham, 3-1 at home to Wolves, 1-0 at home to Chelsea and 2-1 at West Brom. The first rope to unfurl on the side of the good ship Old Trafford was that held by Best. The winger had already confessed that football could no longer bring the escapism it once did when things were going wrong and he missed training for the entire week before the Wolves game. It was front page news on 11th January as O'Farrell ordered him to leave his press-hounded home in Bramhall and return to digs with his former landlady Mrs Fullaway in Aycliffe Avenue, Chorlton. George had recently moved into an ultra-modern home in suburban Bramhall but the architect's penchant for floor to ceiling windows meant that the United star was permanently on display and felt like an exhibit at Chester Zoo as tourists and pressmen came to gawp. It was another disastrous, if comic, episode in the player's decline.

Later Best recalled the hat-trick he had scored against West Ham back in September, "If I could have had moments like that every week, I might have felt a lot better. But we were losing more than we were winning, and if I couldn't be bothered with playing matches, I certainly couldn't be bothered with training. One week in January 1972, I didn't manage to get into The Cliff training ground once and O'Farrell fined me two weeks wages. He also ordered me to go back to Mrs Fullaway's, which was no hardship after the circus that was taking place outside my home in Bramhall."

O'Farrell explained his decision. "Loneliness is one of the reasons for George Best's problems at Manchester United, which I have tried to solve by returning him from his luxury home to his former digs," the United boss said. "It's difficult to adjust from a goldfish bowl to an echo chamber. After I had finished talking to George Best, the Press and television last Monday I was looking for quietness if not isolation. But I had forgotten about the post. Show me the size of your club's morning mail and I'll tell you how they are doing. When things aren't going well the number of letters increases, and we've had a lot at Old Trafford lately. There are two reasons: George Best and three points from five League matches. The older correspondents suggested George should be punished severely. No doubt they are influenced by memories of their youth, when they were deprived of what we now take for granted. The youngsters who wrote thought George should get off scot free, arguing that what he does in his spare time is his own business. But footballers need a high standard of fitness. I had to take the middle course. Nobody suggested that, although I am not short of suggestions about who to buy to make Manchester United a winning side again."

O'Farrell later said that he had hoped dropping Best for the Wolves game would have inspired his grumbling team-mates to show they could win without him. They didn't, and O'Farrell admitted it was a 'dilemma'.

Ahead of the last game of the month against West Brom, O'Farrell's *Daily Mirror* column concentrated more on his own job than his wayward star. "When I took over the managership of Manchester United, I knew I would not be short of advice," he said on January 28th. "In addition to my predecessor Sir Matt Busby, there was a stack of experience at boardroom, player and trainers' level. To be surrounded by advisers whose numbers run into double figures is comforting. Being confronted by thousands of amateur advocates can be irritating. Manchester United are one of the few clubs who attract as much attention when they are losing as when they are winning. Six League games without a victory and the advice pours in. The suggestions come from well-meaning people, prompted by an interest in Manchester United, and that is a good thing. But I do know the strengths and weaknesses of the team. And I do know the best players in England. I also know which players are available — and the best aren't. If they were, Manchester

United would be interested. When they are, Manchester United might not be interested, as then the players could be past their best. Despite my short stay at Old Trafford, this experience is not new... Our recent form is frustrating and proves we cannot afford to be complacent. But being one point adrift of the leaders is no cause for panic... I said, early in the season, when things were going well that the team would hit a bad patch. And this has coincided with an outbreak of injuries... I hope our bad patch will end when my players are fit again. If it doesn't, and some of those outstanding men I have been told about are available, we will reappraise the situation."

O'Farrell rang the changes. First of all Paul Edwards, the 24 year-old defender who had spent all season in the reserves after a couple of years where he had made over fifty appearances for the first team, was brought in to replace James. Tommy O'Neil, a rookie 19-year-old full back, was brought in for Dunne, with United's defence against Chelsea reading: O'Neil, Edwards, Sadler, Burns.

Perhaps United's form in the FA Cup was convincing enough for O'Farrell to persist but in the League their displays were getting close to catastrophic. A 2-0 home defeat to Newcastle was the fifth Division One loss in succession. From first place with a three point gap, United were now in fifth and four points behind leaders Manchester City; the seven-point swing looking much worse when put in the context of two points for a win. And slowly but surely United's defensive issues were beginning to look like the root of their problem. All four teams above them had conceded fewer goals than United's 38, with only City on 31 conceding more than 30 in 28 games.

In just three weeks O'Farrell appeared far more uncertain about the ability of his squad to pull themselves together. "Manchester United's losing streak has brought the inevitable clamour for me to go out and buy players," he explained in his *Mirror* column. "But my public advisers are a little late. I was searching for new men long before the present loss of form cost us the First Division leadership. If I had been able to get the players I wanted perhaps the current slump would have been avoided. A new signing at a psychological moment can give a tremendous impetus to a club. That moment can be when you are winning as well as losing… We want the best, and the best are widely known. Yet I am not convinced there is as much wrong with the team as people claim. We sailed five points clear at the top of the table before the New Year, losing only two matches. My team may not be quite as good as that magnificent record suggests. But they cannot be all that bad either… Losing runs are as hard to interrupt as winning ones. The publicity we get adds to the pressure but it shows that people care. Manchester United do not suffer from apathy or indifference by fans or critics. The club is always news. Although I wish the news was better."

United were due to play at second placed Leeds on February 19th; Don Revie's men had been one of the few teams to defeat O'Farrell's side in their purple patch, so the United boss was hoping for a role reversal. "The Leeds game is a rare occasion," said O'Farrell. "Manchester United are the underdogs for once in their history. I expect the players to feel that they have nothing to lose. I see this as an ideal opportunity for them to regain their form. After our recent performances we must be looking for an improvement and I hope for the standard we achieved when they beat us at home 1—0 after scoring an early goal. We deserved a draw that day and I shall be much happier if we play as well as that at Leeds tomorrow."

They didn't. O'Farrell might have taken heart from the goalless scoreline at half-time but he would have been as shell-shocked as his players an hour later as they all tried to find positives from a crushing 5-1 defeat. O'Farrell had recalled the experienced Tony Dunne and the relatively experienced Steve James to no avail and he could no longer hide from the fact that United desperately needed reinforcements in defence.

Ahead of the FA Cup 5th Round tie with Middlesbrough at Old Trafford, O'Farrell was unable to bring any update. "There have been a lot of possible signings linked with Manchester United recently — but not by me," he said. "No doubt United supporters open their morning newspapers hoping for a statement from the club about which players we are going to sign or, at least, would like to sign. And after United's recent slump I would love to be able to tell our supporters something that would cheer them up. But I can't."

United drew 0-0 with the Teesiders to set up a replay on Leap Year Day at Ayresome Park, where they won 3-0 but supporters would have been just as pleased with the news the day before; O'Farrell had finally brought a player in, and a star name at that. Aberdeen captain and Scotland international Martin Buchan arrived for the princely sum of £135,000. O'Farrell's reaction betrayed the urgency with which the defender was needed. "Buchan will be a tremendous asset to the club and we are delighted to sign him."

The Scot was renowned for his loyalty but was delighted to move south. "How could I turn down a chance like this?" he admitted. "United are one of the greatest clubs in the world, and I am really looking forward to playing for them."

Back-to-back clean sheets against Boro might have had some wondering what all the fuss was about but O'Farrell was hopeful that there was a renewed positive mood at the club. "The win has given everyone a confidence boost and I'm hoping this is the turning point after our bad run," he said.

Buchan was even named captain for his debut, demonstrating the fact that he was going into a defence which desperately needed leaders, but he was powerless to stop his new side going down 2-0 at Tottenham, their seventh consecutive league defeat. It was March 4th and United had lost all seven league games they'd played so far in 1972. They'd also drawn a blank in four of those games, so when it became known that Nottingham Forest were in talks to sell highly-rated forward Ian Storey-Moore to Derby County, O'Farrell moved quickly to make an offer.

The saga was played out in the press to much embarrassment for all involved. United thought they had got their man for a record £200,000 before Brian Clough announced to the press that he had in fact signed Moore, a signing apparently confirmed when the Derby boss paraded his new acquisition at the Baseball

Ground before a home game. It prompted United chairman Louis Edwards to tell reporters, "Mr O'Farrell told us he had agreed with Nottingham Forest to sign Moore. Now I learn that agreement has not been honoured. I understand the Forest directors are very embarrassed about the whole business."

Less than 24 hours later the matter was concluded with Moore being unveiled at United. O'Farrell shrugged off the controversy. "As I stated at the weekend, my negotiations for the transfer of Moore were temporarily interrupted," he said. "I am now very happy that those negotiations have been completed, and that I have achieved what I set out to do —to sign Moore. He is a top-class player, and will play a big part in modelling United's future. There is no doubt he will do us a great deal of good."

O'Farrell had spent £330,000 in the space of a week, breaking the club's transfer record twice. It prompted speculation that they would look to raise funds and for the first time it was suggested that they may be tempted to deal with Derby, who clearly had money to spend and in an area of the team they were looking to strengthen, for the shocking £300,000 transfer of George Best.

O'Farrell was quick to quell the talk. "It is ludicrous even to suppose that we would let Best go," he said. "How could I sell such a player — and who could afford him? He is very much a part of my future plans... This is not necessarily the end of United's big spending. If we are informed that any of the top class players we have inquired about are for sale, then we will buy them."

United celebrated by earning their first league point of the year with a goalless draw at home to Everton before Storey-Moore scored on his debut against Huddersfield Town, Best getting the other, in a 2-0 win, their first in the league since December 4th 1971. Perhaps the record signing and the speculation had done enough to remind Best what was at stake because that was the first of four goals he netted in five games. Soon enough the rot sat back in, with United succumbing to three defeats in four games. A 2-1 replay defeat at Stoke in the FA Cup meant that United would be trophyless again while a 3-1 home derby defeat on 12th April left O'Farrell's team plodding along in 8th. Prior to the last game of the season, a newspaper report ran a poll from supporters with the headline "Sell Best, Say Fans!"

Frank O'Farrell insisted that success would follow with a little patience. "There is a lot of work to be done here," he said. "Team work is vital and we are behind in it. I am looking for improvement from the players who will be staying with the club for they now know what is expected of them. I am not too pessimistic about the future. The two players we have signed, Martin Buchan and Ian Moore, have done well and there are one or two players of similar calibre I want. We have probably surpassed some people by being as high in the table as we are. We did exceptionally well before Christmas."

United won their last game of the season 3-0 against the Potters with Best and Storey-Moore again among the goals and in his 'end of term report' a couple of weeks later for the *Daily Mirror*, O'Farrell was quick to try and realign perspective how his first season had gone: "Nobody had a more frustrating time than Manchester United. We lost a five-point lead at the top of the table. Yet I am satisfied with my first season at Old Trafford. We increased our average gate and improved on last season's record by five points. No team scored more away goals and I am pleased that we were the country's top visiting attraction to maintain the club's reputation of refusing to bow to the dull football which is stifling the game's appeal."

But the season had barely finished when there were huge concerns about Best, whose disconnect with the game had gone a stage further than occasionally missing training. In his autobiography 'Blessed', published in 2002, he admitted, "I never minded the taunts I got from opposition fans, it was all part and parcel of the game. Some supporters threw cans of beer on the pitch and I would pick them up and pretend to drink out of them... But when your own fans start turning on you and mocking you, that is hurtful. I began asking myself, 'Do I need all this?' and began answering that I didn't."

Best said he 'didn't have the stomach' to play in the Home International tournament in May 1972 and went to Marbella without telling anyone. The press found out and so on May 20th Best, reasoning that they were only interested in him because he was a professional footballer — and knowing that he would need an excuse to get out of United's post-season friendly against a Maccabi-Hapoel XI in Israel — hastily announced his retirement from the game in an attempt to get some peace and quiet. "In truth, I didn't know what the hell I was going to do but I figured that by giving the press a sensational story, they would leave me alone for a bit," Best said later.

A few weeks later O'Farrell reported to the media that he had talked to his player and that he would be back in time for the new season. "George has told me he wants to play for United," the Irishman said. "I never thought he would quit. Despite some unpredictable actions and misdemeanours from time to time, I felt his great love for football would decide the issue. George has never told me officially that he didn't want to play again. I'm expecting him to report for training in mid-July... When I saw him recently he looked much better, and it may have been that he did not turn up in Israel because he felt he wasn't match fit. But he has his playing kit with him in Majorca."

Best's team-mates were not amused. On the same day as O'Farrell's insistence that Best would return, Willie Morgan told journalists: "I just don't care what George says he is going to do next. I can't believe what he says because he changes his mind so quickly, and so often." Brian Kidd probably summed up the atmosphere in the dressing room best, telling journalist David Meek, "there's one set of rules for George and one for the rest of us."

Bobby Charlton was also openly frustrated; in a contrast to Best's admission that he lost enthusiasm to play when it wasn't fun, Charlton placed the blame for it not being fun squarely at his younger colleague's door. At one point during the summer, Charlton was so upset that he threatened to leave, and reported to Sir Matt Busby that several players had grown unhappy with Best's behaviour. For his part, and perhaps somewhat in retaliation, Best made it clear that he felt Charlton should have already retired, and the seriousness of their rift was revealed when Best refused to play in Charlton's testimonial match in September 1972. O'Farrell gave another example of their disagreements; despite the lengthy training the team would do on set-pieces, Best, as was his wont, would frustrate Charlton and other team-mates by coming up with something completely different on match-day. "Once the free-kick has been taken, I can't do anything about it, it's up to you as captain to push him away and take control," O'Farrell recalled telling Charlton.

By that time, he was of course back at the club. "George Best, Manchester United's repentant runaway, has been given his last chance by the club," reported the *Mirror*'s John Bean on July 22nd. "If he is in breach of his contract again, we would have to take a far more serious action," O'Farrell said. "George knows that he can't go on and on like he has. He knows that he has got to comply with the club discipline. George accepts this and I hope this will be the last incident we'll have to deal with. Whether the action we have taken will work, I don't know. One can never be sure with an unpredictable person like George, but I'm optimistic."

Reasoning that Mrs Fullaway's house hadn't helped, O'Farrell ordered Best to stay with Pat Crerand. "Georgie boy has been given a personal chaperone, Paddy Crerand, with whom he must now live and who must watch over him to make sure Georgie does not stray from the straight and narrow," renowned United fan and journalist Frank Taylor wrote. "What an appalling indictment of a 26-year-old world famous footballer, that he cannot be the guardian of his own destiny."

Best lasted just a week with Crerand, "we tried to get him back on the straight and narrow again but it was too late, he came to stay with me but he only stayed a couple of nights," the Scot said, "he didn't stay all that long with me, why would he, because I had young kids that were school age… no, George had lost it then in actual fact, I think that in particular time he had lost it, as he couldn't handle all the fame. The likes of George, everybody wants to talk to him… you can't talk to everybody and eventually it drives you mad, when you have to go into seclusion to try and get out the way and all that sort of stuff, and it's not because he disliked the fans, he just couldn't handle all the stuff that goes with it."

Then, the United boss advised his player to see a psychiatrist. Despite dominating O'Farrell's summer, Best hadn't played any part of pre-season yet was expecting to line up against Ipswich in the season opener on 12th August.

The manager tried tough love through the press. "George Best's career is at the crossroads," he wrote in his *Mirror* column. "He knows it. I certainly know it. You cannot sweep his problems under the carpet because they have been exposed in screaming headlines all summer. But I wonder if those who are so quick to criticise George know what it can mean to be pitch-forked like him, into a glamorous life for which he wasn't equipped. Sometimes it is hard to live with fame. That, perhaps, has been George Best's biggest problem. But the solution lies with him. This season he must show he has left his wayward habits behind and prove he has at last learned to say NO to fair-weather friends who tend to drag him away from the job he knows best—FOOTBALL. People who have told me what I ought to do about George don't have all the facts. And any decisions I take concerning him or any player are governed by one factor alone. Is it right for Manchester United? Personalities don't enter it... Last season when George began brilliantly and faded after losing his fitness, he still scored 28 goals. He was on song for only half our programme. I would be extremely happy if I had three men who could score 28 goals a season. And that is the crux of my problem. Great scorers are a rare breed. All George has to do is keep fit. Last season he didn't lose his skills, he lost—or surrendered — those razor-sharp reflexes which put him among the aces. Without his speed and acceleration, he gets caught in possession and risks injury."

In later years, O'Farrell would confess on Best: "He was the key, really. He was carrying the team. And once he stopped turning up, it complicated things."

Nonetheless, a rusty Best was selected in a team-sheet for the season's opener at Old Trafford against Ipswich that looked decidedly unbalanced: Stepney; O'Neil, James, Buchan, Dunne;

Morgan, Charlton; Best, Law, Kidd, Storey-Moore. O'Farrell appeared to be talking to his players as much as the supporters as he wrote his programme notes for the game. "Last season was essentially a finding out period in which, as you well know, we soared to the top and then found we couldn't sustain the pace," he explained. "You don't change things overnight, but we have taken a number of positive steps towards putting this right. A period of change from a long established order, which in recent seasons was not being successful, will inevitably cause some discontent among a few players who may find their positions threatened or may have lost their places already. If any player feels he has been unjustly treated by the decisions taken, my office door is always open for him to discuss the matter in the proper place."

Ipswich won 2-1; having established an early lead, they controlled the game and scored again late on before Law's last minute consolation. The visitors found it easier than the score-line suggested, and Ian Collard, told to man-mark Best, spoke of his comfortable afternoon: "I finished up feeling sorry for him. Bobby Robson, our manager, told me to do a tight-marking job on Best. The longer the game went on, the further back he dropped to try to lose me. He was swearing to himself and getting more and more upset. And I reckon it will get worse for him as the season goes on."

Mick Mills, the full-back who had once been linked with a move to United for £120,000, concurred: "Ian was great. But I expected a lot more from Besty. You had the feeling he realised he is playing in a bad side. There is too much being asked of him."

Best knew in his heart that his comeback was doomed. "I'd thought, as usual, that a change of scenery would help me sort out my problems but it hadn't worked, yet it did convince me that I wanted to play again and give my life some purpose," he said. "Again, no one from the club had contacted me and tried to talk me round. Perhaps they knew I would go back when I was ready and if so, they were right. I went back to O'Farrell and began training like a lunatic for the following season. By now I had already done enough damage to my body that training had become an effort. It had become like work, when before it had been more like fun, something that came entirely naturally to me. My good intentions didn't last long. We got off to a terrible start to the 1972-73 season and didn't even win until the tenth League match of the season. I tried to tell myself that I couldn't go on the way I had been, that I had to stay fit and turn up for training every day… My life came completely off the rails in a black November in 1972. Poor results had worn away my determination to stay on track and twice I just couldn't be bothered to get up for training and was dropped."

United followed their opening defeat by succumbing to two 2-0 defeats on Merseyside within days; first to Liverpool, and then to Everton, to put them bottom of the table. From favourites to win the league at the turn of the year, their fortunes had entirely reversed. "Manchester United, perhaps the greatest and certainly the most popular club in England, are now facing up to at least two years of unavoidable mediocrity," wrote Ken Jones of *The Mirror*. "Bottom of the First Division and pointless after a depressing start to the season they know that the way ahead is going to be hard. It is far too early to regard their position as critical. Rich and powerful, United can in no way be regarded as candidates for relegation."

Frank O'Farrell now insisted that the form in the months after he took over was a red herring he was prepared for: "The team did better than I ever expected it to. But I never lost sight of the fact that there was an awful lot to do before this club could regain its former stature. We needed new players and we still need them. Getting those players is another thing. We have to be patient."

Meanwhile, Brian Clough — outspoken, and one of those managers who had apparently resisted United's advances — was asked about his opinion on events at Old Trafford. Speaking at a dinner in London, he said, "no one has a chance at Old Trafford while Sir Matt is still likely to appear around the corner. That isn't Matt's fault. But I think every manager will know what I mean."

To this point, however, there was little O'Farrell could have grumbled about in terms of interference, aside from a moment that had occurred when he first joined the club. As he was presented with his contract by Louis Edwards, he noted the salary was a few thousand pounds higher than that which Busby had offered.

You would not blame O'Farrell for feeling he had few friends inside or outside of Old Trafford. At least, when things were going well, he hadn't had to worry too much about the 'shadow of Busby', although he did have concerns right from their first meeting about the job. The reports in the press at the time were that the incoming manager would get a salary of £10,000. When Busby first met O'Farrell, he offered a five year deal on £12,000 a year. When O'Farrell met Busby and chairman Louis Edwards together, Edwards revealed that the offer was actually £15,000 a year. Perhaps the event helped stiffen O'Farrell's resolved when he arrived for his first day's work to find Busby still in the manager's office. Wilf McGuinness had deferred and instead taken Jimmy Murphy's office, much to the heartbreak of the Welshman but O'Farrell insisted that for the good of how it would look to the media, it would be better if he took the manager's office. Busby relented. Murphy would later ask O'Farrell, "How did you manage to get him out of there!"

O'Farrell had responded to defeat at Anfield by dropping Bobby Charlton for the Everton game. Until now any reservations O'Farrell may have had before accepting the job regarding interference from Sir Matt Busby had proved to be unfounded. Yet this decision would change all that.

O'Farrell was in an impossible situation. Despite his best efforts the rift in the dressing room had made it clear that there was Best on one side and Charlton on another. It was proving too difficult to accommodate both and establish a balance that was to the benefit of the team. On one hand Charlton may have been regarded as a 'moaner' but he was a fine captain and stood for the standards of the football club, even if it was clear he was approaching the end of his playing career. On the other, Best should have been at his peak and had proved that he only needed to well for a part of the season to score 28 goals in 1971/72. Any off the field moral issues were Busby's domain than O'Farrell's who recognised he now had a fight on to keep the job and so the manager backed the younger man and Charlton was dropped.

Soon after making the decision, it became clear just how Sir Matt Busby felt at a club function. "Your husband Frank is a very independent bastard," Ann O'Farrell, Frank's wife, claimed Busby told her, in an RTE documentary made in 2011. "He shouldn't be. He should come to me and ask me about these things and who he's playing and who he's not playing."

"I was annoyed, I shouldn't be hearing these things through my wife," O'Farrell said, before explaining he then confronted Busby on the following Monday. Busby told O'Farrell that he didn't think he should have dropped Charlton. "He was interfering now, he wasn't the junior director, he was interfering with what I was doing," O'Farrell said.

Pat Crerand, now a player edged out onto the coaching staff via the reserves, strongly rejects that. "Matt never interfered at all, I mean, all the time that different people were managing Manchester United when I was there and after I had finishing playing, you would rarely see Matt," Crerand insists. "At Old Trafford he'd disappear, do what he wants and then disappear, he never interfered with anybody. I'm not sure if people were making excuses for not being successful and that was the factor."

Alex Stepney agrees. "There's been a lot of talk about when Matt went upstairs, that he interfered, I don't believe he did," says the former goalkeeper. "I do not believe for one moment that he interfered with anything of the manager picking the team and the way we played... okay, something might have been said, but it never came through to us. I never thought for one moment that he would interfere with anything football wise."

The undermining worked in both directions against O'Farrell. Denis Law, Willie Morgan, Brian Kidd and others were alleged to have complained to Busby when they were dropped just as senior players had done under McGuinness. It hardly helped matters that most of the senior players mixed socially with Busby on golf days. It would never be suggested that these acts purposely undermined O'Farrell's position as manager but it made it a very difficult situation for him.

As it turned out, Best was a shadow of the player of autumn 1971.

His lifestyle had finally caught up with him and O'Farrell had set in train his own demise by backing the Irishman. This misjudgement and lack of insight (for surely everyone in Manchester knew of Best's decline and his off pitch activities) meant the old guard were in turn less trusting of their manager. We were only in August but it already felt like the beginning of the end.

Charlton was absent again (as, indeed, was O'Farrell) as United could only draw at home with Leicester City, and two days after that game, the manager announced he was giving up his *Daily Mirror* column to concentrate on his day job. He did so with a stunning parting shot. "It's going to take close on one million pounds for me to rebuild Manchester United — to make them not only a National institution again, but to bring back the days of glory to Old Trafford. That's a lot of money, but it represents the size of the task ahead of me, and why, when I go into the transfer market, I have to be more certain than most that the player I sign is the right one. Just how long it will take to put United on to the paths of glory again is anybody's guess. So that is why this, for the time being, is my last column for *Mirror Sport*. I'm going into temporary exile, to devote all my time and energy to the kind of task which now does not permit me outside interests or influences.

"Manchester United are bottom of the First Division. The facts speak for themselves. It hurts me to see them there, and it must be heartbreaking too, not only for my players but for the legions who support us all over the country. It is not sufficient to say we are traditionally slow starters, that there is time, and the position is bound to improve. That may be so, but right now I am under the kind of pressure that demands my full time attention. I am suffering too. I inherited a great club, with an ever greater tradition. Suddenly, they are last in the table, so imagine how I feel right now. At times like this the smallest problem becomes magnified, and, the pressure grows alarmingly...

"I know people are talking, writing us off already, saying that this player and that player are past it, and that bleak years lie ahead for United. Well, I have pride... pride in myself and this club. We are going through a transitional period at Old Trafford, trying to re-build, re-think, re-organise. It will take all of my time. I shall miss my link with *Mirror* readers, many of whom are Manchester fans, but, nothing will, nothing MUST distract me from the task ahead. It is I who must make United great again. I missed our home match with Leicester on Wednesday evening. Where was I? Looking at another match, still doing my homework. But we have our first point now, and it's a start. George Best scored his first goal, too, even though it was from the penalty spot. But they all count, and my coach Malcolm Musgrove told me he played very well. I believe we shall start to see the best of George now. His problems, I feel, are now behind him. Certainly if Wednesday was anything to go by. So we can look forward to some vintage Best performances. We shall need them after our depressing start, which is even more disappointing in view of our great opening last season. But I have pledged myself to pull United through. Therefore, I hope it won't be too long before I'm writing again for *Mirror Sport*, and that United have climbed out of the crisis and are on the crest, again."

Journalist Nigel Clarke, reacting to the United boss's statement, commented "The £1,000,000 that Frank O'Farrell admits he must spend to re-shape Manchester United, represents at least four new players, who must be drafted into the side. But it may not even be enough, for his top priorities are a defender, a centre half, and one or two full backs. A midfield man and striker will also be required."

To put the escalating transfer fees into context, David Nish, the Leicester defender, signed for Derby for £225,000. Clarke reasoned that with Charlton's best days behind him, Kidd's future unclear and Law plagued with injury the club were in need of three top class forwards. "Steve James, at centre half, rarely looks solid enough," Clarke continued, "right-back Tommy O'Neil is handicapped by a lack of height, Tony Dunne is nearing the veteran stage and David Sadler is inconsistent. There have been question marks against goalkeeper Alex Stepney and rumours of part exchange deals, one involving Bryan King of Millwall. Stepney has always been unsure on crosses, and O'Farrell has never disguised his admiration for Leicester's Peter Shilton."

By Clarke's reckoning that was as many as eight players United needed, and that number was reliant on George Best remaining reliable and Ian Moore proving to be good enough. Only Martin Buchan seemed safe and reliable. If Nish's fee was anything to go by, United's need was more likely to be around £1.5m-2m of investment.

The first signing was £65,000 30-year-old Wyn Davies from Manchester City. "I was down for light training this morning and I was about to leave the ground for lunch when Malcolm Allison called me into his office," Davies explained. "I thought he was going to ask me about my broken nose and if I would be fit for Saturday. To my surprise he told me there wasn't a first team spot for me at Maine Road any more. I sat stunned and then he said, 'But there is a chance for you to sign for Manchester United and I think you should take it.' If you had told me a few months ago I would be going to Old Trafford I'd have laughed. But after the way Malcolm explained the situation I thought 'this is it... I must have a look at United and see how keen they are.' Mr. O'Farrell impressed me very much. He quickly convinced me I would be making the right move. I am sorry to leave City where I've been treated wonderfully. But this is a new chance for me and I am looking forward to it. What a day it's been!"

Two weeks later Bournemouth striker Ted MacDougall also signed for £220,000. "By lunch-time today my dearest wish should have come true — I'll be a Manchester United player," he told *The Mirror* on September 28th. "Manchester United... the very mention of the name leaves me numb right now. I have to keep telling myself that I really will soon be pulling on a red jersey and running out on to the Old Trafford pitch. I have always wanted to play for them. To me, they are the biggest name in football and I am proud that such people as Sir Matt Busby and manager Frank O'Farrell should think I can do a job for them. That's why I'll be the happiest man in the world if as I expect—I pass my medical examination at their ground this morning. I won't be able to get my signature on those transfer documents fast enough!"

O'Farrell said he had been a long time admirer: "I have wanted Ted since I was at Leicester. He is a player who is associated with goals and Manchester United have a similar association."

There was competition for places now amongst United's forwards and Denis Law, who had described Wyn Davies as "the sort of player I think we've needed ever since David Herd left," also welcomed MacDougall, saying, "A new name can do nothing but good for the side. Everyone is going to raise his performance."

Bobby Charlton, since recalled to the side, agreed. "The manager has to strengthen the side as he feels fit," he said. "There has always been fierce competition for a first team place here."

O'Farrell had made internal changes too, having Malcolm Musgrove 'draw lots' to change hotel room sharing arrangements for away games in order to break up alliances that the manager felt were contributing towards dressing room rifts. The manager may well have felt some as United achieved their first league win of the season in some style against Derby on 23rd September. Ian Storey-Moore and Wyn Davies were both on the scoresheet in a 3-0 win.

MacDougall's first goal came in a 1-0 win over fellow strugglers Birmingham City on 14th October. The unconvincing win did at least keep United off bottom place but only by goal difference; now they were third from bottom, but on nine points like four other teams. It prompted a column from Frank McGhee of *The Mirror* and for the first time O'Farrell's leadership was called into serious question.

"What has O'Farrell done to MY team?" asked McGhee, continuing, "…what HAVE you done to my club, Frank? What HAS he done to my team, Matt? MY team, and MY club? It is possibly safe, now that I no longer live in Manchester, to confess that Old Trafford under Busby was the place where I learned to love Soccer—and to admire the way I still believe it should be played. United don't play it that way any longer… It is a popular theory that poor old Frank O'Farrell inherited all his troubles from Sir Matt Busby. Certainly, he inherited some, but let's redress the balance a bit. He did not inherit Ted MacDougall (£220,000), Ian Moore (£220,000), Wyn Davies (£60,000) or Martin Buchan (£100,000). He bought them with the money inherited from Sir Matt's mainly-marvellous management. To go hitting below the belt, O'Farrell also inherited money that could have bought Alan Ball. It is an open secret that, had United acted more swiftly, they—not Arsenal—would have been Ball's first choice."

That much was true. Ball's father regularly went to Old Trafford and would beg the club to sign his son. Alan junior said that he had made it 'common knowledge' that he would have 'jumped at the chance' to sign for United. Only on the morning of Ball's move to Arsenal did O'Farrell make an overture and by then it was too late. It was the first true aberration from the United boss, taking place as it did over Christmas 1971, when the cracks in his first team were only just beginning to show. At that point he was being heralded as the best coach in the country; less than a year on, it seemed as if every decision he made was to the detriment of his team.

With more than half a million pounds invested in the team, the Old Trafford board might have expected results. They might have been entitled to expect them just as much as one would expect them to demonstrate patience. But United lost 2-1 at Newcastle and were then humiliated at home against Tottenham when Martin Peters became the second visiting player in little over a year to score four goals at Old Trafford.

One report of the game slammed the manager, "Cyril Knowles and Jimmy Pearce cruelly exposed and exploited the flank virtually unchallenged, while John Pratt and Steve Perryman won the midfield with hardly a whisper from United... Wherever (Martin) Peters appeared, there was no-one to challenge him. That, I believe, is as much a reflection on Frank O'Farrell's direction as it is a condemnation of the United players."

The United boss was equally critical of the performance but seemed to indicate that the problems needed more financial assistance. "We were shocking," admitted O'Farrell. "We lost some terrible goals. How can you give a team like Spurs the breaks that we did... I am certainly not going to buy players in a panic. I have the money and would sign certain players tomorrow if only they were available, but the board know I shall not buy for buying's sake. One expects to be criticised when things are going badly. But what I object to is the way some people, completely unaware of our set-up, are going all out to crucify me. I knew, when I took over at United, that it was not going to be easy. I am fully aware we are going through a really bad spell. But it is not over yet."

A fortnight after that humbling against Spurs, United won 2-0 against Liverpool, with Davies and MacDougall the scorers. Brief hope was extinguished the following week when O'Farrell watched his team fall to a shambolic 3-0 defeat at Manchester City. United conceded early and never looked like they were in the game; their rivals scored two late goals with O'Farrell's side all over the place. Worst still, the defeat put United bottom of the table.

It was the straw which broke the camel's back in the case of George Best. He played in United's next game, a 2-1 win at home to Southampton but couldn't muster up enthusiasm. "The football was so poor that I soon drifted back into the old drinking routine, drowning my sorrows, I suppose, and it didn't occur to me that my behaviour was in any way to blame for the club's position," he later admitted. "I put it all down to the poor quality of the players around me and the back-biting in the dressing room."

One night Best was confronted in one of his friend's nightclubs; a woman threw a drink over him and she was about to do it again when Best, in his own words, "smacked her with the back of my hand. I didn't punch her, just clipped her to keep her off me, like you would a wasp or a fly." However the woman suffered a hairline fracture of her nose. A hearing was set for January 1973 and Best had even more reason, or excuse, to go off the rails. He missed training and was dropped from the team to face Norwich at Carrow Road.

Clearly still of the belief that George was his best player, the manager commented, "some people have criticised me for the way I deal with the situations when Best is in trouble. My reply to those who say 'Throw him out' is that I have a duty as manager to put the finest possible team into the field. Best, when fit, is one of the finest players in the world. Unfortunately not even he can display his many talents unless he is superbly fit. Having missed training this week, he would not have been fit, mentally and physically for Saturday's game. He will do extra training this weekend and continue through next week, so that he will be in condition for the game against Stoke. Best's attitude was one of genuine regret. He was clearly sorry for the trouble he had caused. It all stems from the nightclub incident, but again, he should not have been there in the first place. He should have explained his troubles to the club instead of staying away for two days, but who knows the mind of George Best?"

For some of the players at the club, O'Farrell's handling of Best had now not only caused division but exposed a lack of control. "He certainly baffled Frank O'Farrell whose strait-laced approach to life must have led to his own, private condemnation of George's activities," Alex Stepney said. "Frank tried reasoning and tried outbursts of temper. I have seen this outwardly urbane man, in his white collar and dark tie, almost go berserk with George in the dressing-room... I am sure that Frank will always regret that he had to be the manager of Manchester United during the decline and fall of the greatest football talent the British Isles has ever produced... Frank's attitude to George had revealed a weakness. He had lost his grip and it was beginning to show. He was hiding from everyone and I believe he began to think that even the Press were gunning for him. As was usual, four journalists accompanied us on our pre-season tour of Copenhagen and West Berlin; Frank's paranoia showed at the team-talk before one match when he actually said: 'Remember, there are Pressmen out there who have come to knock you.'"

A Best-less United won 2-0 at Norwich. Whether he was confessing he had previously been wrong to be so supportive of the Irishman or whether he had finally had enough or whether he now tried to appease the anti-Best section of his dressing room, O'Farrell placed Best on the transfer list in early December.

"Worried about the hearing, which went to court in January 1973, I had been drinking even more," Best recalled. "In December, I had skipped training to go down to London for a change of scenery and was enjoying myself so much, I didn't come back for a few days. For once, I felt O'Farrell might have had some sympathy but he was under enough pressure for his own job and obviously didn't feel he could keep worrying about where I was… He went to the board and I was told that I was not only suspended for two weeks but that I was now available for transfer for £300,000. Seeing that it was to be another five years before United were to pay more than that for a player, it seemed a pretty high fee. And at the state I was in at the time, I probably wasn't worth £3,000. Even so, my pride was hurt and I went to see Sir Matt and the chairman Louis Edwards."

Before that, however, came a spell where it seemed certain Best would finally leave the only club he'd known. Derby County tested the water by talking up their interest. Sam Longson, chairman of the League champions, said: "Our manager, Brian Clough, has already said his club would join the bidding for Best. A £300,000 fee wouldn't necessarily be beyond us. We've transacted some pretty big transfers in the past."

Then a BBC radio report stated that Best had actually signed for Chelsea, forcing O'Farrell to deny it. "Personally I feel very sad about what has happened." the United boss said. "The plain truth is that you can't keep a ball and chain on Best. It is a thousand pities that we should have this problem at Old Trafford. In my view it is a human problem as well as a football problem. Best has delighted millions of fans all over the world, yet he has never been able, while I have been here, to realise the responsibility he has to himself, the manager, his colleagues and the club's young players. The problem existed with the two previous managers — Sir Matt Busby and Wilf McGuinness — before I took over at Old Trafford. Who knows Best's mind? Certainly no-one seems able to get through to him, and the board simply had no alternative but to place him on the transfer list. We are losing a great footballer, but the decision is final."

As usual, Best's name was all over the press. Football League secretary Alan Hardaker was not interested. "I'm fed up to the teeth with all this about George Best," he told reporters. "In fact, I don't even want to hear the name of George Best again. Too much time and thought has already been given to this young man."

The footballing public in general hadn't heard enough, just

yet. Everyone from Real Madrid to Bournemouth were interested in signing Best. That isn't just a figure of speech; both clubs made their interest known. There was a ban on foreign players playing in Spain but it didn't stop Real manager Miguel Muñoz from thinking they would try and find a way to make it work. "any club would want George as a player and that includes us" he said. On the same day, there were reports that Third Division Bournemouth would make a £250,000 bid. Cherries manager John Bond said: "I do not want people to regard this as just a gimmick. We are genuinely interested."

Just about the only party in the entire saga to not yet signal their intentions was George himself; though reports on the 8th December, the day before United's home game with Stoke City, said sources close to the player had revealed his preference was to move to Chelsea. O'Farrell responded, "Since the trouble blew up, I have been available in my office all day, but despite all the talk about his future nobody has been in touch."

O'Farrell continued to talk about Best in the match programme that weekend. "So many people have been willing to help him, but even this week he ran off again from an opportunity for the board to hear his problems," he said. "There has been little response from him in answer to appeals and advice. It is all very perplexing... In the final analysis we believe the decision taken will be for the good of Manchester United."

If it seemed that the United boss had enemies everywhere, then at least journalist David Meek served as a contrary voice, keen to point out that the issues were greater than the manager. "There has never been any doubt in my mind that while one would still like the club to return to the transfer market at least once more, there is already enough talent at Old Trafford to steer away from the relegation area," Meek wrote in his column for the match programme. "The main problems have been a matter of blend, of settling in the new signings, and above all else, imbuing the team with a spirit of endeavour and confidence."

Yet Meek went one step further. He wrote a newspaper column with the headline "BE FAIR TO FRANK" saying that the players and the board must also share the blame for United's troubles. The article earned Meek, the Manchester Evening News United reporter since 1958, a ban from the team coach. O'Farrell's case wasn't helped by United losing 2-0 to Stoke, and unbeknown to him it would be the last time he took charge of a home game. He prepared for the Crystal Palace game as normal but was floored by a bombshell two days before the game when it was revealed to him that George Best was returning to the club.

BEST IS NOT FOR SALE reported *The Express*. "I have seen George Best and discussed recent happenings with him," said Chairman Louis Edwards. "He only wants to play for Manchester United. I've spoken to the directors and to our manager Frank O'Farrell. Best will start training as soon as possible."

The Mirror take on the story began, "George Best and Manchester United made their peace last night. And today Soccer's hottest property will be officially taken off the transfer list. The sudden, dramatic reconciliation came when the truant Irish star changed his itinerary yesterday and settled for home. Instead of flying to Majorca for the weekend as planned, Best had talks with United chairman Louis Edwards at the Chorlton-cum-Hardy home of director Sir Matt Busby," reported Bob Russell.

"I know nothing about it. Nothing at all," O'Farrell said when asked of the meeting by the *Mirror*, though he did tell the *Express*, "I have been kept fully informed about Best but beyond that I have no comment to make." Best turned up for training on Thursday 14th December and was seen after training in a pub with a 'half pint of beer' according to the *Express*.

On the day of United's game at Palace, *The Mirror* commented on the controversial chain of events with the memorable back page which bore the headline, "NOWT! NOWT! NOWT!" Bob Russell reported, "Manchester United, once the undisputed masters of both football and public relations, left a trail of question marks behind yesterday... What United aren't revealing — though there are rumours galore — is who or what prompted the sudden and dramatic policy change towards a player they had washed their hands of less than two weeks earlier. And since there has so clearly has been a top-level policy change, who and what does it affect apart from George Best? Manager Frank O'Farrell isn't saying what he thinks of the business, and the players are under orders not to talk about George. But we have a fair idea that they are in a state of confusion, judging from the bewildered faces seen at their London hotel. It's an expression also written over the faces of the thousands who care and campaign for Manchester United week in, week out, home and away."

Having spent so long caught in the political battle between Charlton and Best, neither were selected to play at Selhurst Park. Denis Law was on the bench, with O'Farrell favouring his signed forwards MacDougall, Davies and Storey-Moore.

As O'Farrell got off the team bus, he bumped into Tommy Docherty, the Scotland manager. Docherty was annoyed that he had been let down for tickets and was trying to sort it out. O'Farrell promptly handed his old friend tickets to sit behind Matt Busby and Louis Edwards and watch the game. United were a goal down by the tenth minute. Goals either side of half-time put the game out of reach. The final score-line of Crystal Palace 5 Manchester United 0 still ranks as one of the biggest shocks in English football, more so because Palace only scored 41 goals all season and were relegated.

"It was a dark day", Alex Stepney recalls, "the inevitable crunch came just before Christmas... The laughter had gone out of the club. There was no spark, no enthusiasm, no earnestness coming from Frank. And so we went to Crystal Palace for the most humiliating experience of my entire career. I have never played in a team that was so lacking in spirit and fighting quality. We lost 5-0, and the score-line could easily have been double that... We all knew that night that something had to be done about the stewardship of the club we loved. We had grown completely away from Frank."

On 18th December, Frank O'Farrell spoke to the press about a board meeting the following day. "The meeting will be a long one. The position of George Best will be discussed but that is only one of the items on the agenda" while insisting that he wasn't as in the dark as his comments the week before had suggested. "We heard nothing from Best after the club announcement that he had been suspended and placed on the transfer list. The chairman was anxious that a stalemate should not develop and he said he thought it in the club's interest to have a talk to Best and to find out what was on his mind. When I arrived home on Thursday evening after that meeting had taken place I was told that the chairman had been trying to contact me, but when I rang him back the line was engaged. A few minutes later a reporter phoned me and I had to say that I didn't know what had taken place. It was just unfortunate, but the chairman had definitely tried to contact me."

That night O'Farrell attended a testimonial dinner in honour of Bobby Charlton but was denied a place at the top table. The instability of his position at Old Trafford was obvious. Still, from the tone of his conversation, one must presume that O'Farrell was in for a huge shock when he learned of the agenda of the board meeting the next day. "Matt didn't say anything at the board meeting," O'Farrell remembered. "The chairman said, 'We're terminating your contract' and I said, 'For what reason?' He told me 'no reason' and I said 'I can't go out of this room not knowing why I'm sacked'. He said 'we are bottom' but we weren't, we were third from bottom."

Of less concern to O'Farrell, but of equal significance to the press, was the future of George Best, which was also determined in the same meeting. United's directors clearly saw the demise of the club through the perspective that O'Farrell and Best were almost inextricably linked. One wasn't equipped to lead them off the pitch, the other couldn't do it on it, and so they took the decision that a clean break was necessary. George Best, like Frank O'Farrell, was sacked.

The now ex-manager tried to be philosophical as he spoke to the press. "I've enjoyed working at Manchester United and I hope that whoever takes over will eventually achieve the success the club wants," he said. "But he will need time to do what needs to be done. It's not my way to criticise, I don't fear relegation for United. They have players with enough ability to keep them up... I was called in and spent only a minute or two with the board. When I asked for the reason for my dismissal the club chairman would not give me one at first. When I pressed him, Mr. Edwards said: 'We're at the bottom of the First Division.' I asked about Malcolm Musgrove. I regret very much other people have gone as well. Malcolm is a good coach, but these days it seems when a manager goes so does the coach. I was surprised to hear about John Aston who was appointed by Sir Matt Busby when he was in charge. For a man like John, who has given so much of his time to Manchester United, it must be very upsetting."

The news hit Best even harder, he announced his retirement from the game for the second time that year. "I am finished with the game," he declared. "I shall never play again."

A day later he wrote a letter which was sent to the club and circulated to the press.

"Dear Sirs,

"I had thought seriously of coming personally and asking for a chance to speak at the board meeting, but once again, I am afraid, when it comes to saying things face to face, I might not have been completely honest. I am afraid, through my somewhat unorthodox ways of trying to sort my own problems out, I have caused Manchester United even bigger problems. I wanted you to read this letter before the board meeting commenced, so as to let you know my feelings before any decisions or statements are issued following the meeting.

"When I said last summer I was going to quit football, contrary to what many people said or thought, I seriously meant it because I had lost interest in the game for various reasons. While in Spain I received a lot of letters from both friends and well-wishers, quite a few asking me to reconsider. I did so and after weeks of thinking it over I decided to give it another try. It was an even harder decision to make than the original one. I came back hoping my appetite for the game would return and even though in every game I like to think I gave one hundred per cent, there was something missing. Even now I am not sure what. Therefore I have decided not to play football again and this time no one will change my mind.

"In conclusion I would like to wish the club the best of luck for the remainder of the season and for the future. Because even though I personally have tarnished the club's name in recent times, to me and thousands of others, Manchester United still means something special."

Surprisingly, given the circumstances, Matt Busby was far less gracious when talking to reporters about the Northern Irish star. "We've finally had enough of George," he said. "We've finally had to decide to get him out of our hair once and for all. All of us on the board were at the end of our tether. We've had enough of George and his nightclubs and his way of life."

It was reflective of the general tone with which the club had dealt with the entire situation. As Frank McGhee of *The Mirror* reported: "George Best's latest announcement of his retirement from football — and how we must all hope that this time it is final — had a significant difference. This time some good men went with him. No one can seriously believe that his decision to get out of the game had nothing to do with yesterday's sacking by Manchester United of manager Frank O'Farrell, his assistant Malcolm Musgrove and chief scout John Aston. The most surprising thing about it all is that Frank O'Farrell was apparently surprised when the roof finally fell in and buried him... I am told that O'Farrell, when he was given the news, was also told to hand over the keys of his club-owned car and had to be given a lift away from the ground by Malcolm Musgrove."

★

"Frank came as a stranger and left as a stranger."

Pat Crerand's famous epitaph of the O'Farrell regime has gone down in United folklore. One of Busby's closest aides continued, "I think the job was too big for Frank at that particular time, and I think maybe nerves played a part a big part with him but he was a bit lost at Old Trafford, and I think if you ask any of the players at that time they would probably agree with me."

"Frank was a nice enough guy," recalls Willie Morgan. "He

had a lad called Malcolm Musgrove, a very nice person, absolutely lovely… he got us all together and said, 'Alex when you get the ball I want you to throw it out to Tony Dunne, Tony when you get the ball, Bobby you break off there and Tony will pass it and Paddy… when Bobby gets in, you move in and George'…we're all looking at each other, 'what's he talking about', football's not like that, he was the wrong man, simple… he was a nice guy though, nothing wrong with him as a person, but he was just the wrong man completely."

Alex Stepney believes if Martin Buchan had been signed just four months earlier, history might have been very different. "They (O'Farrell and Musgrove) came in and we didn't know what to expect, but we soon realised that it was a good team to be honest, you know, the two of them. We played a (good) style of football until Christmas, I think we were five points ahead at the top of the league, when we went and beat Southampton but, I think we won 5-2 but we were winning 3-2, 3-1… we were conceding… the fans were wanting Frank to buy somebody but it was too late, I think he waited until March before he brought probably one of the greatest players that I have had in front of me, Martin Buchan. Now if that had happened say, in early October, I think we would have changed that season in respect that we could have finished near enough at the top."

If the manner in which O'Farrell was sacked seemed ruthless, United had at least identified the man to, eventually, lead them out of the mire. However the character of that man ensured that the headline grabbing, soap opera nature of United's decline would continue for some time yet.

CALL THE DOC

SIR MATT BUSBY BRIEFLY TOOK CHARGE of affairs in the wake of Frank O'Farrell's sacking. By briefly, we are talking about a matter of hours, and yet it was still a long enough period of time to provide an element of confusion in the chronology of events.

On the morning of December 21st 1972, chairman Louis Edwards and Sir Matt Busby — and all of the club's directors — went to the Cliff training ground to meet the players.

"We wanted to give them all our vote of confidence," said Busby. "We have some good players who can help us through. I believe they can get us out of trouble… Somebody has to be around the players. The board have asked me for my help. They are calling on my experience and will accept my advice with regard to team selection. Until we get another manager, somebody has to fill the gap — the board has put it on my shoulders and I have accepted the situation." Indeed, *The Mirror* said that Busby was 'in effect' the club's manager for the third time.

Alex Stepney told reporters that the players were impressed by the club's reaction. "The meeting was brilliantly done," said Stepney, "The morale of the players had been low— naturally enough when you consider the last few weeks. But today's meeting wiped away all that. Everybody was given back respect. I'm sure it will make a difference to the atmosphere in the team."

Both O'Farrell and Wilf McGuinness could claim to have fallen foul of interference from Busby; there is the suggestion that Busby couldn't let go of the club he had built. This is complicated by the blunt rejection of such a theory by senior players who, by their own admission, would go to Busby themselves if either McGuinness or O'Farrell gave them a problem. It was a complicated political situation that might have put off prospective candidates.

The fate of Matt's great friend and rival Bill Shankly would be informed by the post-1968 events at Old Trafford. In seeking to avoid their own long, rancorous decline, the Anfield board simply banished Shanks after his resignation in 1974. Not only was he barred from any decision making role at the club but he was excluded completely to the extent that he was banned from Liverpool's training ground. The virtue of that decision was the club's seamless transition into their most successful era. Yet it is a decision not without controversy. Shankly was dead by 1981, with many claiming he'd died of a broken heart caused by the break up with the love of his life, Liverpool Football Club.

Busby biographer Paddy Barclay, reflecting on whether United should have pre-empted Liverpool's example says, "Given what Busby had done, making Manchester United into a global institution, it would have been very harsh doing what Liverpool did, in effect side-lining Bill Shankly on his resignation and bringing in his erstwhile assistant Bob Paisley. History would say 'well done Liverpool, you were tough, but you did the right thing' and that club will always have the trophies to prove it. Manchester United was very different in that the board, as headed by Louis Edwards the long-time chairman, was a long-term friend of Matt's [indeed Busby co-opted Edwards on to the board]. The friendship may have become strained but in the real world it would have been impossible for Louis to do that to the man who'd created Manchester United. So he (Busby) was always going to stay. In hindsight, would it have been better if Louis Edwards had knifed the greatest man in the history of Manchester United to this day? And you may say, that seems a bit odd when this is the club of Sir Alex Ferguson. But Sir Alex would never have dreamed of going to Manchester United before Matt Busby took over. Matt Busby created that job for Sir Alex Ferguson and he was the inspiration. So, the man who'd really built this club from scratch, couldn't be moved. With the benefit of hindsight, you could argue maybe they should have advised Matt 'Listen I'm sorry mate, you can have an office but no power. And we're going to bring in Don Revie, Jock Stein whatever'. Maybe that would have been better. They did try. Matt tried to replace himself with Jock Stein but it wasn't successful."

So while keeping Busby around was good for the romantic heritage of the club, even Barclay admits it was not in the best interests of the managers who succeeded him and by extension the club's competitiveness on the pitch. Of his immediate successors Barclay explains, "the players always had this court of appeal that was Matt Busby. They could go above the manager's head to Matt and the chairman and at that period, because of what those players had done for him in giving him the first European Cup ever by an English club in 1968 exactly 10 years after Munich had nearly killed him… Manchester United was everything in his life and those players, Law, Best, Charlton, David Sadler, Alex Stepney, all the others, they'd given him what he'd so desperately wanted in 1968 in becoming the first English champions of Europe. And he just could not bring himself to stick the knife in. He just could not do it. You might say that's good. But it wasn't good for Manchester United."

Or Frank O'Farrell, who had grown so used to the uncertainty around his position that he can not have been surprised to see news of his dismissal play out in the paper. O'Farrell had become so embittered that it was written in Michael Crick and David Smith's 'Betrayal of a Legend' he kept a newspaper clipping in which Busby had once referred to O'Farrell as his "last great signing, possibly the greatest of the lot". The sincerity seems obvious, although to O'Farrell it was a reminder that Busby still called the shots.

No one emerged from the events of December 1972 with any credit. The thrashing at Selhurst Park was arguably the club's most humiliating since the war. Palace were relative top flight newcomers, with their first experience of Division One football coming back in August 1969. They had survived for three seasons in the top flight finishing 20th, 18th and 20th again. United may have been beaten by as many goals in other games since 1945 but when one thinks of Everton's 5-0 victory at Goodison in 1984 or City's 6-1 win at Old Trafford in 2011, both teams went on to win the championship. Crystal Palace finished second from bottom in 1972/73 and the five goals they scored that afternoon represented

12% of their end of season total.

All of the issues afflicting United seemed to culminate in one horrendous afternoon down in London. Dissent ran freely through a dressing room who knew they had more power at the club than the manager. The manager had staked his reputation on Best over the elderly Charlton and lost spectacularly. O'Farrell's hugely unpopular decision to drop Charlton again that afternoon was the final straw.

However, as Paddy Barclay explains, the knives were already being sharpened as political intrigue played out in the Selhurst Park boardroom. "Frank O'Farrell went the same way as Wilf McGuinness," explains Paddy Barclay. "He was strung up by the players. Wilf obviously had been unsuccessful in moving on the old guard. Bobby Charlton, George... but Frank O'Farrell really faced the same sorts of problems that Wilf had done, which was to get rid of players that still had a direct route to Matt. And Matt, even after the failure of the McGuinness experiment, still behaved as a general manager. Matt would do transfer deals under Frank O'Farrell. Frank, I'm sure he was asked for his opinion, but Matt would sign the players and decide their salaries and so on. Frank basically was done by the players in the same way that Wilf had been. And I mean really, it was impossible to argue after the 5-0 defeat at Crystal Palace, which was totally humiliating, but the writing was on the wall before that because in the boardroom at Crystal Palace at Selhurst Park that day was the manager of Scotland Tommy Docherty and Matt introduced him to Louis Edwards the chairman 'as Manchester United's next manager'. And so Frank O'Farrell's hold on the players had been loosened long before."

Martin Edwards insists that Busby's control wasn't quite as dominating as that. "Well, I think it was difficult for Wilf, and I think it turned out to be difficult for Frank, I think Tommy Doc was a different kettle of fish, I don't know how much he worried about Matt being in the background.

"I think when O'Farrell arrived, he wanted the responsibility (of transfers) for himself, and I think by the time Tommy Doc arrived, Tommy would have had previous experience of managing so I'm not sure that Matt would have interfered with the buying and selling. I think those managers would have made the request in their own right and those requests were really accepted by the board or not, but certainly on the board, Matt would have had some ideas, more ideas than anybody else being a football man, of the players that were being recommended, so he would have had some input but more in the 'yea' or 'nay' category than actually suggesting or going out and buying the players."

"It was just dreadful, that's the only way you could say it," admits Cliff Butler about the game at Selhurst Park. "You couldn't believe that Manchester United were playing that game and they looked so resplendent that day as well in all white. I loved that all white kit because they looked really smart and I still look back on that game and think, how did that happen, Manchester United losing to Crystal Palace 5-0?"

The result was made all the more staggering by how well O'Farrell had started in the job. "One year earlier we're top of the league by five points and then you know, you get to this situation where you're losing to Crystal Palace and things weren't going right," recalls Alex Stepney. "He was a lovely man Frank, but we didn't know a lot about him, because when he came in — like any manager would be — he would come in and make you welcome, there was a mutual respect by talking to each other and things like that, but we started losing that high point in the league, we lost and lost and lost… the gulf widened, he wouldn't speak to you. When a manager doesn't speak to you, not only one person or one player, but doesn't speak to a few players, it becomes a problem."

In his 1981 book "Alex Stepney", the former goalkeeper revealed a resistance in the dressing room which might have explained some of the difficulties faced by the manager and his signings. "The atmosphere in the dressing-room was not helped by the arrival of Frank's first big signing, Martin Buchan," Stepney said, "when he first landed at Old Trafford from Aberdeen he was a very different, and difficult, character indeed. He was Frank's man, and it was as thought he had been told not to get too close in friendship with the other players. I sensed that he had been told we were all bad types and that he was not to allow us to influence his thinking. He rarely spoke. He went his own way and his manner was extremely cold. There was none of the devil-may-care spontaneity from him that I normally expected to find from professional footballers. Whenever anyone tackled him about this supercilious approach he delivered a reply of chilling premeditation. He said that he had been brought up differently from us and that he intended doing things his way. On reflection now I realise that possibly we were unfair to Martin. In our insecurity we probably read too deeply into his relationship with O'Farrell and as we sought to 'take the mickey' out of Martin at every opportunity. Martin's early attitude backfired on him somewhat, because the revenge that his team-mates sought came in a series of Buchan stories, mostly apocryphal, but told with great relish by those who felt they had an axe to grind. For a time Buchan stories took over from Irish jokes in the United dressing-room."

Few players would have loyalty to O'Farrell; those who had their careers at Old Trafford to thank him for were naturally top of the list. Take Sammy McIlroy, who almost reluctantly admits that the defeat had made change inevitable. "I remember the game, Crystal Palace away, we got beat by five and things were looking a little bit grim because of that sort of run," he says. "There was a bit of unrest around the squad at the time. I think after that defeat, I think the board then realised that something had to be done. For me, Frank gave me my debut, I'll always be very grateful for him and you know, he helped me in every way into the first team, himself and Malcolm Musgrove, who was a coach at the time… so I was a little bit disappointed that the manager that gave me my debut lost his job but on the other side, in football terms, you could see something had to change because the results were going the other way."

It was a low point for the board. "That was horrendous because Crystal Palace were near the bottom of the league, as were we at the time, and they absolutely slaughtered us," recalls Martin Edwards. "I just remember it being a totally miserable day and getting absolutely stuffed by Palace... that was the end."

The end for O'Farrell but in some respects the Palace game was the start of an altogether more serious and rapid decline that would take some 18 months to unravel. It was hoped that the club had a solid succession plan. "In his (Frank's) first season we started off very well, we went to the top of league and by the end of the season we dropped back and the second season we had a fairly disastrous first half of the season," remembers Edwards. "By Christmas the board had decided things weren't getting any better... in fact if anything they were getting worse, and of course we had that 5-0 drubbing at Crystal Palace, so the board got together and said that we needed to make a change. Tommy Docherty was managing Scotland at the time and doing a very good job. I don't think there were any other candidates at that stage, I think it was very much you know, 'Can we get Tommy Docherty to come and run United?' so I don't remember there being a lot of debate about other candidates at that time, it was decided quite early on that Tommy was the man."

It appeared to play out in the press in a much more protracted manner than other recollections would have you believe. Docherty, of course, had been at Selhurst Park, sitting close to Sir Matt Busby and Louis Edwards. "I had just gone up to go for a cup of tea and I caught Sir Matt Busby and he made a hand gesture that meant he wanted to see me," Docherty recalls. "So at half time... 'Embarrassing,' he said, and I said it was, it was only 3-0 at that particular time and it finished up 5-0, he said 'What do you think?'

"I said 'the attitude is poor in a lot of the players, too many prima donnas in the team'.

"So he said 'Could I see you at full time out in the boardroom?'

"I said 'Yeah, of course you can'...

"So the score finished at 5-0 for Crystal Palace so he said 'What do you think?'

"I said (it's) 'disastrous really, a club that's in that position, it's very poor'.

"Then he asked 'would I be interested in the job'.

"I said 'Well I've got a job with Scotland and you've got a manager in Frank O'Farrell who ironically enough is Godfather to two of my boys'

"He said 'Yeah he may be the manager now, but he won't be the manager next week.' This is Busby telling me that O'Farrell is gonna get the sack which I didn't think…I didn't take too kindly to the way it was done. Anyway, Frank O'Farrell got the sack during the week and I got a phone call on Thursday morning from Wullie Allen, the secretary of the Scottish FA… Matt Busby wanted to speak to me."

According to Willie Morgan, overtures were made that week via him. "I was playing golf at Mere with the Gaffer (Busby). Afterwards, we had a cup of tea and he just said 'What did you think about Tommy Docherty when you were away?' and obviously I thought he was great, you know, did this, did that, improvised here and I said he was great, a good motivator and he said 'Do you think he'll do a job for us?' I said, 'I think he would be good, yeah.' That was on the Thursday and a couple hours later the gaffer rang me at home and asked me if I had Tommy's number and I did, he lived up at Scotland at the time and he got the job… the reason he came was because obviously we weren't good enough, it started with Wilf and then some of the older players; some had gone, some had retired, Tony Dunne had moved on, Bill Foulkes had retired… it wasn't easy so the squad he took over were okay but not a great team per se, but then he brought himself and he bought other players in and he played great football, his team were playing attacking football, he was a good judge."

In Docherty's autobiography 'Hallowed Be Thy Game' he stated that Busby in fact chased him up the day after the Palace game for an answer. Docherty, attracted mostly by United but also by the return of day-to-day work with players, had already made his mind up. After the official announcement of O'Farrell's sacking, he was a heavy favourite in the press but there was still a little time for the press to link Ron Saunders of Norwich City to the role in the event United were unable to get their first choice. "Tommy had done very well at Chelsea, he'd been at Villa, where he was probably not as so successful, so he had a slightly a chequered career, but had managed an exciting Chelsea team and he was managing an exciting Scottish team, so I think the feeling was that he was the right ingredient for Manchester United, his style of play would suit the United brand, as you might call it, so you know, I think at the time, he was the right decision," Martin Edwards recalls. "I thought he was exhilarating at the time because sometimes the football club needs a bit of a football character and I thought that his character was sometimes reflected in the teams, a bit like say when Ron Atkinson arrived. Tom's teams tended to reflect his personality, he liked attacking football and the rest of it so I never minded that, I thought it was quite exciting."

On Friday 22nd December Docherty was announced as Manchester United manager. "As the Mafia say, he (Louis Edwards) made me an offer I could not refuse," Docherty told reporters. "The signing will be at Old Trafford after United's game against Leeds tomorrow. I am delighted at the way things have turned out. It's great to be here in charge of a great club… First, I have to find what has gone wrong. In my opinion, there are too many good players for the side to be in the position they are. My job will be to help them find their confidence again. That seems to be their big problem at the moment. I don't know about new signings yet. It takes time to find out who you need. A more important job is to get the best out of the players I have. To run a team successfully, you have to mix with the players; to find if they are unhappy, not only at the ground but in their domestic life too. There has to be discipline too." Docherty was keen to address speculation about Busby's presence. "Sir Matt is everything a football manager should be," the new manager insisted. "He has a tremendous knowledge of the game and knows how to get the best out of players. It has been suggested that Sir Matt's influence has been too strong. What rubbish! I will not hesitate to seek his advice — and I know it will be warmly given — in my efforts to take this great club back to the top."

Docherty offered no comment on Best's future. Pat Crerand was tipped to become his assistant, at Busby's suggestion. "Well he managed Scotland, and had done a great job for Scotland," Crerand remembers. "I didn't really know Tommy Docherty at all to tell you the truth, I don't think I'd ever spoke to him, I didn't know him as a person, what his personality was like and all that sort of stuff."

The idea of establishing a link between the senior players seemed straightforward enough, given the issues which had beset the previous managers. Docherty was no stranger to discipline or falling out with his players. In the 1964/65 season, while manager at Chelsea, he was leading a very young side on a championship charge, ironically enough against United. They were due to play three critical games in Lancashire so were stationed in the area; some of his young players broke a curfew in Blackpool and Docherty made the stunning decision to send all eight of them home to London (seven were crucial first team players). Chelsea lost 6-2 at Burnley with a team that included two players who made their only appearance for the club. It was a result which ended their title hopes. Clearly Docherty was a man not to be messed with, and a man not afraid of making very big decisions.

Alex Stepney — who had briefly spent time with Docherty at Stamford Bridge — welcomed the move, "The club had to get back the way we played under Sir Matt Busby basically, for the fans and for ourselves," he says. "I remember Tommy back in the 60s with Chelsea, he had a young team that did very well in the First Division. He was the kind of guy that you'd say 'Well okay, let's see if we can carry on that tradition', because don't forget, back in the 50s, Busby had the 'Busby Babes' and thought about the young players coming through, and he (Docherty) had a fantastic team at Chelsea so (we thought) let's see what he can do."

Stepney's open mind seems slightly at odds with the 'apprehension' he described feeling in his 1981 autobiography. Back then he wrote: "I was filled with apprehension. I had briefly experienced some of his idiosyncrasies at Chelsea, his occasionally juvenile behaviour… Somehow I could not envisage him as the manager of such a great and revered empire as that with its seat at Old Trafford."

United drew 1-1 with Leeds in Docherty's opening match, with the ink still drying on that contract, before three games on the road over Christmas and the New Year revealed the difficulty facing the new man. 3-1 defeats at Derby and Arsenal (both of them comprehensive, with United grabbing late consolation goals) in the league were followed by a 1-0 loss at Wolves which knocked the club out of the FA Cup at the third round stage.

By the time Docherty prepared to take charge of his first proper game at Old Trafford against West Ham on January 20th, 1973, there had already been big changes. First of all, Docherty brought in Tommy Cavanagh, a coach he had worked alongside at Hull City, and a familiar face he knew he could trust. It was the sort of move every manager makes — Frank O'Farrell had done just the same — although naturally, with Pat Crerand serving as the assistant manager in name, it didn't feel like that title was accurate. "I think he listened to Tommy Cavanagh more than he listened to me because they both came from Hull City," Crerand says. "I had an opinion, whether he listened to it or not was another matter, but their ideas of football were totally different from my ideas. I just spoke to him about the style of play of Manchester United, and all the time we were at Manchester United, Matt was a great believer of 4-2-4 or 4-4-2 whatever way you wanted to play it… two wide players, always two wingers, two midfield players and two strikers. I was a great believer in that system and when Tommy Doc come in, he changed all that and I think quite a few people have done it since. They changed (to) that more defensive system which the Manchester United fans do not like, they do not like defensive systems, they like to see teams that charge forward… United were always a team that charge forward and that's why people wanted to watch Manchester United play." It is an argument that still echoes today in complaints about the club under van Gaal and Mourinho.

Docherty would have to deal with internal expectations as time wore on but, with United's need pressing, he had to make a number of judgement calls based on his assessment of the issues of the club as an outsider. It could be said that there were issues throughout the team and Crerand concurs, "I just think maybe the age group was a little bit older, over the hill, there was a lot of the players there that weren't good enough to play for Manchester

United, I thought that anyway and probably maybe Tommy Doc got that belief eventually as well" but Docherty had to prioritise what he deemed were the most critical weaknesses. They appeared to be in defence, with a full-back and a centre-half on his shopping list and midfield where United had lacked a real presence since Crerand and Stiles had been phased out.

Docherty hadn't been at the club for a week before he'd spent £120,000 trying to address that midfield chasm. Arsenal double winner George Graham was identified as the solution. "As soon as I asked George if he would join United, he jumped at the chance," Docherty told reporters. "He is a great midfield player, an arrogant man who inspires confidence in those around him. When he comes through with the ball he is like Gunther Netzer, the German who destroyed England at Wembley. United have always had great players. George Graham is a great player—and if I go for any other players, they will have to have quality."

Graham admitted he was glad to move. "It's a great move for me," he said, "the contract Tommy offered me was almost too good to be true. I know Doc as well as anyone in football and it's good to be linking up with him again."

Before the turn of the year Docherty had also signed right back Alex Forsyth for £100,000, taking the club's expenditure in 1972 to £875,000. The spending would not stop there, with links to Celtic's Lou Macari. First, though, came that centre-half. Former United goalkeeper Harry Gregg, former manager of Shrewsbury Town, had recommended uncapped Scottish defender Jim Holton to Docherty when he was in charge of Scotland. Gregg made further calls once Docherty was installed at Old Trafford to implore him to buy him. Though Docherty didn't watch him, he sent Crerand and Jimmy Murphy in his stead and signed him for £80,000 on their advice. Gregg, now manager of Swansea City — and perhaps feeling he was owed a favour — made a startling offer to take George Best on loan, the club having retained Best's registration despite the 'sacking'. Docherty referred to the move as 'a sick joke' in the press, though Gregg told reporters that he was sure a deal could be struck.

In early January United secured their fourth Scottish player of the Docherty era as Lou Macari arrived at Old Trafford for almost £200,000. Only, on the day he was signed, he almost didn't make it. Docherty and Macari were involved in a car crash just outside Gretna Green. "A big lorry ran into another lorry right behind us and that bumped into us hard," the manager told the press. "The back of the car and the driver's side were smashed. Lou was shaken up and we were lucky that he was not badly hurt. He was sitting in the back seat and if it had not been a big car, the accident could have been serious." On his new signing The Doc said, "I'm delighted to have got him back to Manchester in one piece. Lou will be a big asset... he is a tremendous player. There is a lot of Kevin Keegan in him. He snatches half-chances, is very aggressive, skilful and despite being only 23, has had a lot of experience through Celtic's adventures in European football. I know I have spent a lot of money, but time has not been on our side. The directors have had to be brave, but it shows they nave the welfare of the club at heart, it is disgraceful the abuse they have been under because of our bad results."

Macari was keen to put his turbulent start behind him. "I'm happy to be alive and at Old Trafford," he said. "That accident was some shock. But I've chosen the right time to move and once I've settled in and got used to the training, I think I'll soon start to repay all that money."

That wasn't the only car accident suffered by United staff in January 1973. Youngster Sammy McIlroy was involved in a serious accident that would keep him out of action for some time. Naturally, the midfield schemer worried about his future at the club. "United were in the press every day, Tommy was in the press every day about what he wanted to do, changing the club, bringing players in, obviously some players would have to leave," McIlroy recalls. "Obviously with me in a hospital bed at the time, I was reading all of this and I was a little bit concerned... the club were in a little bit of a free-fall as well. Loads of players were coming in, they brought in Lou Macari, there were other players he (Docherty) brought in as well, I was thinking maybe my time is going to be up here. But, to be fair, he came to see me in hospital and told me that he would wait on my recovery, and give me every chance possible for me to work my way back into his plans, which I was very thankful for."

All four of Docherty's big money buys were in the starting eleven for the game against West Ham, though it did seem there was a narrower shape to the side which read: Stepney: Young, Buchan, Holton, Forsyth; Morgan, Graham, Charlton; Law, Macari, MacDougall.

Docherty's first programme notes addressed the changes he'd made. "For me there is only one job in football... manager of Manchester United, and now I have achieved my ultimate ambition, I am at Old Trafford," he began. "I have always had this love for Manchester United... My regard deepened when Matt Busby took charge of the Scotland team and I played for him. I realised why United were so great and achieved so much. This man has done so much for football, not just for his club, and it is a privilege to follow him. Some people talk about Sir Matt's great achievements and presence as a director as being some kind of handicap for his successor. Perhaps it's a matter of attitude on the part of the man taking over. I regard Sir Matt as an active director as being more of a help than a hindrance and I shall not hesitate to use him if I think he can help with a particular problem... I fully realise that although I have achieved a great personal ambition in my appointment as United manager, this is only the beginning!

"Achieving an ambition might suggest easing up; far from it. For me it is merely the starting signal for a great deal of hard work to try and bring the success that was the regular hallmark of Manchester United. It's going to be difficult but it is not impossible and this view is shared by the men I have gathered around me to tackle the first hurdle of retaining our place in the First Division. My first call went to Tommy Cavanagh... he is now our first team trainer. Pat Crerand is a Scot of course. There's no disguising that fact, but that's not why he was appointed assistant manager. I liked his style as a player and perhaps more to the point now he knows the game and I like his ideas on football. The third staff change was promoting Norman Scholes to chief scout. Jimmy Murphy, who has been scouting on a part-time basis for the club, will play a slightly more active role."

David Meek, who had openly made the case for patience with O'Farrell, gave his own take on the changes in his programme column, "Old Trafford has had a drastic face-lift, ranging from management to players. In the appointment of Tommy Docherty, United have a manager of the times, a forthright, fearless character who is in a hurry... Pat Crerand gave so much to United as a player that he too will be a forceful influence on rebuilding the morale of the players that must now be somewhat shattered. The great quality of Crerand as a player was his sense of responsibility and courage. When things were going badly he wanted more of the ball, not less, and he never 'hid' when the going was difficult. That is the kind of outlook needed now and as assistant manager he is now in a position to help players achieve it."

The pre-match optimism didn't last long. United were 2-0 down inside 25 minutes yet their starting line-up boasting eight Scots showed the required fight to get a result; Bobby Charlton's penalty on 31 minutes was followed by a debut equaliser for Macari ten minutes from the end. It was a nice piece of history for Macari; another indication of the changing tides at Old Trafford. "What I didn't realise when I made my debut - the number 10 shirt, which Denis had worn in the previous game was given to me against West Ham and Denis was given the number 4 jersey," Macari says. "So that was maybe the first little sign from Doc that you know, maybe Denis's days were numbered at Old Trafford."

It had been suggested very early on that Docherty felt Ted MacDougall was nowhere near the standard required. The manager had responded to a London branch of United's supporters club who were planning a 'Don't Sell MacDougall' demonstration before the game at Highbury by telling them he did not plan selling the striker. However just a few weeks later he signed for West Ham and, according to Docherty, MacDougall had been as keen to return south as he had been to sell him.

Denis Law would only play once more for United, in a 1-0 win over Norwich on April 7th, as his knee problems worsened.

By that point Docherty had stabilised the club but it hadn't been pretty. In a game at home to Newcastle, Jim Holton had been sent from the field for an alleged head-butt on Malcolm MacDonald. 'Supermac' was furious, making an outrageous statement to the press saying United's staff were "inciting their players to violence with touchline orders".

United's response was to threaten to report MacDonald to the FA for misconduct; but they couldn't escape the general level of criticism about their style of play. Docherty responded strongly. "I've got the best job in football with the best club in the world," he said. "I wouldn't do anything to jeopardise it. To call us a dirty side is stupid. Jim Holton is an honest, genuine player, who is only interested in winning the ball. Of course I'm not happy about one or two things we are doing... like getting in situations where you see Bobby Charlton hammering the ball away from deep in defence. It's not Bobby's way, but while we are in this position it has to be done. And Bobby understands. We are now harassing other sides when they are on the ball. That is something Leeds and Arsenal do all the time. It has helped make them good sides."

Tommy Cavanagh agreed. "We are fighting for our lives — within the laws of the game," he said. "And nobody could be giving more than Tommy."

It was a back-to-basics approach, then, sacrificing style for substance in the quest to achieve stability. Following United's draw at Spurs on March 24th, Charlton himself came out in support of the manager's approach. "We're in a desperate situation," said the midfielder. "We can start playing the game we want to play next season, once we're safe." United were now two points off the relegation zone in 18th place.

Frank McGhee of *The Mirror* wasn't too sure that those better days would return. "'He (Charlton) was voicing what seems to be the common attitude of anyone of importance at United nowadays, including chairman Louis Edwards, director Sir Matt Busby, and manager Tommy Docherty," McGhee wrote. "They, too, seem to feel everything will come right in the end and, until it does, spirit must have a higher priority than skill. Examining the affect this is having on certain players makes me wonder what justification the club have for the confidence that they can simply shrug off bad habits and start again next season with increased hope. Take Martin Buchan. The Scottish international defender arrived at Old Trafford with a reputation for competence, confidence and leadership. A Buchan interception or tackle carried the immediate threat of a United counter-attack. Now, like too many others, he has become obsessed with safety first. Take George Graham. When Arsenal sold him, he was a swaggering, strolling minstrel of a player… carefree, arrogant, adventurous, always looking for scoring chances. A couple of months at Old Trafford have altered all that. Though Graham hit the vital opening goal in the sixth minute, he never went hunting for another. He was too concerned with reinforcing the defence. Nor is it only the high-price replacements who have been affected. The whole essence and appeal of Bobby Charlton's game, for instance, has always been freedom — the freedom he needs to hit his marvellous passes and memorable shots. Against Tottenham, he was an eagle in a cage."

United were far from impressive but they were stumbling in the right direction. In mid-March, Frank O'Farrell gave his first interview since the sacking, and was described by *The Mirror* as 'Soccer's most famous casualty'.

"The first day after was the worst," he said. "It was the first day of my life that I had been out of work and the first day I'd had off since taking over at United… I was only thinking when I was running this morning that in December life was as bare as the trees. Now the buds are forming. You get over winter."

According to some reports earlier that month, however, O'Farrell might have been thinking about how he could still turn things around at the club. A consortium of five industrialists, an MP and a QC, led by spokesman John Thomson, whose father had previously been a director at the club, launched a takeover bid for United and sent a letter of their proposal to the United directors which included the following: "It has been unanimously agreed that Mr. Frank O'Farrell be invited to take up his duties at Old Trafford again. He would also be given an undertaking that, at no time, would the new board interfere with the running of the club."

The takeover bid came to nothing and in the early days at least, the new manager could not have any complaints about how he had been backed. And, in return, there couldn't be any real grumbles about how Docherty had started life at the club, considering the harshness of that 5-0 defeat to Palace which preceded his arrival. "He had a very good reputation as a charismatic personality manager," Paddy Barclay says. "He was the perfect fit for Manchester United and his impact on the club was instant. Although, if you look at the history books you'd say well, he took a while to get it right… But he revived the football instantly. He invigorated it, he rejuvenated it. Okay, some of the younger players weren't good enough but he identified which were and which weren't… the surgery was rudimentary and done with an axe rather than a scalpel."

That axe was readied before Manchester United were even mathematically safe; plans were set in motion for Tommy Docherty's boldest surgery yet — the removal of the 'Trinity' which had thrilled United's supporters for years.

HATCHET MAN

THERE WAS AN EXPECTATION that at some point in his reign Tommy Docherty would have to deal with the exits of the players known as Manchester United's 'Holy Trinity' — Bobby Charlton, Denis Law and George Best, even if the latter was now contemplating various new careers ranging from nightclub owner and travel agent to NFL goal kicker.

In that respect Docherty probably had a certain level of understanding from supporters and the general footballing public regarding the final chapters of the United careers of Charlton (36), Law (33) and Best (26). There was a crucial point accepted by all — for one reason or another, none of these players could be depended upon by Docherty to rebuild Manchester United. Charlton, derided as he had been for alleged selfishness earlier in his career, was now a physical embodiment of the new spirit of the club, grafting and finding himself in deeper positions on the field than ever before to contribute to the cause of retaining United's place in the First Division. But he was flagging as two decades of service to the club, let alone the physical and emotional toll of surviving the Munich disaster, meant he had passed his peak some time ago.

Charlton and Docherty had a lengthy conversation in the early spring of 1973 where the player informed the manager of his intention to retire at the end of the season. The decision would not be made public until United were safe from relegation; partly to protect against the idea of the most senior player jumping ship, and partly because there seemed to be the tiniest amount of guilt residing in Charlton that should United go down he would have to stay around to help them back up. "I didn't consciously pull back in my effort, but sometimes I had the terrible sense that I was just running for the sake of it," admitted Charlton in his autobiography.

"He was very good about it, he went the right way about it," recalls Docherty. "He said 'I'm just coming to let you know what my plans are and I would like your permission if I could speak to Sir Matt' — not Louis Edwards — 'Sir Matt and Louis Edwards' not Louis Edwards and Sir Matt, so Matt was coming before the Chairman, so I said, 'Well you've got my permission to do that, and thank you very much for letting me know what your plans are' and away he went."

The school of thought was that for whatever reason previous managers had been unwilling or unable to handle the transition of the remaining European Cup winners. So the accusation naturally became that United as a club held on to them for too long. "Maybe a little bit," Martin Edwards admits, "of course they all got a little bit older, even Paddy Crerand (could be) put in that category as well, they were all going to be replaced one day, and maybe because of what they had achieved, and how important they had been, maybe we were a bit slow as a club in replacing them."

Six wins from twelve games had moved United clear of the two-team drop zone and a 2-2 draw at Stoke on 14th April secured the club's First Division future. Two days later Bobby Charlton's retirement was made public. "I'd love to get drunk on a Friday night. And then I'd get up late on Saturday, wrap myself up in a red and white muffler and go to watch the lads at Old Trafford," he told press a news conference. "That is, of course, if I don't land a manager's job somewhere."

Sat beside him Sir Matt Busby was described as having 'tears streaming down his cheeks' on hearing the news. Charlton confirmed "If United had been relegated I would have helped them back into the First Division. Now they are safe. I must look for something new in Soccer."

Charlton would play the last four games of the season. The first game after his announcement was at Leeds whose captain, Billy Bremner, presented Charlton with a clock. The Elland Road crowd were reported as giving Charlton a 'wonderful ovation'. And Charlton's team-mates helped to make the occasion even more memorable, securing a very impressive win which ended their local rival's title hopes. "It's the best result since I took over," Docherty admitted afterwards.

United's last home game of the season was against Sheffield United. In his programme notes Docherty seemed content with the job done. "I think I can safely say that things look a lot different now than when I first arrived four months ago," he wrote. "I am satisfied that the first and most urgent part of my job has been achieved... The club is on the upswing again, and this is what we must maintain. After all, avoiding relegation might seem wonderful at the time, but it is a bit of a negative achievement! We want to be competing at the top end of the table and with the resources available here at Old Trafford I am sure that next season will present a much brighter picture. Success in football can never be guaranteed, but we shall give it a good go. It takes time to build a team, but with only one or two exceptions we have a very young team."

David Meek agreed that things were going in the right direction. "Tommy Docherty is a bold, open personality who has undoubtedly saved Manchester United from relegation this season... Docherty brought vitality to a depressed club."

Charlton bowed out against Chelsea at Stamford Bridge on the final day of the season. He had made life easy for his manager; Docherty had tougher decisions to follow.

★

"At the end of the day a manager is only as good as the players he has at his disposal," Docherty says now. "The only trouble you have with them is when they think they should be in the first team and they're not... the attitude was poor, some of them were dropped out of the team who felt they should have been in the team. That was their opinion, and when they got dropped you get the stirring up in the background about 'The manager is not good enough and he'll never be good enough, he wouldn't be my choice as a manager'... it's the same even today... you've got to make the decisions, and some of the decisions you make are not very popular, they are certainly not popular with the players who you are leaving out"

If Charlton's exit from the club was much smoother than expected, then surely what transpired with Denis Law was the polar opposite. Some parties were still undecided on what the striker had to offer. At 33 and with a history of knee problems, Law had played just once since January. He had a year left on his contract and before leaving for home after the season had ended he went to see Docherty. Half a year into his reign at Old Trafford, Docherty was about to experience one of the most controversial moments of his entire career; a moment which is still open to interpretation.

"Denis was a bit of trouble maker," claims Docherty. "Denis would play on the Saturday, get injured, should have come in for treatment on the Sunday and didn't... that went on for five or six months and I thought no, it can't go on like this at all... so I decided to tell the board that I think the best interest with everyone was that they get rid of Denis, and they transferred him to another club which was at the end of the day was Man City... I called him in the office almost immediately when I had decided what I wanted to do and I told the board what I was going to do, I told them that... are we going to put him on the transfer list, Busby didn't like it."

In his autobiography, Docherty recalls Busby reluctantly agreeing when the United boss explained he'd only been able to pick Law five times since being hired. "I went the right way about it on behalf of the club and behalf of myself and on behalf of Denis," Docherty insists. "He was just understandably annoyed that he was no longer in my plans for the future of the club."

In his autobiography, Law's version of events is as follows. He claims that in the meeting he was told he would be transitioned into the coaching staff during the remaining year of his contract, but that any retirement announcement should be delayed until a testimonial match which was due to be played in September. That evening Law returned home and the following day he was at a pub in Aberdeen with his friends when it was announced on television that he was being given a free transfer.

"It really hurt because I had been with United for eleven years and loved the club," recalled Law. "It will be hard to ever forgive Docherty for what he put my family through at that time. I felt really badly let down... It was totally unexpected. I was only 33 and still had a year left in my contract and felt fit enough to see it through... When it was announced on the television in the pub I was stuck for words. It was a terrible way for the news to be broken that my career with United was over. What made it worse was when I went back to get my boots and personal belongings from Old Trafford everyone else was still on holiday. I didn't even have anyone to say goodbye to. It made walking out of the home dressing room for the last time even harder to take."

Law's former team-mates back his side of the story. "I think he left at the end of the season being told that you know, he's got another year and he was up in Aberdeen, it came on television that he was being released by Manchester United and obviously that didn't go down well with some of the players, and Denis as well," says Alex Stepney. "You've got to be man to man... if Denis had been told that you know, he had another year's contract at the club and went away and then it came on the news that he was you away, you know in the summer, that he'd been released.... well I don't think that's correct... that wasn't the Manchester United way."

Willie Morgan remembers being surprised when he discovered the news. "Denis had gone into see him at the close season to say about a new contract because his contract was up," Morgan says. "Doc said 'Yeah no problem, it'll all be sorted out, just go back and have a nice summer'... so Denis flew up to Aberdeen and on the Saturday morning he is watching, now I can't remember the name of the sports programme in those days, whatever it was on a Saturday morning, it said Denis Law has been placed on the transfer list... and that was the first Denis knew. So that was Docherty... but we didn't know that, we just assumed Denis had asked for a transfer, and he hadn't."

Docherty's assistant, Pat Crerand, was not privy to that conversation but is certain Law's version of events is true. "Denis Law went back to Aberdeen thinking he had another year at Manchester United and he had made an agreement with Tommy

Docherty, I don't know what the agreement was because I wasn't involved in that situation, but Denis went back to Aberdeen, was in a pub with a few pals and it come on at the television that he had been freed by Manchester United, that's how Denis Law found out that he was leaving Manchester United," Crerand explains. "You're talking about one of the greatest players that has ever played for Manchester United finding out he was leaving the club through somebody at the television centre and he spoke to Tommy Docherty a week or so before and got told a totally different story… dreadful… you couldn't believe a word the man said."

Even Martin Edwards isn't able to definitely answer one way or the other. "I think he was disappointed that he hadn't been told face to face… now whether that was actually the true version or not, I don't know. Even though I was a director at the time, I don't know the bottom line of it, all I know is once Tommy made it known that he wasn't in his plans then Denis wouldn't want to be around, but I think he was generally disappointed in the way the whole thing was handled."

How it happened became a matter of who you believed for a while. But in 1979, when Docherty took Willie Morgan to court with an accusation of slander, the then-former United boss's case fell apart over his admission that he had in fact led Law to believe he would have another year at the club, and told the press another story; completely validating Law's version of events and providing further ammunition for those who had negative things to say about Docherty.

The general consensus, though, was that it was probably the right time. Even Crerand admits that. "Probably Denis and Bobby thought their number was up, which probably most people would have agreed with," he says. "You've done your bit, but the problem you had then, how do you replace them? How do you replace Bobby Charlton and Denis Law?"

Paddy Barclay agrees, "In actual fact, it was the right thing to do," he says. "Denis, even though he remained an unbelievably gifted footballer, he couldn't do it. You can't be great if you're not on the field and Denis needed injections in his knees even to get through the games he could, and sometimes even that wasn't enough." Barclay believes that Docherty's act was bold and necessary. "Without a shadow of a doubt, Docherty was the first man who was brave enough," he says. "He was also clever enough. He was political enough. He was big enough. He had a personality, a charisma. He knew how to play the chairman Louis Edwards with a mixture of flattery and force. And he knew that Matt needed him. Matt had finally got the right man, and now Matt's fortunes were now inextricably linked with his. So he was in a position of power and he exerted that power in a way that restored Manchester United and prevented the decline from being even worse. He was brash and forceful, but somehow always gave the impression that he was being forceful for the good of Manchester United. I think the great quality of Docherty that I would liken to (Sir Alex) Ferguson's is that his ego, his force, his power such as it was… his gamesmanship… every trick in the book was being applied for the good of Manchester United, and that was what Docherty definitely achieved."

For all of the misgivings about how these players had been moved out, with only Alex Stepney young enough from the European Cup winning side who could say he would have his best years ahead of him (George Best being another matter) it was time that the board was swept clean. Noses would inevitably be put out of joint but Busby was aware that the cull of the old guard was a necessary evil. At the same time, having been so closely associated with the appointments of McGuinness and O'Farrell, Busby's own reputation was on the line. He was now far enough away to be disassociated with some of the less savoury aspects of that cull, yet not so far away that he wouldn't face criticism should Docherty fail.

Following the departure of Charlton and Law there was a huge hole. In the space of six months, they had left, and there were big shoes to fill for the club's home-grown stars Brian Kidd and the convalescing Sammy McIlroy, as well as senior signings Lou Macari, Wyn Davies and Ian Storey-Moore.

"How can you replace players of that calibre?" asks Sammy

McIlroy. "Absolutely world class on their day, how do you replace them? Storey-Moore came into the club, a fantastic player, had one or two injuries… other players came in, but it was so difficult to try… George Graham, another player who came in, a Scottish international, experienced player, but it was very hard to replace them."

It would be even tougher with the depleted budget Docherty had that summer. Having already invested around £500,000 in just a few months (really, a matter of weeks) to add to the similar amount spent by Frank O'Farrell, Docherty would have to be prudent or get the best out of what he had. It was early days for him to not have faith in George Graham to be a Charlton, or Lou Macari to not be a Law, but replacing Best would be a different matter. And so, of course, in the summer of 1973, the player Tommy Docherty brought in to replace George Best was… George Best.

After leaving Manchester that summer Best had flown to his favourite haunt Marbella, but when he started suffering leg pains, which turned out to be thrombosis, he flew back to England. In hospital back home Best was visited by Sir Matt Busby, who suggested to him, "It's about time you were back playing, isn't it?"

It stands to reason that Busby discussed the matter with Docherty, although Martin Edwards insists the matter wasn't mentioned at board level. "I think that was all to do with Tommy, nothing to do with us in the respect that someone inside the club had mentioned it," Edwards says. "But he was the manager, would it be good for him to bring him back, for the supporters, to get George Best back into the fold would have been a great achievement, that's how I think Tommy would have read it."

Docherty confirms that Best returned to Old Trafford on Busby's request. "Well it was a strange situation because Sir Matt got him back to Old Trafford but the next day he (Best) was back to his old normal ways again," Docherty says. "You never lose the ability that you have as a player and he was world class but you couldn't run the club or the team the way that George was behaving, I mean you didn't know when he was going to come into training and when he came in his attitude in training was a bit laughable. It was a bit of a joke to him but fun you know, doing silly little tricks with the ball or what not and it was just a waste of time."

In his autobiography Docherty elaborated confirming that the season was already underway when he and Best spoke. "Some time in late August I spoke to George and we arranged to meet on 6th September," he said. "He was articulate and easy to talk to and after some social niceties it was George who first brought up the subject of returning to United. This pleased me; perhaps he was even keener to play again than I had first thought. A highly motivated George Best — there was no way I was going to do anything but pave the way for his return and help him all I could." Docherty said the meeting was concluded with him telling Best he was delighted to have him back but this was 'his one and only chance'. Best's account doesn't contradict this but says Docherty also said, "I know you've been having problems but if you miss training, nobody will know about it from me. But if you don't train, you'll have to come back on your own and make up for it." Best says, "We shook hands on it, though I probably agreed to go back to Old Trafford more for Paddy's sake than his." Best said Crerand had been talking to him and had "convinced me that Docherty was a proper United man, who would bring in new players to restore the side to its glory days, and most importantly, that his team would play the United way".

On 7th September the news of George Best's return hit the press. Asked about his previous vow that Best 'would never wear a United shirt again,' he replied: "I was speaking for the board, not myself, when I said those words."

United trainer Tommy Cavanagh told journalists, "George says he is a stone overweight. He told me he wants to get fit for Eusebio's benefit match at the end of this month."

There is, naturally, a slight difference of opinion regarding Best's condition and ability upon return. Perhaps the most generous account is that of Willie Morgan. "He was alright. George was naturally fit, like myself, we were naturally fit both of us. He was fine. It's not easy to come back into a team that's not playing great... he did his best...we all did our best, and that year it wasn't good enough, that's all. But no, he was fine, it was a good move to try to bring him back… but he's not a natural goal scorer, he's not a centre forward, George was… well he started off as a winger, but basically he was an inside forward, yes, he could score goals but he's not your finisher."

Others felt it was obvious his lifestyle was having an impact. "He was an absolutely fantastic trainer you know, he was so slim, he was bright, he was quick, he could do everything," Alex Stepney says of Best's earlier days. "When you get out of that style for a while like he did, obviously he's gonna come back a bit overweight… he tried to work hard at it, but I think really and truthfully, the lifestyle he'd been leading since he left the club and the people that he was with… I didn't think at the end of the day that'll he'd ever get back."

Stepney had been alongside Best in his halcyon days. For others, like Lou Macari and Sammy McIlroy, Best was very much an icon, and that much is clear in their own interpretations. "When George came back the thing that I found was how great of a player he was," Macari says. "When you were training with him, you couldn't get the ball off him, you couldn't get near him… when he played on a Saturday, it was the George Best that people that had talked about for years and years. Not much had deteriorated even though he had been away for a while, he just seemed to be the type of player that could come back, walk through the front door, put his strip on… but of course that's never going to last if you're not training regularly. It didn't last, but I'm glad he did come back, because the memories of him training and playing against me on the training ground are there… I could safely say that he was, for me, the greatest Manchester United player ever. There's been lots of great players at Old Trafford but George was just an incredible footballer, incredible talent, and a character."

Macari's own pedigree was not to be sniffed at. He had of course been a young pup around the Lisbon Lions, Celtic's European Cup winning team of 1967. It might be safe to say that Macari's perception of Best was still one of novelty; he hadn't been through the trials and tribulations of the previous three years in the same way that, for example, McIlroy — who hero-worshipped Best — had.

"George was going through a bad time, he had put on a little bit of weight. I think he was disillusioned with the results as well, there wasn't great press about him, so when George did come back, obviously from the player I knew, and the condition that I'd seen George come back in, I thought it may be a little bit of a struggle," McIlroy says. "But, I was absolutely delighted when he returned because I thought it may lift the club, it may lift the players and you know, really give the club a lift… he had a few games, he showed glimpses of what he could do, but he was nowhere the player that I'd known from when I was 15 or 16 years of age when I first joined the club. He was nowhere near that player but he trained, he tried to train hard, he tried to get back and show the glimpses of what a magnificent player he was, but unfortunately it just wasn't there… I'll always remember going into training, the first day George had come back and all the lads, even the experienced people like Alex Stepney, Martin Buchan and people like that were so pleased that George was actually coming back because we were in a little bit of a dip of form. We needed sort of a lift, and what a lift, a player like Besty… obviously when he came back, looking at him, he wasn't in a great condition but what the Doc had said was 'Listen, train with the lads, come back in the afternoons, give yourself a chance and if you do it, I'll put you straight back in the side', so it sort of gave everyone a lift around the place that Besty was back, and hoping to knuckle down and try and turn us round. Even if he was a fraction of what he used to be, I think that would have given the players and the club a big lift."

That's not to say that Best's return was a complete disaster. As Alex Stepney recalls, there were advantages to having the circus back in town. "As a player you knew that if George Best is in your line-up, the other team is going to be worried about him, it don't matter what sort of state he's in or the way he is, they'll have two probably three players around to mark him which would help you, really, you know," Stepney says.

It also provided a little bit of glamour, that razzmatazz which had been missing so badly at Old Trafford that it made the potential for headaches much more tolerable. "The media was very excited about it all and he came back with very high hopes and I think Tommy Docherty was excited about it too," Martin Edwards says. "At the end of the day it didn't work out."

Perhaps, given the way things had gone for Best in the past, and the reasons which had caused him to lose interest, he should have paid closer attention to how things were shaping up at Old Trafford. Back in August new captain George Graham told the press before the season opener against Arsenal, "the days when Manchester United could be regarded as a soft touch for any reasonable team are definitely over. We're making no apologies for going out and playing it hard because that's the way it has to be if you want success."

United started with a heavily defeat at Arsenal, but won their next two games, both at Old Trafford, against Stoke City and QPR before three successive defeats, at Leicester, Ipswich and in the early return fixture with Leicester which made it patently obvious that this would be another difficult campaign. Gerry Daly had joined from Bohemians for a small fee of £20,000, but other than that Docherty found himself turning to a fairly unimpressive youth and reserve system for squad players, with finances tighter than usual. Defender Steve James became a regular alongside Martin Buchan (who himself was used in various positions along the back line) while Yorkshire duo Arnie Sidebottom and Brian Greenhoff made their own breakthroughs. In the early weeks of the season only Stepney, Young, Buchan, Holton, Macari and Graham seemed like automatic choices. With two wins and just nine goals in the first eleven games, George Best's return couldn't come soon enough.

Best played a reserve game on October 6th against Aston Villa, a 2-0 defeat, and managed 90 minutes in a 1-0 friendly win over European champions Ajax on 3rd Oct 1973. On 15th October he played against Shamrock Rovers in Dublin in a 2-1 win which was abandoned with 10 minutes to go because kids invaded the pitch, most of them trying to reach the Irishman. Docherty, despite being far from convinced, asked Best if he could play against Birmingham

City.

For once Best didn't grab the headlines in a 1-0 win which was more remarkable than the score-line would suggest. Alex Stepney scored the game's only goal from the penalty spot. The decision to allow the goalkeeper to take the spot kicks had been taken by Docherty, much to everyone's surprise, and was based solely on Stepney looking comfortable taking penalties in training. The gimmick was the source of much embarrassment at the club. In scoring the goal Stepney had become the club's leading goalscorer with two goals, on account of him also scoring from the spot in the home defeat to Leicester in September.

Stepney recalls: "It hadn't been discussed with the manager or captain who was taking the penalties and as we were going out when the bell rang, Martin, who was captain, just said to Tommy 'who's taking the penalties?' and he said 'Alex!', he was not thinking it was gonna happen… And, of course, we got a penalty. Course, I don't think Peter Shilton was too happy when I sent him the wrong way! I don't think he's ever spoken to me since! No, it was one of those things but you know, why should I be taking penalties when the manager brought forwards for over one hundred thousand pounds, it didn't seem right to me."

"When Alex started taking penalties that was a strange decision," says Crerand. "If the goalie saved it, there would be panic at the other end. I didn't agree with that in actual fact, if you've got somebody taking a penalty kick that should be a striker, they're used to scoring goals, it should always be a striker, it should never be a goalkeeper, why that idea was thought of, I don't know."

Docherty admits that it wasn't the best idea he's ever had. "Desperation!" he laughs. "We were just clutching at straws, to be honest. It was my choice, we did them in training and he was quite good at them, but no, it was a mistake."

In the next home game against Chelsea, they were two down inside eight minutes. Best, who had started wide, was moved in to a central position. Docherty had observed that the winger's pace was not what it had been and felt his trickery might help get a breakthrough in a more congested area. Journalist Brian Crowther, covering the game, referred to the tactical switch by saying, "A patched-up lifeboat is better than none." It was. On this occasion, anyway. United salvaged a 2-2 draw thanks to an injury-time goal from Brian Greenhoff — his first for the club.

The following week saw another first — Best's first goal since his return — but the strike came in a 2-1 defeat at White Hart Lane which saw United drop to 18th in the table. Even Best's moments of magic weren't enough to help his team anymore. His man-of-the-match performance in a 0-0 draw at home to Norwich City just about said it all. Best confessed that he wasn't playing well and was somewhat distracted by the forthcoming opening of his Manchester city centre nightclub that Christmas.

Still, he kept coming into training, even though Docherty had given him an informal promise that he would keep it quiet if some sessions were missed. Best was not in the best of shape and would often turn up hungover. Crerand, having been so influential in convincing Best to return, was somewhat defensive of his former team-mate. "Paddy was a good lad and although we weren't mates socially he was very protective of me," Best said later. "He would give me bollockings at training, particularly when Docherty was watching, but privately he would try to encourage me. One morning, though, when I turned up reeking of drink, he said to me, 'You stink' and ordered me to have a shower before training."

Best's return was not working out. The win on his return had been the only one he'd enjoyed and Old Trafford gates were dropping with only 28,589 turning out to see a 3-2 home defeat to Coventry on Saturday 15th December. United's winless run stretched to seven games before a trip to Anfield before Christmas. There, Docherty felt that a change was necessary and though he kept George Graham in the side, he relieved him of the captaincy, naming Willie Morgan skipper instead. It didn't help; United lost 2-0, a score-line that flattered them. A Boxing Day home defeat to Sheffield United followed before a win over Ipswich Town on December 29th that gave faint hope that 1974 might bring something better.

On New Year's Day United played at Loftus Road in a game

which would become noteworthy for all the wrong reasons. Docherty's side lost 3-0 to a QPR team on the rise and although Best was by no means the worst player on the pitch — nor was he lacking in effort — journalist David Lacey later reported "Seldom can he (Best) have been caught in possession so often."

That was possibly the kindest description of his performance, according to Sammy McIlroy. "I can remember the press absolutely hammering him and saying it was a shadow of what he used to be," he says. "I found it very sad reading those headlines and those articles of what they were saying about George."

Frank McGhee, reporting for the *Mirror*, made a stunning prediction about United's fate, "I can see little hope of survival for them on this form. They could be at the bottom of the First Division table by the end of the month—and could stay there. Even the man who once reigned unrivalled as football's most glittering genius, George Best, was so overshadowed on the day, so subdued, he played no significant part in the action."

There was nothing remarkable about the game from Alex Stepney's point of view; well, at least in the respect that losing so heavily to another recently promoted side could be considered something you might expect from a Manchester United side. "There were a few grounds around in those days that you know, you were close to the supporters," Stepney recalls. "They're at home, everyone wants to be beat Manchester United and every player is up for it. They absolutely battered us and there's nothing more you can say about it and you know, if you couldn't get the ball to George you know, what chance has he got? At the time he was probably going through an ordeal and thought 'Oh well, this is not for me anymore'."

Though no account of Best, even at his worst, suggests the player ever gave anything less than his best for the club when he was actually around, it was fair to suggest that his behaviour when he wasn't around meant he was rarely in an acceptable condition for a top flight professional footballer.

In his autobiography, Best admitted that the game in London was almost an inconvenient interruption to a party that was still raging at his nightclub, Slack Alice. "As part-owner of the club, and the most famous one, I was naturally expected to be on view most nights and, just as naturally, partake of a drink or several with customers, especially in the first few days of business after we opened at Christmas," he said. "It was fantastically exciting to see the place packed out and, after a New Year's Eve party that I managed to extend into 2nd January 1974, I didn't make it into training the following day, a Thursday. Docherty kept his part of our bargain by not saying anything to the press and I kept my part by calling Paddy and going in to train in the afternoon with him and Bill (Foulkes)."

That missed training episode was picked up by the press. "I don't know where he's got to," Docherty told reporters. "I don't know what's happened to him. He has not bothered to get in touch with me."

Business partner of Best, Malcolm Wagner, did know what happened. "It's simple really," Wagner told reporters. "George was feeling out of sorts when he got up, and he felt he couldn't make it to training. Being George, he just forgot to phone United to tell them."

It could be said, and with some justification, that Docherty was furious with Best's partying over this important period. He felt that Best deserved to be punished. Equally, the manager was giving the player just enough rope...

When George wasn't named in United's team to face Plymouth Argyle in the FA Cup few would have batted an eyelid, so immune had supporters become to the controversy. It was just another George Best episode. Only this time it was, after many threats, the last act. And, somewhat appropriately given the turbulent script, it all seemed to escalate needlessly, with the story following the same pattern of the Denis Law exit as both sides tell contrary accounts.

This time, let's start with George Best's. "After helping the Doc out by playing when I wasn't properly fit, I certainly felt I was ready for this match and he didn't say anything to me about missing training when I went in on Friday, nor during the pre-match meal at midday on Saturday," Best wrote in his autobiography

'Blessed'. "Then, about an hour and a quarter before the game, he and Paddy took me into the referee's room." Docherty told Best he was dropping him because of missing training on Thursday; Best insisted that by training in the afternoon he'd kept to their agreement. "I felt utterly humiliated," Best said. "I knew this time, it was really over." Best says that he went to sit in the stands after the game and tearfully reminisced about better days until a steward came and told him it was time to leave.

Docherty's recollection is slightly different. He says that he gave George the benefit of the doubt after missing training and intended to select him to play against Plymouth; but when he hadn't turned up by 2.15pm when the manager had to submit his team-sheet, he had to omit Best. Docherty claimed Best turned up at 2.35pm 'expecting to play'.

"George didn't turn up for training on the Monday, the next day or the day after that," Docherty wrote. "On 12 January, seven days after the Plymouth game and having had no contact from him, I suspended George for two weeks and placed him on the transfer list. What was the point of suspending George when he wasn't turning up? First of all, I felt his behaviour was intolerable and merited disciplinary action. Second, I didn't want George turning up at the ground or The Cliff as the mood took him, and his presence possibly having an adverse effect on the other players. George never showed up again."

In 2018, in an interview for this book, Docherty elaborated on the pre-game events. "I remember at 2:30pm we got the team sheet done and ready to go into the referee's room to give him," he said. "Who walks through the door at twenty five to three… Besty! He said 'I've come to play!' There was some sort of big bang on the door, I said 'hold on hold on', I opened the door, I saw Besty with a very attractive young lady, he was stoned out of his mind, he said he wanted to play and I said, 'Well you can play, but you're not playing here, I'll see you on Monday, on you go'… I shut the door, and that was the last I saw of him."

Unlike the Law story, however, this incident had witnesses, and they tend to support Best's version.

"I can remember very clearly, George was in the squad," Sammy McIlroy remembers. "We used to report to Old Trafford and we used to go into the player's lounge before the game and then you know, the team would be mentioned and whatever, you know, the players would go in and watch the television and George, I'll always remember, came to me and said 'Listen I'm off, I'm not in the side', I said 'I thought you were' he said 'so did I but he's not picked me'. There were stories about that he'd had a drink and that he turned up with a girl and stuff like that and I honestly didn't see that. George was very disappointed, he said what he had to say to one or two other players and walked out of the club, got in his car and drove away, and that was him, gone."

Pat Crerand, unsurprisingly, concurs. "I remember it very well in actual fact," Crerand says. "Tommy Doc bought him back for that game and Tommy Doc lied after that, he said George turned up an hour from kick-off drunk. There's not a word of truth in it, what Manchester United did in those days, they done it in my day, they used to go Davyhulme Golf Course for a pre-match meal prior to the game, George was at the pre-match meal, same as everybody else, we got to Old Trafford, Tommy Docherty had announced the team and left George out. George just left the stadium and never came back, but there was no drink or anything like that, that is a total lie. Tommy Doc wrote that in his book and I'm surprised George or none of his family sued him because I was a witness and all the players that played in that game were witnesses that George was there for a pre-match meal. There's not a word of truth in it."

Regardless, Crerand couldn't deny the change in Best. "He was desperate to get back, there was no question about that, George when he was a player was a fitness fanatic," he says. "In my day, after training, George would stay behind and get a goalkeeper and go and do all sorts of things, but he loved it, he enjoyed it so much, he would still go out and train after we all had finished training. When he got older, the fitness factor went from him and it wasn't the same for him anymore. I mean, to be a professional footballer, the one thing you have to do, you have to be fit, whether you're a great player, an ordinary player or a poor player, you have to be fit,

George at the end wasn't so he couldn't do it."

Alex Stepney recalls, "I think we got to the ground, I think he was accused of having had a few drinks, I didn't notice that I've got to say. I can't believe George even thought about that, he'd never done that because he was too casual, even when he was at his best, and even when he was coming to the end... I honestly think there was more going on behind the scenes than within the dressing room."

Perhaps the final point in this saga should come from a contemporary his report of the game for the *Sunday Telegraph*. Journalist Bob Greaves said Docherty had told him Best had been dropped for a 'lack of form'. The day before his club suspension — for what it was worth — expired, Best announced his retirement from the game again, although the decision about his future at Old Trafford was probably not really in his own hands anymore. The manager had put his foot down, according to Martin Edwards, when Best — who had been reported as being 'the first in for training' the day after the Plymouth game, missed training on January 10th.

"Somebody phoned to say that Best would not be in for training," Docherty told the press. "The phone message was passed on to me, but there was no explanation. After failing to turn up twice the situation will be discussed by the directors at the next meeting."

"Tommy came with a recommendation that he didn't want George in the side anymore," Martin Edwards says. "I think it's very difficult as a director, no matter what you think about a former player, or whatever else, if the manager feels like he's got to discipline that player or whatever, then you have to support the manager really. Otherwise, where does it end? I think by then, maybe even some of the other players were beginning to think 'Well what's all this about?', you know what I mean, there's one rule for George and one for the others... so the board had to support the manager and once Tommy Doc said that he'd really come to the end of the line with George, we had no option but to support him."

There was no cause for celebration, even if there had been frustration with Best's behaviour. "It was a blow to everyone, you know, whether you're a player or a team mate, best friend, fan or whatever or anyone connected to Manchester United, to see George leave it was something that nobody expected to happen," Lou Macari says. "I certainly didn't expect it to happen but I think he was given a few chances and the management, not just Tommy Doc, I think the management before that had found him a little bit difficult to handle. A decision was made and away you go."

Unlike with McGuinness or O'Farrell, there would be no reprieve for Best under Docherty. And so, in the space of nine months, the Manchester United manager had completed the removal of the only three players, at that point, to have won the European Player of the Year award while playing for the club. It certainly felt like the end of an era.

"Bobby had retired, Denis was moved on and it was the end of the trilogy, the three great world class players had gone and that in itself was sad," club statistician Cliff Butler explains. "Those three great players weren't going to play for us anymore… it just felt inevitable somehow that it was the end of an era. I remember feeling sadness when Best finished, I'd seen him making his debut, watching him develop into what he was, he was fantastic and such a lovely person as well, I was fortunate to meet him a few times and he was just a lovely man to talk to, so humble, genuine, he was a superstar, he was the David Beckham of his day and he was just fantastic and to see his demise wasn't nice. He should have gone out in a blaze of glory, a lap of honour around Old Trafford, it was so sad to see George Best go out like that."

Sad it may well have been; though, as journalist David Meek described it, much like the Denis Law situation, the story had 'an inevitable conclusion' regardless of the events which immediately preceded it.

"Tommy Docherty decided to give George a chance because of his ability but it was even too much for the Doc, after the performance at QPR," remembers Paddy Barclay. "They were beaten 3-0 at QPR, it was just abysmal. Honestly, that was the beginning of the rebuilding of Manchester United. Getting rid of one of the best players in their history."

That much was true. Sitting third from bottom in Division One at the start of 1974, however, things were going to get much worse before they got better.

FROM BAD TO WORSE

MANCHESTER UNITED HAD NOT ended 1973 in good form. In fact, prior to the last game of the year, they had not won in nine games. Critics were everywhere; after a 3-2 defeat at Newcastle United back in November Brian Clough, who had controversially resigned from the Derby job in October 1973 ironically after a win at Old Trafford, laid into the club on ITV's The Big Match, "Manchester United are not doing very well," he said in his trademark straightforward way, "he (Tommy Docherty) bailed them out last year, spending a lot of money, buying a lot of players. This was accepted in the game, because they had to get away from the relegation zone, but of course now it's expected that they go on to improve and they're not improving. They're a mediocre side and I don't fancy them to even finish in the top-half."

Brian Moore asked Clough if he felt United might even finish in the bottom three. "No, he won't be in the bottom three, he's got far too much talent for that," Clough predicted. "He's got a bit of enthusiasm with a couple of young lads as well, but the Best's and the Morgan's and the Kidd's will keep them out of the relegation zone, but it won't get them much further above it."

Moore returned to Clough's earlier description to ask, "A mediocre side with his main problems where?" Clough's response, "his main problems are a lack of startling talent. He's got a lot of players who are much of a muchness, you know when Best abdicated he took something from that side which was irreplaceable, and he hasn't got a star player as such. Kidd's been on the transfer list or available for years. Holton is a big centre-half to get you out of trouble but never will win you anything. Stepney in goal, is on the backlash, so to speak, of everything. I don't think he's got good players."

There was a school of thought that Clough was frustrated that he hadn't been offered the job ahead of Docherty. According to Paddy Crerand, he coveted the position. "He was a great character, and he had a great football brain, he always wanted to be the manager of Manchester United," he says. "Manchester United wouldn't take him, I know there were times when he was expecting that he'd be top of the list for the job at Old Trafford, but they didn't want him at United for whatever reason, I don't know, you need to ask the people that were in charge of the club at that particular time, but I found him great, Brian Clough. I found him a terrific person, he knew his football, he was just a great character."

Paddy Barclay suggests Clough in charge of Manchester United could have been much better than his other highly-publicised role with one of the 'bigger club's of the day. "Clough might have been a great Manchester United manager," Barclay says. "His experience at Leeds makes one wonder whether it might have worked like that. He was very angry not to have been offered it by Matt, but Matt didn't like him very much and that's why he didn't become manager of Manchester United. We can only speculate at what he would have done. Look at what he did with smaller clubs. What could he have done with the unlimited potential of Manchester United? Implode maybe? Or make them Champions of Europe again? You just don't know. But the reason he didn't get the opportunity was Matt thought he was too brash. He didn't like people that talked before they'd done things and he didn't like people that appeared to think that they were bigger than football."

After all that, perhaps Martin Edwards, who was privy to boardroom discussion, is closest to the truth when he bluntly shuts down any suggestion that Clough was considered in December 1972. "No, he wasn't," he says.

A couple of weeks after the Plymouth game, and coming hot on the heels of the announcement that George Best was gone for good, United drew 1-1 with Arsenal at Old Trafford. It was a game which gave a little insight into the on-pitch difficulties faced by Tommy Docherty. The team that day read (in formation rather than number) Stepney; Buchan, James, Holton, Houston; Morgan, Greenhoff, Young, McIlroy; Macari, Martin. Buchan was not a right back, and there were question marks over Steve James ability to be the bedrock of the centre of defence. Jim Holton had promise but his physical style was, at the present time, a negative representation of Docherty's style of play, which would be at odds with his beloved reputation among United fans in years to come. Stewart Houston, a new signing from Brentford, had promise, but this was very much his own integration period.

Brian Greenhoff had been one of the more impressive players since breaking through earlier in the season in a midfield role. He was partnered by Tony Young, a decent utility player whose career to that point had mostly been at full back. He had been drafted into midfield because he was snappy in the tackle and always positive when moving the ball forward. His inclusion was a damning indictment on George Graham's form. On the wings United had Willie Morgan and Sammy McIlroy, arguably their most mercurial talents. Morgan was still adjusting to the position of leader when he had always been perceived as something of a lieutenant to the Trinity and, in their absence, Morgan was now identified by the opposition as the man you would double up on. Sammy Mac was still struggling for fitness due to the lung injuries sustained in the car crash the previous January. Mick Martin would interchange with McIlroy but neither were centre-forwards, nor were they renowned for being great goalscoring midfielders (though McIlroy weighed in with his fair share). That meant the goalscoring expectation weighed heavily on the diminutive shoulders of Lou Macari. Both he and Martin were under 5 foot ten. In all, it meant that arguably seven spaces in this team needed to be more settled, and it suggested that a year into the job, Docherty was still trying to discover his best team. There were good players in reserve. The maligned Graham, Alex Forsyth and Brian Kidd were just three who could come in (although they were, in fact, the three dropped for the game with Arsenal). But even if some of the players were good enough, playing two defensive-minded players in the centre of midfield and two players who were effectively midfield players up front gave a straightforward explanation for why Manchester United were finding goals so hard to come by. The most prolific player in the reserves was Peter Fletcher, whose four goals up to January made him a veritable predator by first team standards, and he would be given the chance in February, but, just as in his previous outings for the first team, he was unable to make the step up.

Both the club and the manager seemed to be struggling to come to terms with their new reality. In trying to make his team more robust, Docherty had foregone the swashbuckling reputation that had landed him the job. His Chelsea side had been entertaining while as Scotland manager he had a winning percentage better than any of his predecessors (and, to date, successors for that matter). The Manchester United team he saw capitulate at Crystal Palace in December 1972 lived up — or down — to a reputation for being soft. For too long they had got by on the chance that one of their big name players would pull them out of the mire. As those star players left, or were absent for whatever reason, the problems only worsened.

Upon his appointment Docherty had to get back to basics to help United survive in the First Division of the early 70s. With teams such as Leeds, Arsenal, Liverpool and Derby dominating with physical and talented teams, it was a rude awakening for a club that had coasted on the back of their greats. Training methods at the club were years behind their rivals while player recruitment had seen a shocking drop in standards. The Doc's early buys were temporary measures to steady a sinking ship. That had just about worked in 1972/73 but the anticipated arrival of replacements for Law and Charlton in the summer of 1973 had not happened. Lou Macari and Martin Buchan aside, many felt Docherty's early teams were filled with players who should never have been within a mile of the Old Trafford stadium, let alone the first team.

With the dismissal of George Best, Docherty clearly hoped that the team could unify during the relegation run-in. This was easier said than done, considering the problems suffered by the previous managers, but many of the hard yards had already been travelled. Docherty had at least proved himself a man capable of making hard decisions. In the case of the exits of Denis Law and George

Best, the manager had also shown he was not afraid of making unpopular decisions in situations where he would inevitably be cast as the villain.

With such symbolic moves, and with his job apparently secure despite United's struggles, the squad realised their futures were more insecure than the manager's. It is doubtful whether such a scenario would have made a significant impression on the senior players but then Docherty had also acknowledged that by changing the captain. It was a bold move to remove George Graham from the team, particularly when his replacement was a home-grown full-back who wasn't even good enough for his natural position at Manchester United, let alone the responsibility of midfield.

After a home 1-0 cup exit to Ipswich and a defeat at Coventry, full-back Alex Forsyth was moved into midfield for the home game against title-chasing Leeds United. The Yorkshiremen's comfortable 2-0 win in front of 60,025 at Old Trafford put United bottom of Division One and made a mockery of claims that Docherty's team were tougher to beat. The ship was sinking quickly and United now seemed to be in a worse state than had been when the Scot took over, even if he could rightly claim that the manner of the defeat against Leeds was not quite on a par with Selhurst Park.

"The lads are sick of losing after playing so well," Willie Morgan told reporters after the match.

"Away from home, we have had to play it a bit tight and go for a point," Docherty told the press. "Now we must go out to win every game." 'Going for a point' was a lot less negative a game plan in the days of two points for a win. And to be fair, 'keeping it tight' had led to at least one impressive record for the United boss. The 36 conceded in the 27 league games so far put them on course for the best defensive record the club had enjoyed since they last won the league in 1967. Yet the 22 goals scored so far that season meant an average of 0.81 goals a game, which, if continued, would give United a total of 34 at season's end. This stood to be the lowest since the club were known as Manchester United, with even Newton Heath's record of 27 goals coming in their first ever season when they played just 12 games. The lowest tally United had ever recorded in a 42 game season was 41 goals on their way to relegation in 1922.

Hopes were rock bottom as United travelled to fourth-placed Derby County and the visitors were 2-0 down at half-time. Their second half fight-back to earn an admirable 2-2 draw couldn't have been any more desperate. Both of United's goals came from speculative, long range efforts from defensive players, with Brian Greenhoff and Stewart Houston both netting to lift their team off the bottom of the table. It represented the last throw of the dice more than it did a team who were playing 'gung ho' football and the Old Trafford supporters gave their response with their attendance in the next game. From the 60,025 who had turned up to watch United play Leeds on February 9, the goalless draw with Wolves on February 23 was witnessed by just 39,260. A 1-0 win at Sheffield United gave Docherty his first win of 1974 but another goalless draw, in a bad-tempered Manchester derby at Maine Road which saw Lou Macari sent off, was followed by a damaging 1-0 defeat to fellow relegation strugglers Birmingham City. United's ill fortune was exemplified by the freak goal they conceded; a defensive clearance ricocheting off Blues centre-half Joe Gallagher and flying past Alex Stepney.

By the time United were back at Old Trafford, they were hopeful that the glamour draw of Tottenham Hotspur would prove that the low turnout for Wolves was a one-off. But the attendance was even lower, as just 36,278 fans turned up to watch Spurs win 1-0. United were rock bottom again and now there was no avoiding the fact that they were knee-deep in the mire, although they had two games in hand on Norwich who were three points above them but only one in hand on Birmingham who were five points ahead.

Manchester United's crisis was reflective of the times; there was a coalminer's strike which had caused the Government to impose a three-day week to conserve electricity. "It was a gloomy time," remembers Paddy Barclay. "The television had to go off at 10.30 at night, floodlights weren't allowed to be used to conserve energy because of the coalminers strike coming so soon after an international oil crisis. So it was a gloomy time, it was a time which, for people that had been through the war, I think it would have reminded them a little bit of rationing, post-war rationing when you could only have three sweets or one bar of chocolate every month or something like that. It was time in which Britain almost seemed on those grey afternoons to be behind the communist bloc. It seemed to have that lack of colour and vividness that you associate with life in Western Europe."

In the late winter it was beginning to dawn on even the most fervent of United supporters that relegation was a possibility. "I don't think we thought we were going to be relegated, it wasn't a good season but I don't think until sort of after Christmas that anybody thought we could go down," Cliff Butler recalls. "Manchester United just didn't get relegated, I think the last time was 1936, even I wasn't born then! We weren't getting terrific crowds which I think gives you some indication, I think the crowd started to drop and again I think that was result of what had gone before. People too easily remembered when we were wiping the floor with teams and winning games regularly. I think the doom and gloom set in when we realised we could go down… I think during that season, there were quite a lot of low points, but losing at home is always more depressing than losing away. There were quite a few home defeats that season and one in particular was against Spurs… I wouldn't say it was a huge crowd, we lost that day in front of quite a modest crowd, which wasn't what happened when Spurs came to Old Trafford. It was always a full house, it was always packed, I think those sort of days when the big clubs came to Old Trafford and there weren't packed terraces, that gave you an indication of where we were heading."

Pat Crerand says that even the great Manchester United weren't immune to a loss of interest from fans. "Of course there was, you get it at most football clubs, the loss of interest when a club is on their way down, and it happened at Manchester United," he says. "We had sixty odd thousand in the glory days, because the ground wasn't big enough to hold any more than that, and obviously it dwindled."

The players were also beginning to accept the inevitable. "We were in the middle of a rot in that time where the games weren't right, we weren't winning games and the crowds were dropping," Sammy McIlroy says. "Even though we still had a fantastic, loyal support, things weren't happening, a lot was going against us… and then we were getting deeper and deeper into the end of the season and your beginning to think, 'Hmm, six weeks to go, we are in a real relegation battle here'. I think a lot players before that knew… the experienced players, big Alex Stepney I think, if you asked big Alex he'd tell you that there was definitely a relegation battle on, maybe a bit earlier than I thought, because I always had this belief that maybe we might just sneak out of it but it was definitely… there was definitely a feeling around the club that we were in a real battle… when you know that you're going to be in a relegation battle, we weren't playing well, you look around the crowds and you see empty seats and you see empty places all round,. I remember a game against Tottenham Hotspur… in my time, even before I played for Manchester United, watching it on television the great players, both sides, it'll be a sell-out. I think we had something like thirty-six thousand against Spurs which we lost 1-0. The fans were beginning to believe that this was a relegation battle, and it was beginning to affect the players as well… we knew we were in a dog fight."

The Spurs game was the seventh time in nine games United had failed to score. For Stepney, it was no surprise that fans turned away, or why the team was struggling. "I think out of the whole season, cup matches as well, I think there were 10 games we lost 1-0. Now that hurts," he explains. "As a player, especially for me being a goalkeeper, you're losing 1-0, what's going wrong?" Stepney's experience as penalty-taker had come to an abrupt end when the inevitable happened; he missed one in the goalless draw with Wolves, sending the side into panic as he rushed to get back into his goal.

Willie Morgan admits that it was tough being so close to the supporters travelling back from away games after tough results. "To see the fans you know, on the platforms in the pouring rain and you're sat in this first class carriage on your way back having just been beat again and they're still loving you, that's the hard bit," he says. "Where we used to go out at night and that, it wasn't like that. It's not the hard-core fans you're out with, it just wasn't like that you know, everyone always 'You'll be alright you know, you'll get a win this week, you'll win this week', everyone was behind the team, it was sad for the supporters more than anyone."

Morgan was not only struggling to come to terms with the extra level of expectation placed on him, he also was carrying an injury. "Prior to going to the World Cup, I played probably three months, January, February, March, April into May with an injury, I had a real bad injury, I had a dead leg and of course they used to strap me," Morgan says. "Of course playing with an injury, it creates more injuries, so I played the whole last half of the season not 100% fit, just resting through the weeks so I could play."

The apathetic nature of the crowd, who were now voting with their feet, was counter-productive for the confidence of the new and younger players. Docherty added £60,000 Jim McCalliog from Wolves (a player he'd known from Chelsea) to his attacking options, to go with the £20,000 he'd spent on Gerry Daly at the start of the season.

Alongside Forsyth and Houston that made four 'Doc' signings against Spurs, while 17-year-old Paul Bielby — a rookie given a chance from the bench against Tottenham following an impressive outing in an oddly-timed (and infamous) friendly against Glasgow Rangers — complemented Kidd, McIlroy, Greenhoff and James as the home-grown players trying to make names for themselves in testing circumstances. Martin Buchan may have started to show flashes of his potential when used in the middle but only Stepney, Kidd and Morgan were now the only members of this squad who knew anything but struggle.

The goalkeeper had some sympathy for his colleagues. "I think some of them possibly were frightened of making mistakes and that's the problem when you're not winning," he says, "instead backing your own talent to get yourself back into the right frame of mind and to be in a winning team. Perhaps there might have been a bit more disorganisation within the dressing room, staff-wise, things like that… it didn't affect me, but it could have affected other players, younger players, the younger element and when you get new players come in you get this problem of you know, 'Are they for themselves, or are they gonna be for the team?' and this is probably what happened."

Stepney feels that the chopping and changing had come at the cost of the side, "There were a lot of players that came in who only played probably played two or three games, young kids and players who thought they had a chance and it didn't materialise… I don't think (some of) the players that were brought in helped the situation to be honest. He brought in quite a lot of players… but the fact is, that doesn't always work you know, you've got to have that camaraderie in the dressing room and when you get that from not only the players but from the managerial side of it, the training side of it that has to be addressed as well to be right."

A look at the squad list from that season bears testament. Twenty-five players were used in the 1973/74 season, and twenty-four of them were outfield players. Two players — Alex Stepney and Martin Buchan — played every game. Willie Morgan missed one. Brian Greenhoff played 36 times in the league, Lou Macari 35 and Jim Holton 34. The following players played between 10 and 30 games — Alex Forsyth, Stewart Houston, Steve James, Tony Young, George Best, Gerry Daly, George Graham, Mick Martin, Jim McCalliog, Sammy McIlroy and Trevor Anderson. Six players made between two and four appearances. There was no consistency in the first team and no consistency in the squad.

One player often unfairly associated with that period is Ian Storey-Moore; the winger automatically suffers by comparison to the likes of George Best, but Paddy Barclay feels it is grossly unfair that he is associated with the demise when he could, and perhaps would, have been responsible for a recovery if circumstances had gone his way. "The factor that nobody ever factors in, that in my opinion was a key one, was that Docherty had lost possibly his best player in Ian Storey-Moore whose career was unfortunately ended by a training injury," Barclay states. "There was a questionable diagnosis or two and he didn't get the right treatment. And this player, for whom United had paid a phenomenal fee from Nottingham Forest, an outstanding goalscoring winger, a real Manchester United player and an exciter, couldn't play. He might have played three matches in the season or something like that. So he'd lost a £100 million player in today's terms, in Ian Storey-Moore, and I wonder if Storey-Moore had played 42 matches that season – he'd probably have scored, quite apart from his wing-play he'd probably have scored 15 goals. That would probably have kept them up."

It's widely acknowledged that United's lack of goalscoring prowess proved costly. "We weren't scoring goals and I think generally we were struggling, there was no question about it, we were struggling but the writing was on the wall the season before, so we knew that we had problems," Martin Edwards says.

Consolidation had been the aim in Docherty's first few months; of course, it wasn't expected that United would suddenly become title contenders in his first full season, but there were still high hopes. "The objectives were to try and buy a couple of players, I was promised there would be money there to purchase those particular players that I wanted," Tommy Docherty says. "Our ambitions were to get a bit better, to get the youth teams strong again, and just really to improve on the situation as it was at the time because it wasn't good enough."

His programme notes at the start of the season suggested that the levels of expectation were actually much higher. "You supported us magnificently through those hectic last few weeks of the season when we had our backs to the wall and the Second Division was dangerously near," Docherty wrote. "I must make a realistic assessment of our chances and I cannot honestly say that we are going to win this and that. But I think I can promise you an improvement, free, I hope, from some of the anxieties of last season. I think we are much stronger at the back for instance which should see us avoid any serious trouble at the wrong end of the table. A good defence is a sound foundation and it is on that department that I want to build. I shall be happy to finish this season in the top six and to achieve that target would I think be satisfactory progress. I am slightly disappointed that we have not kicked off with another big name to take over from Bobby Charlton. It has not been for the lack of inquiries, I assure you, but persuading clubs to part with a top man is naturally not very easy. But although I have become reconciled to starting our programme without a big transfer signing, I do not rate it the end of the world. It does not unduly worry me from the playing point of view because I have a great deal of faith in the players already on the staff. We have an extremely young staff that can only get better. It may take just that little bit longer when you cannot replace a man like Bobby Charlton with mature skill, but get there in the end we will. All our youngsters have talent and it may well be that circumstances will bring some of them on more quickly. Certainly there is nothing more rewarding in football than to find a young player suddenly shooting to the top. I would be the first to be pleased if they forced us to abandon the idea of signing a star altogether."

Cliff Butler says that from the supporter's side, more entertaining football would have been welcome. "We were too close, it was too near in the past, to the era of Law, Best, Charlton, Crerand, this all conquering team that was fantastic to watch," Butler says. "I think however good it would have been, it wouldn't have been good enough, because people would always compare it, you know they'll say it's not like it used to be. I think a lot of the time it was okay, the football was okay, they used to be good in attack… sometimes they failed a little bit in defence, but it was entertaining."

Before the start of the season the players realised there was some way to go before they could call themselves championship contenders but they felt they were on the right path. "Well we thought it was working," Morgan insists. "We started off… 'We're gonna be alright, are we going to win the league? I don't think so' but, you know, 'We'll do alright' but then it started to go wrong. It's like anything in football, certainly, when it's going for you, you get every break known to man and when it's going against you, you get the opposite. No matter what we did, how we played, everything… it was always the odd goal or they scored late on and it becomes… it is very difficult you know, losing becomes a habit, and of course your confidence goes… but we tried. We tried hard enough, it wasn't for the lack of trying but no matter what we did, it obviously didn't work at the time."

Pat Crerand surprisingly insists that Docherty's large scale reshaping of the squad did not have a damaging effect on the dressing room, and feels that United's issues were simply down to the loss of brilliant players. "There was nothing wrong with the dressing room," he says. "Everybody seems to think when players play badly or a team plays badly, it's the dressing room, it's not. If you went into the player's dressing room at any time, at training, they were having great fun and great laughs. I think people maybe lose their fitness standard, lose their ability and get too old, which plays a big factor and that's that, but to get players in, which United certainly had to do at that time, like George, Bobby, Denis to get quality players like that, where do you get them? Where could you get three players that were as good as them? You'd probably have to go to Real Madrid or something like that and get them from there, it's very difficult."

Lou Macari says that on top of all the other reasons, a major factor was the strength of the league. "When you talk about relegation back in the 70's, and when you look at the league, it is so unlike nowadays where money rules the Premier League nowadays and vast amounts of money can improve your team," he says. "Manchester United, back in the early 70's for people who obviously weren't around, didn't have that much more money to spend on players than Derby County, Nottingham Forest or Aston Villa… so it was a level playing field, anybody could beat you, home or away, teams who'd come to Old Trafford… if you didn't perform well for a number of weeks you could get yourself into a little bit of trouble, which we did, obviously."

Tommy Docherty agrees that momentum seemed to play a part in United's issues. "You know, success breeds success and if you're playing well and winning games you're home and dry," he says. "If it's the other way, and things are not going well, it goes from bad to worse… players who were confident all of a sudden lose that confidence."

Willie Morgan agrees that it was a combination of issues. "He (Docherty) tried all sorts and it just didn't work no matter what we did," he says. "At the time it's very sad, I can tell you, you were frightened to go out the bloody house at the weekend! We just had to take it on the chin. The one thing that was phenomenal throughout that season, when we played away from home, certainly in London, we used to go on the train in those days and all the fans... inevitably, we'd been beaten again and no matter whether it was snow, rain or whatever, they were there, and that was the hard bit. We felt so sorry for the fans, I mean it was heart-breaking. Manchester United have great supporters and it was heart breaking for me, because they still loved you."

It was the support which provided the lifeline. Docherty's comments after the Leeds defeat indicated that he appreciated that the time for caution had been and gone. United had become tougher to beat under him than under O'Farrell, however until now O'Farrell's team had entertained far more than Docherty's had.

One thing Docherty rejects is that he accepted United's fate or that he ever sent out a United team not to win. "I actually never ever had the attitude ever as a manager to accept the fact that we will go down or we will lose this particular cup tie," he insists. "Every game as a manager, and as a player, I played to win. If the team played well I gave them the credit, and if they didn't play well, well, we discussed it at a proper time."

It was said — though those post-Leeds comments suggest he didn't need telling — that Sir Matt Busby took Docherty aside some point in the spring to tell him that if United were going down, they 'should go down with dignity'. This was according to Busby's own words in an interview with the *Sunday Times* in 1976. Crerand corroborates this. "Matt said to him at the time, 'If we're gonna go down, let's go down with a bit of glamour, let's attack, attack, attack', you hear the Manchester United fans saying that all the time now when things aren't right 'attack, attack, attack' it did change but it proved to be too little too late. Maybe if they had started that way they might have finished in the top 3 or 4 in actual fact… all that defensive-minded thing is not a Manchester United way of life," Crerand says. "I was up the stairs with Tommy Docherty and I remember Matt coming up the stairs and Matt never interfered, I don't know anything about the conversations that Tommy Doc had with Matt Busby, I don't know because I wasn't there, but I was there when this conversation happened. Matt spoke about playing with wide players and attacking football and all of this sort of thing. Matt had accepted the fact that United were likely to get relegated, he had accepted the fact, but (was saying) 'let's go down with a bit of glory, let's have a go at people' and all of this sort of thing, and it changed and they nearly got out of it. United won four out of five games, something like that, the last few games, but it was too late… but I had been pushing for all of that for so long but nobody was listening, nobody was listening."

Not only does Docherty flatly reject that — saying "Busby never, ever discussed with me how the team should play, ever, because I wouldn't have paid any attention anyway" — but the players too generally have no recollection of any point where Docherty addressed the style of play. Martin Edwards believes that it is feasible the conversation took place. "I've heard the story and I don't know because I wasn't there, you know, I can believe that could have happened. I think we tried to be more adventurous towards the back end, we tried to score goals and obviously we were in a situation where we were going down and if we didn't do anything, we would have drifted down anyway, so we might as well, there's an element (of), 'let's have a go here, let's try and survive in the right way' and it nearly came off, didn't it? It nearly came off and I think just the way that we went down, the style of play that they were playing, gave everybody the encouragement that things would come right the following season."

If Docherty had a moment of reflection after that Leeds game, it would take another seven weeks for either the penny to drop or the pendulum to swing. By that point things had gone from bad to worse; four out of five games without a goal suggested the players had not heeded the comments at all. The Tottenham game was a nadir for the club. They were going down and the fans seemed resigned to it. The pressure of playing at Old Trafford was taking its toll, whether full or half-empty. They'd scored just one goal at the ground in 1974, through defender Steve James. Ronald O'Connor, reporting for the *Telegraph*, summarised the situation, "In his 15 months at United, Tommy Docherty has produced defensive stability, but this has been achieved at the expense of midfield artistry and attacking skills. The quality of forwards now at Old Trafford is clearly not good enough."

Perhaps, then, it needed things to be as bad as they were; a five-point gap to safety meaning United would have to claw at least three wins from their last nine games (after winning just six in their first 33) to make up the current gap, let alone what else Birmingham City might pick up between now and the end of the season.

Next up for United was a trip to Stamford Bridge. It was the one game every season that George Best relished, a real glamour tie in English football, canonised by the sight of Best being chased by Ron "Chopper" Harris. Docherty's old side had the opportunity to inflict a savage wound on his new club. It would be United's last trip to the capital that season. Perhaps his own pride had been hurt, but this was an afternoon when Willie Morgan led by example. His team-mates responded.

"At 29,000, it was a good and respectful turn-out for the funeral," wrote *Telegraph* journalist Desmond Marsh in his match report spectacularly headlined 'Sad Chelsea stumble over corpse'. "But, lo and behold, the corpse was seen to be twitching and every mourner left in great good cheer. Although it is far too late for Manchester United to save themselves from next season's Second Division, they said their big-time farewell to London with a flourish and swagger that was both touching and exciting. After an edgy, neurotic first half they quite demoralised a tawdry Chelsea side. Throughout the game they were wonderfully inspired by their captain, Morgan. After just six minutes Morgan was blessed with the sort of luck that United have been short of for months; Greenhoff fastened on a muffed clearance, set McIlroy clear on the left and Morgan was given space and time to take aim before letting loose a swirling drive from all of 30 yards that found Phillips off his line and helpless.

"It was a thrilling stroke and the preface for the estimable Morgan to start his marvellous one-man show… on the hour United went two ahead when McIlroy chased a nondescript ball to the by-line and Daly clipped home his centre; seven minutes later Morgan again turned Harris and Houseman inside out and McIlroy joyously walloped home the cross. Three-nil and still United twinkled. But after Martin had hit the upright and Morgan missed a glorious fourth by a whisker, Garner saved a bit of face for the woebegone Chelsea by pulling one goal back when he swept in Houseman's centre. But, by then, United's travelling army were singing their chaps home — muted only at the very last by the announcement of West Ham's two points."

Maybe United's young players hadn't known what to expect. Who knows if, for example, the support had been as reluctant as it had been at home to Spurs? They appeared galvanised by the raucous support and got the breaks their neat build up play deserved. Desmond Marsh had effectively written off the result as irrelevant in the grander scheme of things, but Cliff Butler says the win gave the fans hope. "I thought to myself, we might have a chance here."

Man-of-the-match Morgan said a good result made a big impact. "You know it's like anything, you get a break, and you get a win and then you're not thinking about losing," Morgan says. "The next match then, you look forward to rather than think, 'ah I hope we don't get beat' you know, it's a different mind-set." Lou Macari agrees but also feels that it was a cyclical thing rather than a turning point which could be attributed to anything in particular. "We started to pick up with one or two results that came our way, not through anybody saying anything, not through anybody doing anything except the players getting the results on a Saturday that got you two points," he says. "That probably gives you a little bit more confidence; spirits are a little bit higher in the camp and then you have a sort of grandstand finish to the season."

Sammy McIlroy also played a big part in the win and remembers the game well. "Chelsea at Stamford Bridge was always a game where there was an atmosphere, you're up against decent players like Chopper Harris as well, you knew you were in a battle," he says. "I always remember getting a result that day, beating Chelsea... and that was a great boost for us, games like that gave us confidence that's why I always say, in that season, I was always thinking after getting a result like that we might sort of stay up." McIlroy's recollection is slightly different to Macari's; he felt that there was a new mood coming from the big win. "There was a feeling going around the club, if we're gonna go down, let's go down trying to play the United way, try to play you know, entertaining, going for goals, if they scored two we get three sort of attitude," he says. "We won a game and the next thing everywhere was lifted, the club were lifted, the fans were lifted, we went on a sort of run of four or five games winning and then you begin to believe, we may get out of this, winning breeds confidence."

It didn't immediately translate to the Old Trafford crowd. The following Wednesday United played in front of just 33,336 at home to Burnley. The result was a disappointing 3-3 draw but it still felt like a positive step for a side who had been struggling for goals in front of their own fans all season. So there was still some optimism when United went to Carrow Road to take on fellow strugglers Norwich City. Three points from two games had put them above the Canaries on goal difference and they had pulled a point back on Birmingham to reduce that gap to four with seven games remaining.

After a difficult hour of football, Lou Macari — back in the side after missing the last three games because of the suspension for his derby red card — grabbed a crucial goal. Five minutes from the end Brian Greenhoff raced away to score a second. "Well when you're in trouble towards the end of the season, there are always going to be games that are really important, probably a bit more than others, when you're playing a team down at the bottom and Norwich were down there with us," Macari recalls. "We realised the importance of the game and it was one of those games where if you won it, it could give you a big chance of staying in the league."

It was smash–and–grab. Norwich had dominated the game but United had secured a crucial 2-0 win. For once luck had gone for them, and after the game Docherty ordered the United players to go and thank the fans. On the train journey back to Manchester, Docherty mingled with fans and was so emotional he made promises to them that if the club went down, they would come straight back into the First Division.

"The Norwich win made training that week better and there was a little of the old laughter with the lads," McIlroy remembers. "We had games coming up that we could win, there were important games, so training was good, the banter was good around the dressing room and we started looking forward to these teams that were coming, especially the ones that were around us, having that a little bit of self-belief again." It started to show in the manager, too. "Tommy Docherty, even in the relegation battle, as a manager himself was always up for a fight, always up for it, thinking we had the players to get us out of trouble," McIlroy says. "Never once was he negative, never once was he thinking, listen were playing so and so today. We very rarely — even in relegation battles — we rarely looked at a team who we were playing against, it was all about us, if we performed on the day, we'll get a result and when the Doc come into the club actually, it was exactly his way."

Paddy Barclay believes that United's plight gave them no choice but to come out fighting. "I didn't think Docherty needed any lessons in aggressive, attacking football," Barclay says. "I think that, to an extent, desperation put an edge in United's football and some good performances were recorded. A surge of good form began just before Easter and the crowd was a good barometer... over Easter they played home matches against Newcastle and won 1-0 and the crowd rose to nearly fifty thousand for the home game against Everton, and they won 3-0. I think there was a feeling that, to paraphrase that newspaper report, the corpse had risen, that was an exciting time."

The gates did seem curious. 44,571 watched United get a 1-0 win over Newcastle and 48,424 were inside Old Trafford for that

3-0 win over the Toffees. The victory over Newcastle was another example of United getting the rub of the green; Jim McCalliog scored his first goal for the club after misjudging the bounce of the ball. He had planned to swing a leg at it, but the ball bounced too high. Despite still not being high enough for a proper header, McCalliog stooped to head past the Magpies keeper. He then scored two goals in the Everton win; United's biggest of the season.

In between the games Alex Stepney had told reporters, "Suddenly the lads are starting to play for each other. There is a chance. They are talking on the field, shouting to each other. Helping each other." The team that had faced Newcastle read: Stepney, Forsyth, Houston, Greenhoff, Holton, Buchan, Morgan, Daly, McCalliog, Macari, McIlroy. Six of those were Docherty signings, two were young players who had come through the club's youth system, leaving Stepney, Buchan and Morgan as the leaders of the side. One can imagine the difficulty facing Buchan and Morgan when their own performances were under such scrutiny. This team still lacked a player who could be described as a goal-poacher but in Morgan, Daly, McCalliog, Macari and McIlroy they were not wanting for invention or goalscoring midfielders. They just had to hope that their purple patch could continue until the end of the season and maybe, just maybe, pull them out of danger.

It was no longer a completely unrealistic aim. The win over Everton had seen United move above Birmingham on goal difference and they were now just two points behind Southampton with a game in hand. And their next game was at the Dell. Docherty named an unchanged side from the team that had swept Everton aside. It was not an exaggeration to say they could have scored double the amount of goals they actually scored in their last two games. They started well against the Saints and in the 20th minute were awarded a penalty when McIlroy was brought down by the goalkeeper. For a brief moment the 30,789 packed into this tiny south coast venue looked over at the Manchester United goal; Alex Stepney was not striding forward for this one, though.

"One of the funniest things happened was, we were on the coach going there to the Dell in Southampton and I was sat beside

Willie Morgan and we were talking," Jim McCalliog remembers. "And because of me kind of moving in pretty quickly into Manchester United, I didn't know who took the penalties. And I said to Willie, 'Who takes the penalties?' Alex Stepney I think had been taking them. He said no, I'll take the penalty today and I thought that's okay, fair enough. Funnily enough, the game was twenty minutes old and we got a penalty, and all I could feel is Willie pushing me forward from behind saying 'go on Jim, you can go and take the penalty!' And I thought 'Thanks very much Willie!' So I took the penalty, and to my advantage I scored the penalty. I was quite happy, but I thought thanks very much Willie for dropping me in it!" The new signing needn't have been so anxious. His penalty kick comfortably beat the goalkeeper to give United a precious lead.

If every good story needs a protagonist then you might be left scratching your head by the insistence of most associated with United at the time that the team just needed the rub of the green; that they were playing well enough. Certainly, Jim McCalliog's modest career before and after his brief sojourn at Manchester United does not automatically place him in the company of the likes of Eric Cantona when we consider individuals who made a big impression on the club. Yet Jim's contribution to the cause was bigger than a United career that lasted just 31 games.

On the face of it, McCalliog appeared to be another in a long line of the Doc's tartan invasion, but he might have ended up at Old Trafford much earlier. "I'd just made my debut for Scotland with England at Wembley (in 1967) and I'd asked for a transfer from Sheffield Wednesday for various reasons," he says, "and it was in the paper straight-away that Sir Matt Busby was looking for players... they'd won the league, they were looking for players for the European Cup next year, that season. And obviously the papers were saying I could come into that category which was very flattering, and I was absolutely delighted and then I was actually told by somebody, not to sign for anybody. Sir Matt would come and sign me. When it fell through, I was totally devastated."

McCalliog had starred in a Wolves win over United earlier in the '73/74 season but, as the campaign wore on, it was clear his future was away from Molineux. "I had fallen out with (Wolves manager) Bill McGarry and it was just coming up to the transfer deadline," he recalls. "I'd spoken to Aston Villa and Vic Crowe. Manchester United got wind that I was going to go Villa and they threw their hat in and they offered the same money as Villa… I had the opportunity to go and talk to Tommy Docherty at Manchester United. With me being a Man United fan and the stature of Manchester United, I think it was a no-brainer. No disrespect to Aston Villa but I couldn't wait to go to Old Trafford. It was a very exciting day for me, I remember driving from Wolverhampton to Manchester and meeting the boss Tommy Docherty and I think it was all over and done in about two minutes and I was a United player. That was a special day." To Jim, it didn't matter that the club were in a relegation dogfight. "I thought there were some decent players there and I thought if there's any kind of team spirit there, they'll pull out of it," he says. "So as far as I was concerned, I wanted to go to Manchester United and hopefully help as much as I could, to keep us in the First Division."

The forward was entering a split dressing room; sure, there was Martin Buchan from the O'Farrell reign but him aside, the team at Southampton was five players (including Greenhoff and McIlroy) from the first Busby era and five signed by Docherty. Of course, McCalliog was already familiar with some players at the club. "Well one of my best friends was at the club, which was Willie Morgan so that was great," he says. "I didn't actually talk to Willie (about the transfer) because I didn't have a lot of time. I also knew George Graham, George was at Chelsea when I was at Chelsea. So there were people that I knew there, so I wasn't going to be a stranger in the camp. Straight away the dressing room was like nothing I'd actually experienced before. Except for a little bit when I was at Chelsea as a young player but, the atmosphere, you could cut it with a knife. There didn't seem to be a leader in the dressing room and there seemed to be a lot of cliques. So you had to be very careful what you were saying. I didn't really go into any of the cliques. All I did was talk to everybody. That's the way

I've always been in the dressing room. I think the dressing room is so important in a football club, so it was just a wee bit sad, that side of things. But at the same time I was looking at some of the players that were in the dressing room, and thinking 'These are good players. If we can pull together, I think we'll be okay.'

"It's always that wee bit difficult sometimes for managers, because they see us all as a group, but when we're away from the football club and when we're travelling together, then you can see people that are in cliques. And it's very difficult to break them down. But usually if you get some success or maybe get a cup run, it makes a difference and it pulls the team together. But I think Tommy Docherty had ways and means of finding out what was going on in the dressing room!"

Perhaps a new forward, unburdened by the pressure of having tried and failed to score for United that season, was just what the team needed. McCalliog's penalty was his fourth goal in five games since arriving at the club and he was far from a prolific scorer so his form must surely have inspired the likes of Macari and McIlroy that they too might get the rub of the green. It must have been a very difficult time for McCalliog; to do the job he was brought in to do, and it still not be enough. "I think I scored about 4 in 5 games, which were striker's figures really so I think that helped to bring about a bit more spirit and I think we could see a bit more light at the end of the tunnel," he says. "And in all fairness we shouldn't have gone down, we really shouldn't have, because at Easter time we'd got into 4th from bottom, and it was all for us there… but nobody's got a divine right to stay in the First Division. Manchester United were always known for being an entertaining side. I think that would come eventually but we were going to have to go through this dodgy period to get back to where they were before."

In the space of just a few weeks, the mood of the club appeared to have been completely transformed. "I felt pretty good, I seen a lot of the guys, looking at them, they had a bit more of a skip in their step," McCalliog says. "Whereas, when I first arrived, there was quite a lot of disharmony… just a terrible atmosphere. The results helped, but maybe they came too late." There is a temptation — particularly in the pursuit of storytelling — to detail every nook and cranny, building up certain moments that, in other areas of the tale, seemed insignificant. Southampton were struggling, yes, but they had a decent side. They certainly had a more than decent striker in Mick Channon, who scored an equaliser for his team on the hour mark. Despite the Saints ultimately being relegated, Channon would finish as the division's top scorer and was so highly rated that he would be capped for England and linked with a move to United in the coming summer.

The 1-1 draw was not a disaster in normal terms — after all the tight confines of The Dell always seemed like a bogey ground for United — and even journalist David Lacey's match report seemed optimistic. "Manchester United are playing with much more composure now," he wrote. "Their football still has little of the individual excellence or the emotive, surging movement of previous Old Trafford teams, but at least they have shed, for good one hopes, the dour, desperate image which was so tarnishing the club's reputation."

The result, however, halted United's momentum at a crucial point. The dropped point against a rival, and the lost opportunity to get out of the relegation zone had a damaging effect on morale. "We failed to win at Southampton and then I think that was it, that was probably the day most people thought, we are doomed now, we're not gonna pull out of this," Cliff Butler explains. "In particular, I keep referring to this game at Chelsea. Chelsea were a good team at the time and we were brilliant there that day, it was really good football and to win 3-1, to win at Chelsea I thought it might have been a turning point… but it was the Southampton one that tipped the scales."

There was still hope. Birmingham and Norwich still had to play each other and so what was then known as a 'relegation four-pointer' really had far greater implications. Next up for United, though, was a trip to Everton. After beating them so handsomely just the previous week, Docherty bullishly predicted that his team would 'murder' the Toffees at Goodison Park. But Everton had only been beaten once at home all season and had a plan to man-mark Morgan out of the game. It made it difficult for United to create, and although they defended admirably, that had not been in question as the season wore on.

At half-time, having played so well, scores from other games were read out. Birmingham were 2-0 up against QPR. It was another blow for United's young team, and one that you have to think was on their minds as they conceded a goal less than sixty seconds after the interval. As the manager tried to inspire his charges to a late revival from the touchline, they were all dealt another body blow when the Birmingham result was announced before the game had finished. They had maintained their advantage. United, crestfallen, limped to a 1-0 defeat.

"The announcement was made in bad taste," Docherty complained afterwards. "It came as the players were still on the pitch. My players hear the score and right away they go bump. We wouldn't have told them the Birmingham score because we were in with a chance of winning our own match and we wouldn't have wanted to dampen their spirits… I still feel we can make it."

"I thought that was a wee bit classless," Jim McCalliog admitted. "It come over just before the end of the game and it kind of rubbed it in a bit. I don't think it demoralised us but it was so unusual to hear an announcement while the game was on."

THE DAY THE MUSIC DIED

I F THERE WAS ANY FIXTURE that could galvanise the club it would surely be the Manchester derby, which just so happened to be the penultimate fixture of the season, and United's last of the campaign at Old Trafford. The previous round of results had left West Ham in 18th place on 36 points, Birmingham in 19th on 35, and Southampton in 20th — the first relegation spot — on 34. United, in 21st, were on 32 points, and had a game in hand over all those sides, but needed to win both of their remaining games and still hope that results in the other games went their way. Norwich were bottom on 29 points and already relegated.

Docherty kept faith with the team which had lost at Everton. His programme notes ahead of the derby were far more optimistic than the mood of the day. "Don't fear for the future of Manchester United!" he wrote. "That's my message to you on this our last home game of the season against our friends, neighbours and keen rivals from across the city... Changes had to be made and they have been considerable. Since my appointment at Old Trafford, I have released 31 players from various levels and signed 11. I felt I had to streamline the staff with the accent on quality rather than quantity and at the same time make way for young players coming up from the junior ranks... Whatever the outcome of our efforts this season we certainly cannot complain of a lack of interest (referring to supporters). It has been one of the factors behind the splendid spirit that exists among the players and it will only spur them on to greater efforts next season. I only hope that the improvement of recent weeks has been some small reward for the supporters' faith and that like me you can sense that there are infinitely better times ahead for Manchester United."

David Meek, in his column for the programme, was also positive. "Relegation has a nasty ring to it... but the threat has been considerably softened these last few anxious weeks by the way club and fans have reacted," he said. "The team have responded with their best football of the season, a sense of sporting responsibility and a hope for the future… as far as Manchester United have been concerned, their football has never been as attack-minded or as clean."

City had not enjoyed a fantastic season themselves. They had recently sacked manager Ron Saunders and replaced him with Tony Book, who had himself faced a fight to secure City's place in the top flight. They had nothing to play for but pride. That, and of course contributing to United's demise. "You've got a local derby and you've got two clubs here in Manchester, the fans don't like each other, no question about that, so if you got a chance to put United down, what a bonus that was," Pat Crerand recalls.

City manager Tony Book — perhaps indulging in a little Machiavellian humour — made Denis Law the City captain. The erstwhile King of the Stretford End had played twenty-three times in the league for the blues that season and scored nine goals; he was going to retire after that summer's World Cup, meaning this game would be his last in English football. Whilst not quite an emphatic statement that Docherty had made a mistake letting him go, the fact that United's leading goalscorer in the league, Sammy McIlroy, had just six goals gave weight to the theory that it may have been worth it to have retained Law.

There was tension in the air. One eye or ear would inevitably be kept on the game between Birmingham and already relegated Norwich. A win for Birmingham would consign United to the drop regardless. "A game against Man City, you're always treating that different to a normal game," remembers Lou Macari. "Add in to that we were in serious trouble and needed the points… I think we arrived at Old Trafford more nervous than I'd been in any of the previous games I'd played in. It was your biggest rival at the time, Manchester City, it was a game where we could be in serious trouble at the bottom, they could contribute to us being relegated and the rivalry in Manchester between the two clubs… this was the big game unlike nowadays where people would tell you Manchester United versus Liverpool is probably the biggest game, at the time it was Manchester City, so the importance of the game was something we were well aware of before we travelled to Old Trafford. In the build up to the game, I think there were a lot more nerves in the dressing room than ever before."

United, despite the anxiety, started well but immediately it seemed like a return to the days of February and early March; where the build up was neat and tidy, and the patterns of play were attractive, but the ball wasn't breaking kindly for Docherty's side in front of goal. As half-time approached, almost everyone was keen to hear what was happening down at St. Andrew's. Perhaps it had filtered through from the support on to the pitch earlier in the game that Norwich had taken the lead, but, by half-time, Birmingham had not only levelled but gone in front. United came out of the dressing room for the second half knowing that whatever they did it wouldn't make a difference if Birmingham took two points.

The Old Trafford crowd were behind their team and were almost immediately joyous after the interval; Sammy McIlroy beat the goalkeeper with an effort, but his shot was cleared off the line. It was the best opportunity a frustrated United could muster. As the nerves began to show, City, completely relaxed, began to control the game. Dennis Tueart hit the crossbar with an effort from the edge of the area and less than a minute later forced Stepney into a fine save.

There were just under eight minutes left in the match when one of the most iconic events in Manchester football history occurred. Francis Lee dribbled across goal and rolled a low ball into the six yard box - Denis Law, with his back to goal, instinctively flashed a heel at it, flicking the ball past a static Stepney into the United goal. The few City fans present erupted in delight; Law was congratulated by his team-mates but walked downcast toward the sidelines. As he did so, a large number of United fans took to the pitch. Before the game could restart, Law was brought off and walked straight down the tunnel to the dressing room. The game had barely restarted when the referee blew the whistle because of a pitch invader. One became three, with Martin Buchan leading one off the pitch. As City controlled the ball, United fans once again swarmed on to the turf, prompting the referee to blow for time and send the players to the dressing room. The game would not be restarted but the result stood. In truth United were already relegated because Birmingham had won, meaning they were down anyway, but it did not make Law's goal any less symbolic or the myth that City had relegated United any less enduring.

"The day began in gloom and then the sun came out, Denis's back-heel was scored after the sun had come up which may suggest that those up in the heavens supported the sky blue of City," Paddy Barclay says.

"I'm still trying to forget it!" laughs Tommy Docherty. "It's amazing that, it's an old saying in football, ex-players of yours come back to haunt you, it's true… football is riddled with situations like that where ex-players come back and haunt you." This was arguably the most famous example of this football phenomenon.

Lou Macari is the first to argue against the idea that Law's goal actually relegated United. "Well to this day people say it was revenge for Denis and the fact that the Doc was the manager when he left Old Trafford that was never the case, Denis didn't want to see Manchester United relegated and actually as we all know now, his goal didn't relegate us, it was other results that relegated us. So you can imagine back then it was drama on the day, it was Man City, you throw Denis into the equation, it was a massive story."

For the players, it didn't matter anyway. Particularly for someone like Alex Stepney, the sole survivor of the European Cup winning team just six years prior, it was hard to take. "I think we were down anyway but that didn't make any difference, it was the pride of playing in a derby game to win, you know," Stepney says. "Denis did as Denis always did, he was a predator… I mean you could tell by his face what happened, but, it happened, I mean… what more can you do about it?"

Willie Morgan even has begrudging respect for the quality of Law's strike. "It was a great goal by the way, he took it really well!" he says. "We thought we were down because we've been beaten, but we were down anyway because the other result went against us… it wasn't actually Denis that sent us down, so he can sleep at night!"

Pat Crerand, too, had sympathy for his ex-teammate, "I remember when Denis Law scored the goal against United that eventually put them down, Denis didn't know what to do, he told me afterwards that he was afraid to go home in case there been a crowd outside his house or something like that, obviously with having being an ex-United player and one of the greatest ex-United players."

If the older heads could be a little philosophical about it, spare a thought for those young players at the club. The 'Holy Trinity' were hard enough to live up to as it was, with personal accomplishments that have never been matched by any player at the club since, despite the avalanche of trophies that came into the club over the turn of the century. It was one thing not being the next George Best. It was quite another being a player in the team that went down. It's difficult not to feel sorry for the youngsters who were trying in vain to get United going. Sammy McIlroy, who came closer than anyone, remembers, "We had the sort of feeling in that game that even if we had won, we were looking over our shoulders at other clubs results. Okay, the game was stopped that day with Denis's goal, the back heel, but that didn't really matter anyway because other results went against us. A lot of people said about Denis sent us down, which he didn't... he walked off that field that day once he scored, he didn't even celebrate. Denis was a great player for Manchester United and I had the great privilege to play with him and against him when he played for Scotland. A proven goal scorer you know, when the ball comes into the box, not many players would have actually thought to try and back-heel it into the corner of the net. It fooled all of us, it fooled even our goalkeeper who was a great goalkeeper, Alex Stepney, and once the ball hit the back of the net, Denis's face right away... no celebration... off the park. But we knew later on in the dressing room, when we got the results, it didn't matter what happened, we were already down. I was very sad, with the crowd invasion as well, it wasn't a nice day to be a Manchester United player."

It seems almost as much for Law's own benefit as anyone

else's, that people are so keen to point out the semantics of the goal not actually relegating United. But the symbolism and all of the various elements surrounding it — the seismic nature of the event in British sport, the chronological series of events which had set up Docherty and Law as such major players in the story, the passage of time, and even the scarcity of footage in comparison to the over-saturation of football today, makes it impossible to consider Manchester United being relegated without, at the same time, seeing a crestfallen Law trudging away from goal, the only Manchester City player to be upset for scoring a goal in a derby.

"It was awful," Law later said. "I was very sad. It was an absolute fluke."

For the fans, it meant just the same. "United could have won that day and they were still relegated because of results elsewhere," says Cliff Butler. "But it's never stopped Manchester City supporters saying Denis did send us down, and it still feels like that to be honest, even now and at the time, I think on the day of the game when the ball went in, I think I thought to myself, this is incredible – Denis Law has relegated us... he was my hero then and he'll always be one of my heroes, there was just something about him, from day one, he was fantastic Denis, he was just so brave, he wasn't the biggest of lads, quite slim but going in where it hurts, he was just terrific and to see him score... he didn't even know he'd scored it to be honest, I don't think... he didn't realise and I think it spoke volumes on that day, that there's no celebration, there's no punching the air, he just put his head down and I thought that was quite poignant, really, you know, he was showing respect to United, I thought that was really something."

If you were to subscribe to the idea that relegation was a necessary hurdle for Manchester United's regeneration, then you might liken Denis Law's role in the episode as that of Travis Coates in the story 'Old Yeller'. Ironically, United were showing signs of being the healthiest they had been for a number of years. Although at the time there was no hiding from the shame of being a player in the team who was relegated at the world's most famous football club.

The newest of the bunch was the first to get back to the United dressing room. Or so he thought. "I remember the game really quite vividly, thinking if we can get a goal here first then we might have a wee chance," Jim McCalliog says. "Then of course the incident that everybody talks about was Denis Law's back-heeler. Once that happened, and Denis walked off the field…. that was quite a surreal moment. You kind of felt 'Is this a dream?' It just didn't feel right. Then of course, before the game finished, the game got abandoned. Then I think I was one of the first off the pitch and I went in the dressing room and who's in the dressing room? In the corner, with his head down in the corner, still in his strip. It's Denis Law. So I went over to see Denis and embraced him, to see if he was okay and obviously he wasn't. I think that's the only time I've ever seen Denis not celebrate a goal. Obviously he had big affection for both clubs, City and Man United having played for them both. So it was quite amazing watching our players walking in the dressing room and Denis in our dressing room in the corner."

"I was a young player at the time, I actually thought at that stage of the season, I didn't think we would get relegated, I always thought that something that would happen, that we would stay up," Sammy McIlroy says. "I couldn't believe Manchester United were playing in Division Two as it was called in those days… not many years after winning the European Cup, as well you know, it was a massive, massive blow. I mean I can remember, after the City game when we found out we were relegated… I remember looking around the dressing room and it was just disbelief. I'm looking at you know, Alex Stepney and Martin Buchan especially Martin, he'd come down from Aberdeen, a successful player up there and there was just this disbelief that we are actually in the second division. It was hard to take, and even when you go home and you see people and… well for days and days it was in that 'Manchester United have been relegated to division two' and it was so hard to take at that time."

Lou Macari agrees. "Oh it's a nightmare, you go down a league and you've played in the team all season, the first thing that's in your mind is what can you do to compensate everybody for that happening? Of course, once it's happened, you can't," Macari says. "The only thing you can do is next season is hope that things can go well, hope that you can bounce back at the first attempt and re-pay everyone who has followed you and been loyal and stuck with the team and back then supporters were loyal and stuck with the team… I never thought there was going to be a case of people deserting Manchester United, it's Manchester United, people didn't do that."

It was difficult for people to comprehend that Manchester United went down. "Funnily enough there was a bit of sadness for the fallen giant," Paddy Barclay says. "Of course there was an element of gloating at the fall of a giant but there was also an element that was rather sad because it's Manchester United, the Manchester United that Matt Busby built. There was the usual criticism at that time, no more, no less. I do feel that there was a lack of cackling, the kind of cackling you'd expect now if Manchester United were relegated, which, of course, they'd never be."

It is incomprehensible; but it was no less incomprehensible back then, especially if you were to have asked anyone in the summer of 1968 about the club being relegated. And so the saying "Too Good To Go Down" comes in to play. And unsurprisingly it's a saying that the players reject, realising they have to take it on the chin. "I think you're never too good to go down, the league table never lies. 48 goals against, 38 goals scored, it's simple as that. Ten games lost 1-0, the answer is there," Alex Stepney says. "It hurts, it hurt most of the time, when you've won the First Division and you've conquered Europe and nearly got to winning the FA Cup and things like that you know, and your life was Manchester United. I was bought by, at the time, the best manager in the world as far as I'm concerned… and the people around him and the people within the club, there was so much respect that it hurt. It eventually takes time, days, it might have been weeks for you to turn round to yourself to say, 'I've got to be a part of this to get us back'… fortunately not only for me, but from even the manager that stayed on and also the players that were brought in, the players that also had this horrible time of relegation… Sometimes that helps, you know, it digs deeps in there, 'that's not gonna happen again, we're gonna get out of this'."

Willie Morgan agrees with that sense of responsibility. "The fans were fantastic you know, they just wanted to hug you and say it's okay, which makes it even worse," he admits. "If they come on and say 'Ah you're useless, and you've let us down'… but it's the opposite when they're hugging you… it makes you feel a thousand times worse, absolutely dreadful, so, it was a hard time, it was a hard time that year for myself. It was even harder because I played nearly three months with getting strapped up just to go out and play, and it was just like, at the end of it all, it didn't make any difference… but you get over it, as you do, you get over it and just get on with things, you have to… it's just dejection you know, you're so dejected and it's very difficult to explain, getting relegated is not easy because you feel ashamed. The biggest thing is you've let all the fans down you know, there's still sixty three and a half thousand in and you let them all down and you just feel ashamed. I think it's slightly different nowadays, I think if you get relegated you go on the telly and talk about it, we didn't, we'd hide, it's a different mentality and a different thing but you felt ashamed. I certainly did because I felt I'd let everyone down."

The then-captain Willie Morgan is blunt in his assessment of why United were relegated. "There were just too many average players in the team," he says. "You can carry one, maybe two, but then it's hard and we just had too many. We had four or five, maybe six, who just weren't good enough and it's just a fact. It doesn't make them bad people… just that they weren't good enough, no matter what team it is, it doesn't matter where you are, who it is, everyone goes through it, all the great teams through the years… it's a nice distinction though, the only captain to have taken United down!"

There should at least be an asterisk on that point. Whilst the players insist, with some accuracy, assert that it wasn't Denis Law or Manchester City who sent them down, by the same token, as Pat Crerand makes clear, it wasn't the team Manchester United ended the season with that were wholly responsible for their demotion.

"The whole season was a low point, Manchester United didn't get relegated in the City match, the results on the day made them go down anyway but to see Manchester United get relegated was a nightmare in actual fact. No club needs relegation… maybe certain types of clubs, yes, but not United, Manchester United are a world famous club and in those days, they were still a big name, anywhere in the world. When you mentioned Manchester United, everybody knew about them, but no, they didn't have to go down it was just a style of play that they had at that particular time, it was boring, not good to watch, boring is only the word I can use.

"For me, particularly, it was embarrassing to think that United were going to go in the second division while I was at the club, (I'd been there) maybe ten years, maybe more at that particular time, it was just an embarrassment. I did what probably nearly every Manchester United fan did, I went home and never left the house, never went out, never spoke to anybody… we always used to go out on a Saturday after a result, but we never went out that night and we just didn't go out, we didn't do anything. I mean I think to have faced fans would have been embarrassing, that was the main reason why I, in particular, didn't go out, you'd have been too embarrassed to talk to anybody and I can say in all honesty, it wasn't my fault, I'm not going to take any credit for United getting relegated, Tommy Docherty and Cavanagh can accept that for all it's worth, it was not a great deal to do with me, but I was still ashamed that a team like Manchester United should get relegated."

For the players, it was a little harder to absolve themselves of the responsibility. "When you get relegated at a football club, especially at a club like Manchester United, you're a little bit, I don't know if the word embarrassed is the proper word but you don't really want to be seeing a lot of people for a little bit of a time," admits Sammy McIlroy. "Especially fans, and fans forums, and stuff like that and be asked the questions, 'Why did ya get relegated?' The simple reason was… the reason why we got relegated was we weren't good enough and for Manchester United to go down there, it was tragic."

Tragic, but there was still hope. "It was a decently balanced team, but yes it did lack experience," Paddy Barclay explains. "I would not criticise Docherty for that. You know when people say, and they're never the fans of the clubs, but they say 'What that club needs is to go down and have a season in the second division and rebuild'. Now there's no manager in the world brave enough to do that but I wonder if Docherty was brave enough to do that. Obviously that's what happened, whether or not he meant it, I don't know. That was probably the only instance in which a club has almost deliberately done that in order to rejuvenate their team and rebuild. It's the bravest thing on earth. Usually when you go down you lose your job! But Docherty was made of sterner stuff than that."

Of course Tommy Docherty rejects that. Regardless of the whys and the hows, only two facts were now important — Manchester United were relegated and Tommy Docherty was the manager who took them into Division Two. "When we got relegated I obviously died a thousand deaths," Docherty confesses. "You take it… basically you take it on your own skin, so to speak, I still feel we were too good to go down but we went down so you can't argue with that, we weren't good enough." It is searing honesty from Docherty, who at times, even at the ripe old age of 90 years old, appears impervious to anything bad you could say to him. So, did he doubt his ability in the job? "There was never any self-doubt but I just felt that we were too good to down, but we went down, and you've got to accept that the thing was, were we good enough to come straight back up again?"

There was another question on his mind. "I didn't think I would keep the job in fairness," he admits. "I was embarrassed, what I was praying for was for the season to start as quickly as possible, the new season. If you get relegated you expect to be sacked. It depends on the board, how strong they are. I had a great board at Chelsea who stood by me when we got relegated at Chelsea and we'd come straight back up again and the same applies. The club have got to have the confidence and the self-belief in you as you've got yourself and the players as well."

The story goes that Sir Matt Busby called Docherty soon after relegation and offered him a case of champagne as a show of support and solidarity. "It was a marvellous gesture on his part," Docherty said of Busby in his autobiography. Certainly from the words of Martin Edwards it never seemed as if sacking Docherty was ever a consideration. "It was very depressing," Edwards says of the events of April 1974, "anybody's reaction to going down is always the same, your first reaction is one of depression, but then when you start to think it through your mood improves, you get better and you think 'well, you know we have got some good players in that squad there is no reason why we can't get back with a little bit of strengthening here and there' and all the rest of it, yeah, you know, we'll come back… there weren't big discussions whether he should go or not. I think everybody felt that he had inherited a situation which was difficult the year before and he saved us, okay, things have been on the downward trend for a while. There was almost a bit of inevitability about it, but we all privately wondered 'Do we still have confidence that he can get us back?' and the answer to that was yes. At no stage then did we ever propose that we make a change or that Tommy Docherty wasn't the right man. We went down and he had Matt's full support so that's all I can say really."

"I knew that he wasn't gonna get sacked anyway," Pat Crerand says. "I knew that wasn't on the menu for him. Matt was a gentleman and an understanding man, maybe he saw something in the last half a dozen games."

Others remember being similarly certain. "Sackings didn't happen regularly in the 1970s the way it happens now, so no, I don't think anybody expected him to be sacked," Lou Macari says.

"No, I didn't think he would get sacked at all," concurs Willie Morgan. "It was the right decision to keep him at the time."

Perhaps those were different times and the board were more considerate. Then again, this was the same board that had dispensed with McGuinness and O'Farrell for lesser failures. Or, should that be, considering the implication of the statements, the same man. It wasn't universally accepted that Docherty would stay. It wasn't universally accepted that anyone would be safe.

"Normally if you are a manager of a team that got relegated, you'd get the bullet so I think 75-80% of me was saying I think he's gonna go," Alex Stepney says. "He didn't, it didn't happen and now I was in a situation, I know Tommy had said something about he was gonna get Peter Shilton and things like that, but I had played 42 games and we got relegated, I let in 48 goals now I think the teams that went down with us were probably letting in over 60 goals, so I thought I had a chance of being part of that team to bring us back."

Sammy McIlroy remembers being concerned that the boss might get the bullet. "When you get relegated a club this size, the stature of Manchester United you're beginning to think what is going to happen to the manager," he says. "But because of that little run at the end I think the board realised that it was a job he had to take of sort of rebuilding when he first got the job... players like Denis, Bobby, George, experienced players, who were in the side under Sir Matt, and Frank O'Farrell... I think Tommy Docherty had told the board, 'Listen, I can rebuild this squad' and he had the confidence to tell the board that we will come straight back and I think the board, especially Sir Matt at the time, believed in that and he kept the job. There was only one way to go and that was up and if the manager was embarrassed at that stage he definitely didn't let us know it on the training field and on the match days cos he drummed it into us that this club was too good to be in the second division, we have to get out of it."

Before that, there was the formality of closing out the First Division campaign against Stoke City - a game nobody wanted to play in. Nobody, that was, except Brian Greenhoff. If any individual gave an indication to a brighter future it was the lad from Barnsley who would be named supporter's player of the year and made captain for the club's last game in the top flight in opposition to Stoke City's captain, his elder brother Jimmy. It was an intriguing and thoughtful gesture from Docherty that he hadn't needed to make, one which revealed the strength of his relationships with his younger players. Things were looking bright. But Manchester United lost that game 1-0; their eleventh defeat by that same score that season, it was the 21st time they had failed to score. Try telling anyone connected with the club that their time in Division Two was going to be enjoyable.

LIFE IN DIVISION TWO

"YEAH, THEY'VE HAD a lot of problems," Bobby Charlton admitted in a sit-down interview with the BBC's Barry Davies upon his retirement in April 1973.

"Who do you blame?" asks Davies.

"I would think it stems from the fact that United were on top for so long, that unless you're in the position to recognise that you need change, you're going to fail, and I'm afraid that's what happened with United. Fortunately we won the European Cup in 1968. Everything since then seems to have been an anti-climax. Possibly Sir Matt Busby should have changed the team, possibly even prior to that. I think possibly for the last three or four years there have been lots of occasions where I could have been left out of the team really. But maybe reputation swayed his decisions. I think it should have been changed a lot earlier than it has been, though. It's very sad to see the club going down like that. I hope they do better."

As Charlton himself says, perhaps there is some truth in the suggestion that United should have been part way through a process of regeneration before Wembley, 1968 but it's difficult to point the finger at Sir Matt Busby, without whom there would have been none of the club's success or identity. If the great man had an indication of his own decision to retire before he made it public, then at least he gave plenty of notice. After such a long period of time, what would have been the best state to leave the club in for a successor? Or, to put it a different way, was there a better way? To answer that question you have to get inside the mind of those successors because surely each individual has their own perception of the perfect situation to inherit at a football club. Certainly, Wilf McGuinness couldn't have expected or hoped that Busby would handle a large outgoing transition. It wouldn't have been deemed necessary at the time. Denis Law was not even 30. George Best was the reigning European Footballer of the Year and Bobby Charlton was still a giant of the game, a central figure in England's attempt to retain the World Cup in Mexico in 1970.

McGuinness now concedes that he could have kept Jimmy Murphy's counsel and from the accounts of the players it feels like this would have probably made the most significant difference. However, at some point it always felt McGuinness' relative inexperience as a top level player would prove to be his downfall. How could McGuinness have planned for the players going to Busby instead of him? Sometimes you have to say that a plan was put in place for all the right reasons but just didn't work out. The ideas were right, and perhaps with a little luck in semi-finals, a Cup Final appearance might have added sufficient lustre to McGuinness's reputation to earn the respect of his peers whose careers were now coming to an end.

Then, as with most United managerial appointments down the years, the pendulum swung to the other extreme. After the greenhorn McGuinness, Busby clearly wanted the vastly experienced and successful Jock Stein to replace him. The second choice appeared to be Dave Sexton. When Frank O'Farrell was appointed, it very much felt like United had waited until the last minute and been stuck with a consolation prize. More than one lesson was learned through this appointment. While O'Farrell had enjoyed success in the lower leagues and at Leicester City it soon became apparent that the Manchester United manager had to have a certain stature to be able to go toe-to-toe with big name players. He also had to have a pedigree to justify taking tough decisions. If he was to be successful then he would have to be able to handle a transition. Just as they did with McGuinness, the players felt able to undermine O'Farrell. It could never work. Therefore the only hope of transition in such a scenario would be when the veteran player admitted their time at the top level was over or if it was made publicly obvious for them, as in the case of Bill Foulkes. When O'Farrell tried to ease a veteran player out, as in the case of Charlton, that became a black mark against the manager as the club closed ranks, simply because he lacked the standing (over and above his title) to make such a call. A similar thing happened in summer 2013 when Wayne Rooney dictated the terms of a new contract to incoming manager David Moyes after Sir Alex Ferguson had clearly left the door ajar for the Liverpudlian's exit before his retirement.

If the looming figure of Matt Busby is to blame at all, in the respect that the players felt they could go to him if they didn't like an answer from the manager, then his role in acknowledging that shouldn't be underestimated either. It seems that when Tommy Docherty was hired, even Busby had realised enough was enough, and that only one man must be trusted to sweep the deck. Considering the club had been through the doldrums anyway, the act of providing a fresh start became more important than the players, the style of play or trophies. Busby's absence from the discussion is notable when it came to Charlton and Law's exits, likewise with Best's eventual, and final, farewell.

The closest we have to a suggestion of interference is the alleged conversation between Busby and Docherty some time in the early 1974 about the style of play. Regardless of whether or not that happened we can know some things to be true without question. One is that United were not playing the sort of free-flowing football their supporters had been used to, another is that the reason for that was partly intentional by Docherty. The manner of Manchester United's defeats had become worrying; Best's attitude in a losing team was concerning enough, and the indiscipline that had been prominent in the side in the Sixties was becoming more of an issue. That had transformed from retaliation, to petulance, to frustration. From a flash point, it had almost become diluted over the years, where the players had been aggressive but were now easy to play against. For years, Manchester United hadn't needed to work hard to win games. Now they did, and Tommy Docherty's principle job was instilling that attitude into the players.

If one needs a modern example then look no further than Louis van Gaal's first months at the club. He had a fantastic pre-season, but when it came to competitive football United were found wanting.

He then made a number of high-profile, glamorous signings. The first game after these players arrived was a home destruction of a poor Queens Park Rangers side. They went to Leicester City and lost 5-3 after leading 3-1; it was an illustration that Van Gaal would have to get back to basics and protect that defence, at the cost of attacking football. Unlike Docherty he never won the crowd over as his reign became characterised by soporific performances, particularly at home and he became the first United manager to be sacked for football reasons after winning a major trophy.

In early 1974 Docherty had been successful in making United hard to beat. He now needed to trust that his players were capable and responsible enough in their defensive duties that they would not forget those responsibilities as he tried to make them a more attacking side. Considering that Docherty's Manchester United are remembered fondly for their kamikaze attacking style, and how the man himself would be so flippant towards the construction and instruction of it, these early days should not be discounted when it comes to explaining how the team developed.

Perhaps the seeds of Docherty's Dare Devils were sown in that Chelsea game in March 1974. Galvanised by their surroundings and their away support, there was also a change in formation that day. Centre-half Steve James was forced to come off after an incident in which he lost some teeth; Brian Greenhoff was moved from midfield to defence, but maintained his positive attitude with the ball, bringing it out and pushing his team-mates up field. Defenders who actually appeared to like playing football as opposed to preferring the physical combat side of the game were still a relatively rare breed in England yet they were revered on the continent. Docherty had cause to think. If he could have the industry further back, he could complement it with the skill and entertainment he'd had with his previous teams. It would be a gradual process. He just needed the time and the players.

Time appeared to be on his side after the genuine vote of confidence he had received following the club's relegation. Getting the players would be another thing. United were linked with a move for Mick Channon but the Doc returned to his former club

Hull City and made a move for Stuart Pearson — he arrived at Old Trafford for £170,000 with youth player Peter Fletcher going the other way as a make weight. Pearson's arrival raised eyebrows but in a rare instance of the manager and his then coach being in sync, Paddy Crerand had been to watch Pearson and gave his thumbs up to the signing. Here was a striker deemed good enough to play for the club and not just because he had experience of playing at the potentially more physical lower level. "He was a terrific player," Crerand says. "He was too good for the second division, in actual fact, I saw him play for Hull and he was too good for Hull City, he should have been in the First Division."

Docherty didn't really need the vindication, having been aware of Pearson from his time at Boothferry Park. "Chris Chilton was the centre forward for Hull City at the time, he was a good established First Division player and he kept Pearson out of the team. I used to go with the reserve team on a Saturday morning and Pancho was playing in the reserves and I thought the first team centre forward must be a good player if he's keeping this fella out, you know... of course when I went and got the United job properly one of my first targets was Pancho."

Pearson's previous experience with Docherty had been positive. "He was a bubbly character, he's always been like that, I know," he says. "It was a bit of a comedown probably for him (at Hull) because he came as Terry Neill's assistant. But what he helped Terry with was amazing because we went on a run at Hull City that year and we weren't far off promotion... Tommy always said to me he'd come back and sign me, which I didn't believe. It was a bit of a surprise when I got the phone call from the secretary saying you're going down to London to meet Tommy at the Russell Hotel. I had a chat with TD and I signed straight away. It wasn't about money for me. It was about joining arguably the best club in the world. So, the chat was over a cup of tea and by the time I'd finished my tea I signed... The story that he gave me was that I was the first one to help us rebuild and that they're going to get a lot of talent in, he didn't mention any other names... but I knew that Tommy was going to be ruthless getting them back to the top."

Docherty and Crerand might have been convinced but for Martin Edwards and the other members of the board, Pearson was a gamble, a show of faith in their troubled manager. "In all fairness the board wouldn't have known a lot about Stuart Pearson because Hull weren't in the same division," Edwards admits. "He had scored a lot of goals for them, and he was Tommy Doc's choice, and of course Tommy Cavanagh was from Hull, Tommy's assistant, so he came with a very strong recommendation and he was prolific for them, so we felt he had a good chance in the First Division so you know, he came with a lot of hope."

The sizeable fee was also a reflection of the fact United would not be financially troubled by relegation. So long as the public interest, and the crowds, remained high (with the latter point related to the former) then, in the short term at least, the demotion wouldn't be too restrictive on the club's spending capability. These were the days before mega-rich owners caused disparity in competition within the league; the days before eye-watering television deals caused disparity in competition between the leagues; and the days before 'parachute payments', which were designed to make life easier for clubs relegated from the Premier League, in effect helped cause a disparity in the lower divisions too. With that, there was an innocence, and particularly at Manchester United, where all of their greatest successes had been achieved with a side comprised of players developed by the club. That meant when United did spend, there was perhaps a greater concentration on justifying high transfer fees.

It was also an important commitment by the board because demotion could become a financial problem if the club were stuck in the second tier for more than a season or two. Liverpool had spent eight seasons in the Second Division as recently as 1954 to 1962, so it wasn't unknown for clubs to sink without trace, just as Leeds United have disappeared from top class football in the past two decades after being a force to be reckoned with in the 90s.

As far as Willie Morgan was concerned, Pearson's arrival meant that United had the one thing they'd been lacking. "The potential was there the year before when we got relegated, because we actually played good football — we just couldn't score goals," Morgan says. "We think okay, close season, he's going to sign a centre forward, that's what we need because we're creating chances... we were creating so many chances we just couldn't put the ball in the net."

One person who it had been hoped would fill that role was Brian Kidd. After disputes with managers, Kidd couldn't argue that Docherty hadn't given him a fair crack of the whip. But in 21 games in 1973/74, Kidd had scored only two goals, and they both came in the same game. His reputation remained intact despite United's demotion and his own form and Arsenal came in with an offer of just over £100,000. There was no doubting that Kidd had all the tools to be a top striker, but that would have to be away from Old Trafford where he had been brought into a team of leaders and was unable, when the time came, to take the mantle himself. This is no slight against Kidd; it was a pressure that even turned George Best away from the club. The teenager who had scored in the European Cup Final on his birthday was on his way to Highbury.

Also deemed surplus to requirements was George Graham. The former Arsenal midfielder refused to put in a transfer request and so the man appointed captain at the start of the 1973/74 season was demoted to the reserves a year later. He would move to Portsmouth in November after he realised his time at the club was over. Docherty's hope that his shared history with the midfielder at Stamford Bridge would translate into leadership material for his former charge at Old Trafford had failed; it wouldn't be the last time a former player of Docherty's would not get on with him later in his career. Another player with a similar story was Jim McCalliog who had only just signed for the club but upon relegation considered handing in a transfer request before deciding to stick it out.

At least now there was somebody to share the goalscoring burden with him. Pearson was not a poacher in the same sense as Denis Law but he was certainly a finisher. He was also a figurehead; despite not being six foot, he could lead the line and had the strength to hold the ball up to bring other players into the game.

He was perfect to play in front of United's industrious midfielders. From the collection of individuals Tommy Docherty had inherited, there was now the indication that a real side was coming together. "In the closing weeks of the '73/74 season I could see the green shoots of a team forming," Cliff Butler recalls. "Gerry Daly and Sammy McIlroy were becoming class players. We had a defence that was forming with Alex Forsyth, Stuart Houston and the two centre halves Martin Buchan and Brian Greenhoff, and that season I think we had 10 players who played more than 30 games, I think we had four that played more than 40 games, so it rolled over from the 73/74 season, it was gaining momentum."

If there was finally some familiarity within the United dressing room then that would have been a welcome consistency against the culture shock that awaited them in Division Two. The opening day of the 1974/75 season could not have presented a bigger contrast than the club's first game in 1973/74. Instead of striding out at aristocratic Highbury before 51,501 fans, United began lower division life at humble Brisbane Road, home of Leyton Orient. An official crowd of 17,772 managed to squeeze inside (and in some cases above and around) to watch the historic game on Saturday August 17th, 1974.

As the United coach pulled up there were hordes of supporters asking the players and even the manager for tickets. "We had fifty complimentary tickets, the police were throwing them out with anger, and I was giving them complimentary tickets to get them back in again," Docherty laughs.

"When we left Division One the majority of the stadiums were great," Sammy McIlroy says. "It's a culture shock when you go into Division Two when you drive up to the stadium, especially Leyton Orient, Brisbane Road, such a small stadium and you're thinking 'Oh my God, what's happening here?' You see fans outside it, waiting for you to come off the bus, Leyton Orient fans you know, shouting and screaming at you. Tommy Cavanagh, our coach at the time, used to say when we went to the ground, 'Go straight out, don't go into the dressing room, straight out, have a look at the pitch and see exactly what you're going to play.' That first game was definitely a shock because it wasn't a great stadium, the fans were right on top of you, it was a boiling hot day, first game of the season, away from home at Leyton Orient and you're thinking 'Oh dear, this is going to be a battle.'"

If all Sammy McIlroy had ever known was United, all Lou Macari had ever known was the big time with United and Celtic. "I've got to be honest, when the first game came along which was Orient, I didn't know what to expect, I didn't know what to expect crowd-wise, I didn't know what to expect from the opposition," Macari admits. "We were going to Orient and it was unknown territory for us. Everything we were walking into was sort of unknown, a minute after the team bus arrived at the Orient ground and there was... oh my God... there were thousands outside. I think the thousands outside were ticketless, because a lot of my pals were there, and I was on the bus. There they were outside, making gestures to me, they needed a ticket and I said I haven't got any tickets. About an hour later I realised my pals that were outside the ground were now inside the ground and how they got in I don't know, but they didn't have tickets! That was the start of a rollercoaster season, in terms of, excitement, drama, and everything you want to be involved in as a footballer in that division. It was chaos, pandemonium and when you won the games... I mean my pals at the game didn't return to Manchester for three or four days because they used to go out, I was going to say they'd make a weekend out of it but it was more than a weekend, it was as long as they could stay away and celebrate and enjoy the occasion."

Unlike Macari, whose domestic form counted against him, Willie Morgan had spent the summer with Scotland at the World Cup. From the biggest football stage, he stepped into the unknown. "It was amazing, you know, because you don't know what to expect, and we go down there and they've got bunting out on the streets saying 'Welcome'," he laughs. "We just... without walking around saying 'How great are we, we're Manchester United, we know we're gonna beat ya', you didn't start beating your chest... you just believed that you were better... the nice thing was the pitch was lovely and obviously for us it was bonus, a beautiful pitch.

To win the first game and to be received so well, you know, the home supporters were very appreciative of us being there, even though we beat them, which is nice, it's a nice feeling and it was the start of a great year."

Morgan scored in a 2-0 win. It was as comfortable as could have been hoped. A change was noted in Docherty, possibly inspired by the performance of his team and settled by the knowledge that he would have time to bring them back. "If anybody knows Tommy Docherty they will realise that what I'm saying is true," Lou Macari explains. "He was funny, he was witty and he relaxed you, he got into that dressing room with the team before the game, that was his input, people may think 'Well, that's surely not enough', but all managers have different strengths and the Doc's biggest strength was he was very funny, to this day he's funny. That brought a relaxation to the dressing room, it brought calm to every game before he went out and I really do believe that that was the main ingredient why we won the league and headed back to the top league."

The conservatism had disappeared. The thought process was clear and understandable. If United were good enough to put three goals past the likes of Chelsea and Everton in the First Division then they should have more than enough to deal with the Second Division. "Tommy Docherty's motto in them days was 'Because of who you are, you're Manchester United, every team in this league is going to try and beat you, home or away they will do their utmost to beat a club like you, so you're going to have to match them with their fight early on, you've got more quality than them, go out and show that'," Sammy McIlroy remembers. "We had a great start at Leyton Orient and right away after the first game we had that sort of confidence. The fans that day were unbelievable, the supporters we brought from Manchester were unbelievable and were thinking 'right, let's get a run going, after a good start away from home, let's get a run going' which we did."

There is a temptation to neglect the more insightful work Docherty had already done. As this period marked his own transition from worrier to the flamboyant, quotable character people grew to love or hate, the idea of him as a master tactician is forgotten. He is perceived mostly — and to some, only — as a great motivator, who did little in the way of the meticulous planning of his side. Yet that perception completely devalues all the good Docherty did in his first 18 months, even if it ended in relegation. Of course, relegation was enough of a sting to the pride of the players who took them down, to instil the fight within them to bounce back but a lot of the foundations for the recovery were already in place. Certainly, taking Lou Macari's comments at face value leaves you with that impression.

"I think the inspiration was just, we had let everyone down, the club itself had felt the effect of being relegated," he says. "It was big news… Manchester United has always been big news and you can imagine how big it was when we got relegated, and you know, how much we were in the spot light. I think as players and management at the club at the time we realised what we had to do."

But big teams with soft underbellies make for rich pickings in the Second Division so it was critical that Manchester United had, at their core, a fighting spirit. Even though Docherty was now urging his team to express themselves and dominate the opposition, there was still something present in his reminder to the players — as McIlroy attests — to let them know that the bare minimum expected was matching the commitment of the opposition. Whereas as recently as early 1974 such commitment had been almost the entire personality of the side, it was now becoming only a part of what United had to offer.

The opening day victory provided a much-needed bounce but there was no boastfulness as United prepared for the first home game of the season against Millwall the following Saturday. "Everyone at Old Trafford is deeply conscious of the debt we owe you for your loyal support and it will be our support and it will be our inspiration in the months ahead," Docherty wrote in his programme notes.

"It makes me very sad to write a message for the first time as Chairman of a Second Division Club especially as it is some 36 years since we were last in this position," Louis Edwards wrote.

"I can only assure you that every possible effort is being and will be made by everyone at the Club to achieve a change of fortune and, if at all possible, to get back in the First Division at the first attempt... I would now like to say a word to those supporters who travel to away matches. It seems to me that many of them think they are defending the honour of the Club when they cause trouble but all I can say is that there is no credit in being known as the worst behaved football followers in the country... Forget the 'United Aggro' and make yourselves the best behaved supporters in the land. If you are unwilling to do this then all I can say is that we don't want you and would prefer to get along without you."

United's punishment for the pitch invasion against City the previous season was to have fences installed behind the goals, separating the fans from the pitch. That it was Millwall, with their own lurid reputation, who were the first visitors, was somewhat ironic but the day passed without drama. Winger Gordon Hill was in the Millwall line-up and his memories of the game give some insight into the mindset of the Second Division players who were now coming up against the biggest team in the country. "It came as quite as a surprise to us because we had been used to playing in front of eight to twelve thousand people and twelve thousand on a good day," Hill recalls. "We were going up to fifty-five thousand people and five thousand people standing outside waiting to get in... we went up there and we just got absolutely blitzed. I mean we were the Lions, Millwall had the big lion on their chest and all that, we went up there, and we were more like Christians because we lost 4-0. I was very fortunate to have a decent game, but it was deafening to say the least, it was so deafening that you couldn't hear people talk on the field."

And so the stage was set for United to begin their season in style. Seven wins and two draws from their first nine games made it clear that the second tier's illustrious visitors did not intend to stick around. "Straight away you felt something was different, we won comfortably and there was a flair about it, there was an excitement about the way they were playing the game," says Cliff Butler. "It was very cavalier, the emphasis was on attack and it felt good, I think it was about ten games before we lost so after 9 games and we're undefeated, we're at the top of the division and people think we're gonna do it"

"From that opening day at Brisbane Road we realised what we had to try and set out to do, was to take Manchester United back to the top league," Macari says. "We had a great team spirit, I think the team spirit we had, I don't think there's any comparisons to any club in the country, I just don't see the same camaraderie between a lot of players nowadays and the way we were."

What easily could have been a year of understated embarrassment became a time fondly remembered by everyone at the club. Even Paddy Crerand, who was haunted by the demotion, reminisces fondly of the time. "It was incredible," Crerand says. "There was thousands locked out at every ground... at nearly every away ground there wouldn't be much more than twenty thousand allowed in. I would think in those days United would travel with at least twenty thousand, there were massive crowds following United all over the country in those days, loads of them couldn't even get near the stadium because they wouldn't get in or the gates would be closed, there were so many times that the gates were closed, it was incredible. I mean it just showed you the support that United had, going into the Second Division. With lots of clubs, the support dies away to a great degree, but United actually got stronger and stronger and it just showed you what the fans thought about the club at that particular time."

Willie Morgan agrees. "Everywhere we went it was like a party, a circus," he says. "Would I like to get relegated again? No. Would I liked to have that season in the Second Division, yeah, because it was fantastic, everywhere we went, it was like a circus, everybody wanted to see us, it was fabulous and it was a breath of fresh air... I saw places that I'd never seen before."

It would be a stretch to say relegation was a good thing for Manchester United just as it would be for any football club. But once you look at the circumstances and consider the benefits, it's clear that Docherty made the most of it. "In retrospect, relegation and the way United responded to it, in particular Tommy Docherty, was one of the best things that happened to the club," author Paddy Barclay contends. "They went back to proper Manchester United football... it was proved by the fact that the crowds actually went up when United started the next season in the Second Division and not just because they were expecting United to go through the division, but because they knew the football was good and getting better."

Perhaps the high point, certainly in the first part of the season, was a game up at Blackpool on a very memorable day for United. Docherty was transitioning his team into a 4-2-4 shape, with Morgan on the right and Gerry Daly on the left. Normally Stuart Pearson would lead the line but was absent at Bloomfield Road and so Lou Macari, who had been playing in midfield, was up front with Jim McCalliog. Docherty would eventually have the headache of who to leave out until he came up with the bright idea of moving Greenhoff into defence. Until that point, he had the luxury of being able to choose from McIlroy, Macari and Greenhoff in the middle of the park, and often a player would be missing elsewhere which meant the player who would usually miss out would retain his own place. The defence that day was Forsyth, Buchan, Holton and Houston, an all-Scot and all-conquering backline. Alex Stepney, the goalkeeper, could stand back and admire as his colleagues put in a tremendous display to win 3-0.

"It just changed overnight, we had flair back, we had wingers, we were scoring goals," Stepney says. "We had Stuart Pearson come in and you know, it was a great attack with Lou and Sammy you know, defensively we were strong, we had Stewart Houston, Alex Forsyth who had come in, there were quite a few players that had gone but the guys had been replaced brilliantly... the change was that young players came in, experienced players became stronger because of what happened as well... we had flair, and once you start scoring, they (the players) start showing their own talent and skills and the manager sees that, the coaching staff see that, 'Don't stop it, just keep it going', and that's what happened. In the Second Division, we had record crowds you know, that season, it'd never been known in the Second Division, but we were playing attractive football, not playing the way that happened in the 60s, but we were playing attacking, flair football and we had players that couldn't care less, they went out and attacked."

"He didn't get overly into tactics," Stuart Pearson says of Docherty. "He wanted a pattern of play and that's all we ever did. We did a set pattern of play. Alex Stepney got the ball, the two full backs had to sprint wide and we had to throw it to them. His first port of call was looking for me up front. They pinged it into me and then everybody released themselves off me. We used to do that for hours, early doors. Left back into me, everybody join me. If it went through the middle, it had always had to go wide. We never did any of what you see now, when the ball goes to the midfield player, he knocks it back to the centre half, he knocks it out to the winger, he knocks it back to the midfield player and he knocks it back to the centre half. It does my head in, I think it does the fans head in as well. So, it was fantastic for me being the main man. I was the one that everyone was looking for. And we all got used to it, so when anybody was in a good position, whether it was Louie or Sammy coming to join me. I knocked it off first time for them and then we started playing."

It would be a little while yet before Docherty signed the two or three players who most people associate most closely with this style of play — and those players of course brought their own abilities and personalities to the mix — but it was fair to say that most of the ingredients were already there and that the turnaround really did appear as if it was overnight. Perhaps, though, that perception is altered by the simple fact that United were now winning games as opposed to drawing or losing narrowly. Docherty insists that his approach never changed, although he concedes that the players' growing confidence both in themselves and in the approach also had some effect. "At the time we played it better than anyone else," Docherty says. "We played push and run, two-touch football, you know, play the ball, control the ball, pass it, control, pass, control, pass and when you lose it, get back at the opposition as quickly as you possibly can, and make them move quickly, and they will make more mistakes than you will. I knew my style of football, that United fans would love it. We were great to watch at Man United, usually managers play the way that they played themselves as players. I mean Busby was a very good midfielder, an excellent midfield player and the team played that way as well, and Jimmy Murphy with the Welsh side, his team was playing good football as well. I'm not saying it's always the right thing or the wrong thing but that's what usually happens and every club I've been with as a manager we've played push and run, two touch." Nowhere, though, as effectively or as memorably as when The Doc put the smiles back on the faces of United fans.

And being there to witness it, in its early flowering, especially considering the circumstances, lent itself to the idea of a rebirth of the club. "It was just a breath of fresh air," Cliff Butler says. "They started beating teams every week and so the euphoria started growing among the fans, and they started enjoying it again. I'll never forget the number of people, the support was astonishing; every match, in fact, it became a problem at one point, there was that many going to games, they were just everywhere."

Blackpool was a case in point. "The more games we won in the league, the more the support grew," Macari says. "You would see thousands of thousands of people with red scarves on supporting Manchester United, who didn't have tickets, who couldn't get in and this became a regular theme. At Blackpool, if my memory serves me right, we went out on the pitch… I thought are those tangerine scarves or are they red scarves? Or have we got that many supporters here that three quarters of the ground is full up of United support? Three quarters of the crowd had travelled from Manchester and were desperate to see their team! I think there was a belief that it was their team that was heading back to the top league and I think they had a great belief in us early on watching the team play, watching them develop, how quick we were… it was up and down and it was non-stop."

It was memorable, too, for Sammy McIlroy. "We played some fantastic football even though we were away from home," he says. "The atmosphere was unbelievable with Man United fans right round from the half way line, right round to the other side, it was all red, singing, getting behind you and I think the supporters then, watching us play against Blackpool were believing even then, that we were gonna come straight back because the football was unbelievable and that we were scoring goals as well. You had little thoughts back to the end of that last season when we got relegated, how we were feeling then to how we were feeling at this stage of the season, in October at Blackpool... what a difference, and what it was, was confidence and winning. Everyone wanted the ball, the forwards were having shots, the midfield players were getting involved, the defenders were doing their job, everyone was confident and that day coming off after the Blackpool game we were beginning to believe this is the way to do it. The fans were loving the way we were playing, the papers were loving how we were playing, every away ground was getting sold out, and the crowds were coming back at home as well, the atmosphere was beginning to sort of really come good."

United had got the fear factor back, in some diluted fashion. It was a nice feeling for Willie Morgan. "Manchester United is a massive name and you know that people are going to be frightened to come to Old Trafford," he says. "You know they are, they're all second division teams, so you know they're going to be frightened, so you've got a great start even before kick off, and then going away from home, we always thought we could beat anyone."

It was a new feeling, though, for Stuart Pearson, who scored a hat-trick on his return to the team two weeks later. "Well in the end, they had a proper professional side to everything," Pearson says of United. "I'm not saying Hull didn't, but when you turn up at Old Trafford and you're getting ready to go down that tunnel and there's 50-55,000 people there... even though they'd just got relegated the year before, they were just amazing. And I honestly believe, they talk about you're worth a goal start but you know I think it was probably a two goal start because they're just amazing people. It was just an amazing feeling to score a hat-trick at Old Trafford... after the first season, they used to give me the chant so when we got on the pitch it's 'Oh, Stuart we would walk a million miles for one of your goals', and you wouldn't believe how I felt when I heard that… it just lifted me."

The confidence in the team had come on leaps and bounds after the League Cup draw at the start of October pitted them against Manchester City. It was a chance for revenge so soon after April; an opportunity for the players to show that their form was good enough to take on anyone.

"We wanted a game like that," says McIlroy, "Because people were saying 'Oh we are doing well because were in the second division, the standard ain't great you know, wait to we see if you do come back' what's it going to be like? We beat City at Old Trafford, and deservedly, again the crowd were fantastic but that result against Manchester City when our neighbours, last game of last season, when Denis Law's back-heel sent us down… whatever, we got our sort of little bit of revenge against them and showed that we were capable of playing the top teams… I could see the confidence running right through the side and the football that we played, the one touch football, the goals we scored, the chances we created on pitches that you're not seeing today, really bad pitches, but this team was playing some unbelievable football, I think it's one of the best and I could understand why the fans loved that season because records were broken home and away. It was a fantastic team to play in."

The feeling of wanting to prove something against their local rivals was shared by McIlroy's team-mates. "When you're playing against City and you remember relegation and you remember one or two other results that have gone against you, you're desperate to beat them," Macari says. "You know it's going to be a massive achievement, you know it can help you get that one step closer to Wembley, it was a great night for us and the big crowd was fantastic. It would have given everyone a belief that this was a different Manchester United now, a different team, and that team could hold their own against anybody."

The clean sheet in a 1-0 win was the first of six consecutive shut-outs to mark an equally impressive run of nine in eleven games. United were as miserly at the back as they were proficient up front. But the 4-0 win in the league against Oxford saw the last clean sheet for five league games, in which United only won twice. The last of those games, a 4-4 draw at Sheffield Wednesday, was notable for Jim Holton suffering a broken leg. In the short term Docherty would try and plug that game first with rookie Arnie Sidebottom and then with Steve James, who had of course previously played regularly. It was a combination which survived United's roughest period of form, over the winter, although Docherty's side held firm to their place at the top of the table.

In late February, after a defeat to Aston Villa, Docherty made one of his most significant signings when he acquired the services of Steve Coppell from Tranmere Rovers. It was a timely boost. United had just endured a run of four goalless games in five. Pearson was absent for the first three of them but better was expected. It was nothing more than a wobble but the period saw the first real signs of a problem under Docherty's leadership.

Willie Morgan had suffered an eye injury in 1974 and Docherty, on observing his form, felt he was no longer the same player. In a game against Portsmouth, Docherty had substituted Morgan with the game at 0-0; perhaps the approach to substitutions has changed over the years, but with teams limited to just one in those days, it was more symbolic. One thing that has never changed is how disappointed an attacking player is bound to be, when taken from the field in such a situation, because of the message it sends. Morgan was dropped from the team at various points over the coming months and was a high-profile casualty of a defeat at Oxford, two weeks before that loss to Villa. A week before the Oxford game United had lost at home to Bristol City; it turned out to be Jim McCalliog's last outing in a United shirt after a year in which he had scored a respectable seven times in 31 games. He would be sold shortly afterwards to Southampton, with Docherty explaining the transfer was a means of recouping the money spent to sign Coppell.

"A problem started mid-way through the season I think," Willie Morgan says. "I just signed a new six year contract a year before my problem started with Jim McCalliog... he was my best friend and Doc shafted him. Jim told me and I went to see Doc on his behalf and then went back to see Jim and said, 'Don't go in and say anything but this is what he's gonna do, he's gonna get rid of you and do all that stuff, don't tell him because he'll know I've told you'. That was the start of getting me out, which wasn't going to be that easy but he did, it took him a while, but he did."

McCalliog claimed that he had an issue with Tommy Cavanagh which led to his exit. "I had a wee problem with Tommy Cavanagh and that was it," he said in Sean Egan's excellent book The Doc's Devils, although he didn't elaborate.

Although it is never mentioned in his own autobiography, Docherty reportedly called the senior statesmen in his team, Willie Morgan and Alex Stepney, into his office for a meeting about the future of his coach. "The champagne flowed, but some disquieting things were happening within the privacy of Old Trafford," Stepney said. "I was sickened by one stroke the Doc tried to pull. He sent for Willie and me and called us into his office. He wanted to talk about Tommy Cavanagh, Cav, the coach he had brought from Hull City. I knew Cav to be one of football's great enthusiasts. He knew everybody in the game. He would talk football with anyone all day long. Winning matches for whichever team he happened to be with was all that interested him. Docherty looked at Willie and me and said that he had received complaints from younger players about Cavanagh's language and attitude towards them. Docherty said it was his feeling, and that of the youngsters who had made the complaints, that Cav had been out of order on a few occasions. He wanted to hear what we thought about it. He said: 'I want to know whether you think I should sack him, because we cannot have this kind of thing going on.' I said that I thought that Tommy Cavanagh had enormous heart for the game and for the club. He was honest, he called a spade a spade and he was very good for the morale of the team. I told the Doc he could do what he liked, say what he liked but that he should not ask me and Willie to give the go ahead to sack Tommy Cavanagh. Willie, who was nodding in agreement as I spoke, backed me up again and we left the office together."

Morgan doesn't mention Stepney but recalls a meeting. "He called me in and asked me to make a complaint about Tommy

Cavanagh so the board could sack him. I said 'no I'm not doing that. Sack him by all means, I didn't like him, that would have been great to get rid of him, but I'm not going to do that.'"

Morgan was substituted in the March 1st win over Cardiff City. His replacement was Steve Coppell, who was making his debut. Morgan would play again for United, but his spot on the right-wing was now taken by the young, quietly-spoken Liverpudlian. Stuart Pearson's goal in the 1-0 win at Bolton on March 8th gave United a five point lead over Sunderland and seven over Norwich, who were in fourth (the top three were promoted, with no play-offs). With nine games remaining, promotion prospects were looking really good. United drew at home to Norwich then won at Nottingham Forest — under the stewardship of Brian Clough since January — before a 1-1 draw at Bristol Rovers.

That game on Good Friday was the first of three in four days over the Easter period; after a 1-1 draw at Bristol Rovers on Good Friday, United defeated York City 2-1 on Easter Saturday in an encounter which saw the start of what would truly become known as the Docherty shape. Steve James had picked up an injury at Bristol and so Brian Greenhoff moved into defence. It meant a recall for Morgan on the left wing, with Gerry Daly partnering Sammy McIlroy in the middle of the park. Lou Macari played alongside Pearson up front. With two players who were clearly intended to play wide, it was the boldest move yet from Docherty, and a show of confidence in his side to impose themselves on the game without an extra body in midfield. The switch was not yet permanent — the idea of Greenhoff in defence was still an emergency measure — but before too long it would be. The hiccup was well and truly over, United won beat Oldham at home to set up a game at Southampton that felt just as important, for other reasons, as their last trip to the Dell a year earlier. A win would seal United's return to the top flight; it was quite the turnaround from the draw in the same fixture last season which caused irreparable damage to momentum and confidence. Docherty's team resisted temptation to get involved in a physical encounter — a remarkable testament to the composure of a team with an average outfield age of 22 years and 9 months — and Lou Macari scored with 14 minutes remaining.

The former Celtic man's response to promotion was relief, and it was somewhat fitting that it was achieved on the road. "When you arrived at the grounds and you see so many supporters — and there were thousands of supporters at every away game that couldn't get in — it made you realise and believe how important it was to the support who hadn't deserted you," he says. "Whether it was down in London, wherever it was in the country, they were gonna attempt to be there to cheer you on and the best way to repay them was to do what they wanted us to do which was go and win the second division and I think we won it in a little bit of style as well."

The Championship was also decided away from home; cries of 'Champions, Champions' echoed on the Old Trafford terraces in a narrow win over Fulham but Aston Villa still had a slim chance of overtaking Docherty's team. The title was assured in United's penultimate game, they went 2-0 up at Notts County with goals from Stewart Houston and Brian Greenhoff. County fought back to earn a draw but it didn't stop the celebrations. Again, it was fitting that it was achieved away from home, at a ground United hadn't played at for almost forty years. Meadow Lane would soon be a regular venue for league matches between the clubs in the higher division; but only United's 1992 visit would bring a higher crowd than the 17,320 who were packed in to see Docherty's team secure the title.

It didn't matter that it was a division lower, there was a genuine buzz; Manchester United were back. "It was fantastic," says Paddy Barclay. "It was reminiscent of what it must have been like when people flocked to see the Busby Babes, it was something new, something young, something free and exciting and entertaining. People were keen to be lifted by something and Tommy Docherty's Manchester United in the Second Division... I can still remember the excitement that they caused and people actually started following Second Division football, looking at the Second Division results first ahead of the First Division almost because of the stir that they caused and the excitement they brought to places, where they've never probably seen such… they've might have seen a lot of good football before but they've never seen such glamour. Manchester United is a glamorous club and that restored the glamour of Manchester United."

It was an interesting experience in terms of how United's exposure would be affected, particularly after a period when attendances had fallen. If there were concerns about the club's profile, then they were quickly put to one side. If anything, as Barclay says, there was an increased spotlight on the league because of United. Martin Edwards: "We weren't out of the limelight because of the way that it went and because of the way we started off, we were still always big news. But it was a good thing, you know, in hindsight, it's easy isn't it? But I actually believed it was one of the best things that could have happened. I think it re-established the Busby era and the rest, it was like a new era. Here we are… okay we've been successful, we won the European Cup a few years ago, here we are, we are relegated and we are coming back with a brand new team playing an exciting brand of football… it couldn't have worked out better really."

Any reservations Pat Crerand had about United's attacking style under Tommy Docherty had been calmed. "United were in this attacking mode and they just blew teams away, I think teams might have been nervous of United as well because of the size of the club," Crerand says. "Certainly they must have got nervous when they saw the crowds that turned up at away matches, particularly the crowds outside the ground, never mind inside the ground. Probably players in those teams in that particular time, they knew about United but didn't understand what United was, and it must have been a great thrill for them to come and play at Old Trafford in front of sixty odd thousand which was what the ground held in those days. So it was great for players as well in those days."

The season was rounded off in celebratory style, with a 4-0 win over Blackpool. United had scored 66 goals — almost twice as many as the previous season — and conceded just 30, in 42 games, a defensive record made more impressive by the twenty-two clean sheets that were kept.

The match programme for the game contained very optimistic views of the future. "United supporters everywhere will be delighted that the Club have won promotion back to Division One at the first attempt and this is a great moment for everyone connected with our Club," chairman Louis Edwards wrote. "They have achieved this in first class style and have led the table all the way. Behind the players and staff at all times have been you, our supporters and my fellow directors join me in giving a hearty vote of thanks to you for the way you have rallied round at a time when you were badly needed."

It is said that Docherty now felt completely settled in his role. He had delivered a team playing football worthy of the club's reputation and his notes in the programme suggested he felt positive in his own role in the success. "I am delighted that we shall be going back to the First Division with the title because it is the way Manchester United have tended to do things over the years," he said.

Stuart Pearson, scorer of two goals on the final day, certainly felt the benefit of playing in front of a more settled team. "We kept winning and winning and winning," Pearson says. "We were playing well, and you get a bit of confidence. Even though we weren't the finished article, we knew that we were hard to beat. That's basically what happened week in and week out. The more you win games, the more confident you are. Even if you have 3 or 4 of your best players out of the team the guys that come into replace them – they feel confident as well. But you see it's so different nowadays. We only had 11, 12, 13, 14 players that could go and do that. We had a few reserves that at a pinch could come into the team. Whereas now you look at the programme, there's about 40 names on it, so you've got too many. I think that obviously, after winning the European Cup the supporters had a few years that weren't great and then it came to this in the end. The problem is, I think, you can't always blame Tommy, I think the club didn't invest enough in players. The recruitment of the kids maybe wasn't good enough. So I think they had to have a full overhaul in the end and when they get relegated, you've got to think about everything. I think TD had a great relationship with Mr Edwards, Louis. And you also had Martin on the board, who was a young lad at the time and he was fantastic. So TD had that relationship with them, and in the end he probably had to twist their arm and say 'look, the only way we're going to do this is to invest' and that's what he ended up doing in the end.

"Everybody was so disappointed the year before but to win that title, you knew that you were progressing and that was the start of great things. I think we all knew that we were going to go on and be better. We deserved it that year... for TD to do for what he did, and change it all round and get the team playing how he wanted them to play... to win that Second Division title, I thought it was amazing, so I really treasure that Second Division medal. To win the league against Blackpool in the home game and to be Champions... that crowd, the Stretford End alone, it went up for miles, and the Scoreboard end even competed with them, but the actual noise... it was just deafening and for us to go through all that we'd been through that year, going to all those away grounds and the fans being with us all the time, it was just nice to be able to go to Old Trafford in front of 60,000 I think there was, and reward them with the trophy, it was just an amazing feeling."

It was not quite that for some of the more time-served players. "I could see a sigh of relief from everyone that we'd done it," Sammy McIlroy says. "But, also, a belief that this team is gonna get better. I could see that as well and it was fantastic feeling when we did clinch it, not only clinch it, but we were Champions as well, which that mattered as well to the players. We didn't just want to come up we wanted to come up as 'Champions', you know, and that made the icing on the cake. The atmosphere was fantastic, we did a lap of honour as well with the cup around the ground, and the fans were absolutely delighted, delirious that we were back in Division One again and as champions and they could sense that this young team was going to get better." For McIlroy, there is some substance in the suggestion that relegation was at least a positive in the way it helped United generate their momentum. "The way we came back, the way we played football, the team that was coming together, would that team have come together if we had stayed in Division One, I'm not too sure," he says, "I don't think it would."

McIlroy and Macari have often been found on opposing sides on the difficultly of that season was and how much of a good thing demotion was. They do at least both see the benefits of that year. "I think when you get relegated, it's doom and gloom," Lou says. "You probably don't realise that it could actually do you a little bit of a favour, because obviously we weren't good enough at the time, which is why you get relegated from that division. You go down a division, you win football matches and it gave us a new lease of life... but the big question was if we got back to the top league, how would we perform then, had we matured into a different bunch of players than got relegated from the top division, all that again was the next stage of the unknown which we were soon going to find out once we got back into the top league. It was a spring board, life in Division Two was a spring board to bigger and better things for us all when we went back. When you get promoted from the Second Division and you go back to the top league you've really got it all to do to... What we quickly found out was because we had so many games in the league below playing a certain way scoring goals, winning most of the games, we had developed a way of playing, and I think that's fair to say, if you speak to any United supporter they'll tell you, the style of play didn't change in the top league to what it had been in Division Two."

From a financial point of view demotion hadn't been quite the catastrophe it would be today. The main difference in terms of finances between clubs was gate receipts and United still attracted the biggest crowds in English football, despite being in the Second Division. TV rights deals were derisory and live televised football was still a decade away. To underline the point, alongside United in Division Two that season were Nottingham Forest and Aston Villa, two clubs who would win the League championship and European Cup in the near future. It was a good breeding ground, as United would prove the following season.

ONE HUNDRED MILES AN HOUR

THE NEXT TWO YEARS WERE a whirlwind for Manchester United, exemplified by their lightning quick football which took the First Division by storm but also by the huge numbers following the team all over the country in numbers never seen before inspiring a whole new generation of supporters too young to have seen the Busby Babes or even George Best in his pomp. Before that though there was some genuine turbulence behind the scenes as Tommy Docherty sought to assert control.

First of all there was the controversy of Willie Morgan's exit from the club. It was another acrimonious parting of the ways and another example of Docherty's ruthlessness which would build a dangerous quorum against him at boardroom level. United were set to go on a post-season tour of the Far East and Australia. Morgan says that he was told he was being left off the tour with Docherty telling him to go on holiday. The following day the front page of the *Manchester Evening News* bore the headline "Morgan Refuses To Go On Tour". Within weeks the Scot was sold back to Burnley for the surprisingly low fee of £35,000.

He was replaced as captain by Martin Buchan, himself a prime candidate for conflict with Docherty. On the pre-season tour of 1974 Buchan had refused to hand over his passport for the club's trip to Belgium saying he 'wasn't a child'. Pictures of the championship celebrations against Blackpool are notable for Buchan's refusal to be snapped in the club's Umbro shirt; instead, he wore an Adidas jacket as he was sponsored by that brand. It was a bigger deal than it would normally have been considering Buchan was now team captain, having taken over from Morgan, and thus would feature heavily in the images. Buchan's position as captain was never under threat because he was clearly the defensive leader in the team. Another player may not have been so fortunate.

Buchan would temporarily relinquish the captaincy on the 1975 pre-season tour in another example of the standards Docherty set; on a stopover in Switzerland Buchan and some of the players went out for a drink. Although they honoured the curfew Docherty had set, the manager sent Tommy Cavanagh to check up on them and the former Aberdeen man was offended enough to resign the captaincy before being persuaded by team-mates to continue. A far more serious issue developed in Australia when Docherty arranged a head-tennis tournament. He asked Steve Coppell, Brian Greenhoff and Sammy McIlroy to participate with the promise they would be given AUS$150. When he found out Alex Stepney was appalled, as there was an agreement that all monies earned from such activities would go into a pool for equal distribution among the squad.

Stepney would have further cause for concern when he was told he would no longer be first choice, with Docherty saying his new number one would be Paddy Roche, signed earlier in the year. The news was made public and Willie Morgan would tell the press, "Apart from Pat Crerand and Alex Stepney, he's got rid of all Matt Busby's players and Alex is next. That's obvious after recent events. I've just picked up all the cash from bets with supporters who wouldn't accept that Alex wouldn't be first choice after two brilliant seasons."

A sad turn of events meant that Stepney would in fact start the season in goal, when Roche's father passed away on the eve of the Division One campaign and the Irishman took some time off. And Docherty's first team plans were thrown further into disarray in the final pre-season friendly, against Red Star Belgrade at Old Trafford. In the warm up, Jim Holton — returning to action after his broken leg — was struck in the face by a fierce strike from Alex Forsyth. Holton not only suffered concussion, but damaged knee ligaments as he collapsed. He never played for the club again. Docherty had made just one signing in the summer, bringing in veteran midfielder Tommy Jackson on a free transfer from Nottingham Forest with a view to him providing some leadership in the reserve team. Holton's injury meant Jackson was instead called up to the first team for the first part of the season.

The disruptions did not seem to impact on United's momentum, their return to the top flight say back to back 2-0 wins in the Midlands; Lou Macari getting a brace on the opening day at Wolves and three days later Sammy McIlroy getting two at St Andrews, Birmingham.

"I was more than delighted with our start to the season," Docherty wrote in his programme notes ahead of the first home game of the season against Sheffield United. "It was a very tense moment as we waited for the start of our first game back in the top division. In the end I just said to the players that we had been together for two and a half years and that there was really nothing more I could say. I told them that they knew well enough how I wanted them to play and that we had practiced it. So there was no point in a long tactical talk at that late stage. I told them simply to go out and play. That is exactly what they did. We did not try to change our style or approach just because it was our first match back in the First Division... I see no reason now why we should not consolidate our return and prove a useful team in the top grade. I am not making any rash predictions about honours at this stage, because we are a young side and we need experience. But we shall grow and I have no worries about our ability to hold our own this season. I also believe that in the process we shall entertain you with our football and I wish all you fans a happy season."

United won 5-1 against the Blades to go top of the league; a position they maintained after defeating Tottenham in a thrilling game that ended 3-2 on September 6th. A far cry from the last time they'd faced their glamorous London opponents, with over 51,000 at Old Trafford.

The manager had predicted that the forthcoming 'freedom of contract' rules for players — which meant they would be able to move where they wanted at the end of their contract (with a fee that would be determined by tribunal), as opposed to clubs flat-out rejecting offers — would signal the end of big spending from football clubs. One player Docherty did make a move for was Gordon Hill, the Millwall winger who had shown a couple of flashes of brilliance against United the previous season. The story wasn't too dissimilar to the one which saw the club sign Steve Coppell. Then, Tommy Docherty had travelled to Tranmere Rovers with Jimmy Murphy — now chief scout, following in the footsteps of his equally legendary dear friend Joe Armstrong who had sadly passed away in the summer of 1975 — to watch Coppell. Murphy watched just ten·minutes before telling Docherty to sign him. In Hill's case Murphy travelled alone to watch Hill play for Millwall at Chester. The winger was being coveted by Arsenal and Tottenham. The Welshman left the game early and called Docherty imploring him to sign the cockney wide man. When Docherty said he would call Millwall in the morning, Murphy insisted he do it immediately — the manager acted as instructed and Hill was a United player within 48 hours.

It wasn't all rosy. A bumpy run of form in the autumn saw United drop to fifth. During this period Stepney was dropped for Roche after the veteran goalkeeper (Stepney was now 33) was deemed to be at fault for a defeat at West Ham.

"We won at Wolves, we won at Birmingham, we went on a roll where, I think we were on top of the league but after 14 games we got beat at West Ham 2-1," says Stepney. "It was my fault, as a goalkeeper, you've got more chance of it being your fault than most players, outfield anyway, you know, but you've got to be honest about it. You walk into the dressing room after the game and apologise. The Doc called me in before the next game and said 'I haven't been fair to Paddy, I am bringing Paddy Roche back' and of course United unfortunately went on a bit of a bad run. I'm not saying it's Paddy's fault, I'm just saying it was a bad run. (We played) Liverpool, Arsenal and City, I think and then he had to bring me back… fair dos to him, he apologised, he said 'I made a big mistake.' From that day on funnily enough Tommy and I had a better relationship, if you wanna put it that way, a respect sort of thing."

Docherty's transition from the 1968 playing staff was almost complete when he ousted Pat Crerand. Pat had been left in no doubt as to the importance of his input in Docherty's set-up when he was asked to leave the dressing room at half-time in a League Cup tie at Maine Road. City were winning comfortably at the break and Docherty was fuming but Crerand was left humiliated by being so undermined.

"In my mind, that was the end," Crerand confessed, although he would remain at the club until the end of the season before taking the manager's job at Northampton. Crerand was in fact given a testimonial later that month when the European Cup winning side of 1968 (with Francis Burns and Denis Law in for Bill Foulkes and John Aston) would play against the current side, Stepney in the '68 goal and Roche in the present side. That game was played in testimonial spirit, of course, so one must take that into consideration. Nonetheless, the score-line of 7-2 in favour of the younger players was interesting for a few reasons. This was November 1975, only three years since the 'Trinity' had still all been first team players at United. The size of the score-line gave a revealing insight into just how far past their collective peak the team had been allowed to go and perhaps how well-oiled the current United collective were. It also gave Docherty some public vindication about his concern over the goalkeeping position, though it came at the worst possible time.

It didn't help Roche that the run of games he came into included trips to Anfield, Maine Road and Highbury, but he made high-profile errors in all three before Crerand's testimonial. It was obvious the manager would have to make a change in goal for the next league game but the seven conceded by Stepney would not have filled Docherty with optimism about the change. Ultimately, Stepney brought some stability back to the goalkeeping position and United's form improved over the coming weeks. After the November 22nd loss at Arsenal, it would be almost three months before they tasted defeat in the league again.

Gordon Hill's arrival in the side meant a permanent shift to 4-2-4. The genesis of the shape of this side was made almost complete after an FA Cup tie against Wolves in March 1976. Greenhoff was again moved into the centre of defence and was influential in bringing the ball out from the back. United won a thrilling game at Molineux recovering from two down to win 3-2 and that was the start of a run of five games where Docherty's men scored fourteen goals. Hill's unpredictability was a fine contrast to Coppell's unerring consistency on the other side of the pitch and their wing-play emerged as the most eye-catching feature of a team whose collective work-rate seemed non-stop.

"The acquisition of Steve Coppell late in the promotion season was a great coup for United, he was a fabulous winger from Tranmere Rovers and then we got Gordon Hill, and together they were just out-and-out wingers and it was fantastic football," says Cliff Butler. "It really was exciting to watch, it was almost taking you back to George Best on one side and Willie Morgan on the other, we were almost back to where we were. There was an excitement. We had Brian Greenhoff, a ball-playing centre half, that was quite a new phenomenon in those days, alongside him we had Martin Buchan who was also an extremely cultured footballer who never got ruffled and your two full backs… That was formed at the end of the relegation season and I think it just carried forward, as I said, the acquisition of those two wingers was probably the icing on the cake and Stuart Pearson in the middle, they were all technically, really good players."

Hill had taken to the big stage like a duck to water and loved the reputation he and Coppell were establishing. "Stevie was an engine, Stevie would go up and down the field all day long, he was like a piston, he would stop twenty goals and he would score five whereas I'd score twenty-five goals and not defend. I mean it was a great mixture because you could play with each side, we would switch, change or stay and that really threw everybody out."

Hill (Merlin, as he was known by Millwall and then United fans due to his magical ability) was that rare breed of winger — the sort who not only entertain and score more than their fair share of goals, but were productive enough to not infuriate team-mates or coaches with inconsistency. "Merlin yeah, I didn't know what he was going to do actually," Docherty laughs. "He was class, he was actually, he was a great crosser of the ball, his left foot was like a violin, and a terrific goal scorer of course as well, brilliant."

It was a new supply line for Stuart Pearson, whose own reputation was growing as a consequence. "I think obviously the fans, players, manager, the board were delighted we'd gone back up and over the next few years, that's when they started getting quality players in," he says. "We already had Alex, Buchan, I was feeling my way into the club, scoring a few goals, doing quite well. Then we started getting players like Gordon Hill, Stevie Coppell, Brian Greenhoff started playing alongside Martin Buchan, Arthur Albiston got in the team. The team was looking excellent at the time."

United were a team transformed. A club reborn, even.

"After the difficulty of scoring goals and relegation, you then had goals coming from all angles, you had both Hill and Coppell who could score," says Paddy Barclay. "Coppell in fact could have played centre forward and have been a good one. Pearson, as well. You know all of these were huge improvements. It was a lot better and Jimmy Greenhoff later came in to join his brother Brian and, yeah, players that you could still romanticise about. Again you can't underrate the midfield, the work that was done in midfield, it was really a vibrant midfield, the chance-creating culture which came from Mick Martin and especially Gerry Daly who is, in my opinion, one of the most underrated players in the history of Manchester United."

United were due to play Derby County in the FA Cup semi-final at Hillsborough. They'd been to this stage under Wilf McGuinness of course but this felt very different. This was not a tired team who had already tasted greater accomplishments; this was a vibrant side, rampantly escaping the ghosts of the past and making a name for themselves. The game became one of the seminal occasions under Docherty; United won 2-0, with both goals from Hill. The first — a counter attack started by an interception and pass from the marauding Greenhoff and finished by Hill from long range, who had cut in from the right in a display of that unpredictability — showed everything that was so good about Docherty's team.

Hillsborough swarmed with United fans who were rocking the coaches as the players came in. Docherty's recollections of arriving at the ground show just how much the club were embracing the fanaticism. "There were some lads asking me, 'Mr D any chance of getting us a ticket, getting us in?' I said 'no I've not got any tickets, I'm sorry but you can carry this hamper into the dressing room' and about eight of them got hold of the one hamper all got in, 'Thanks Doc!' they said as they put the hamper in the dressing room and out they went onto the terrace."

Up until that point of the season United had exceeded every expectation. Only Derby had scored more than them in the league (by one goal and they'd played a game more) and their defensive record, bar that period with Roche in goal, was comparable with the best in the league. Better still, United were just a point off top spot with a game in hand over leaders Queens Park Rangers.

Even if any genuine concerns of relegation had been put to bed early on, United had made a mockery of predictions that they would be lucky to finish mid-table. Stuart Pearson admits his pre-season expectations were on the optimistic side, "I'd have thought top six, you know, if we could have finished in the top six we'd have done okay. I don't honestly think it felt more difficult, in fact it felt a bit easier because you feel as though you belong there now, and for us to battle every game against the Second Division teams, and then play against top quality teams you felt as though you belonged, you felt as though you can compete with the best."

Pearson's journey was different to the other United players of course. Those who had gone down and come back up had a little more to prove. Few had done that more convincingly than Sammy McIlroy, who had improved into one of the best midfielders in the league. "We had belief, no matter who we played," says McIlroy. "Even though we were a young side coming straight back in again, Tommy Doc drilled into us to be frightened of no-one… we couldn't wait for the first game. We couldn't wait to play, we knew how we were gonna play, we were playing with wingers, we were playing with midfielders, attacking players, we had people who could score, we had people at the back who could defend and also play as well, so everything was sort of in place for us to make a good fist of life back in Division One… we were scoring goals, and winning games, and the football was just like it was in Division Two, but we were doing the same early on against bigger and better teams. I think the fans were a little bit surprised with how well we were doing."

Maybe so, but it should be put into a little perspective. Manchester United were still the biggest club around. Their demotion had been the big shock. Their return, whilst eye-catching, was not completely from the script of *Roy of the Rovers*. It wasn't unusual, in those more meritocratic days, to see promoted sides do so well.

"There wasn't a really a surprise that Manchester United came up and did well," says Paddy Barclay. "After all they'd only been down for a year, people could still remember them being contenders, the force of history was with them. So no, it wasn't surprising in that sense. Also you have to bear in mind that it wasn't unusual in the 60s and 70s for teams to come straight out of the second division and to continue their momentum you know, Ipswich Town under Alf Ramsey, he'd be an example of that and that carried on as late as the late 70s with Brian Clough's Nottingham Forest who came up one season and winning the European Cup it seemed a little over a couple of years later. United came straight up and became a major force, no I don't think it was a surprise then, I mean now when teams come up like Leicester City it's a fairy tale because economics make it much more difficult than was the case then. What Docherty really instituted was attack, attack, attack. It was that attacking style that he'd restored and that is I think why the crowd stayed with them, even after they were relegated. I think the average crowd went up by about 12-15% after relegation. So, once they got back to the top division then the crowds began to approach the national dominance, you know the crowd if Manchester United are at home, they'll be the biggest crowd in the country by a fair distance. You know the crowds began to be dominant over those of any other club in the top division. And that was where Docherty re-positioned Manchester United."

Up until the semi-final, far from a distraction, the FA Cup run had been a fillip for this young United team but with a place at

Wembley now secured — against Second Division Southampton, where United would be genuine favourites— and a favourable position in the league, the reality of United's fairytale return to the top flight kicked in. Docherty's men were beaten heavily by Ipswich Town a week after the Derby game. They bounced back to win both games over Easter but then faced Stoke City two days after Easter Monday.

You could put it down to fatigue, nerves or inexperience, but the truth was United did enough to secure their third consecutive win. Stuart Pearson and Steve Coppell were both missing with injury, forcing United to change shape. Docherty called up Tommy Jackson and young utility player Dave McCreery to play up front, flanked by McIlroy on the right and Hill on the left. Despite the unfamiliarity, United were impressive, but could not beat Peter Shilton in the Stoke goal. Docherty made tactical changes, moving Brian Greenhoff further up field, but the commitment to win came at a cost. With United camped in front of the Stoke City goal, the inevitable counter attack transpired in the 87th minute. United could not recover and lost 1-0.

Even if United's good form hadn't been a ground-shattering shock, they had over-achieved to be in with a shout of winning the league in April. Bobby Charlton had brushed off failure to win the league in 1968 with the attitude of someone with three league title medals behind him. There was every reason for this young team to believe they would have another crack of the whip, and so, in the moment, and particularly because their exciting form had been so unexpected, this young United team did not necessarily have to take the defeat as the body blow a more experienced side might have. Their time, they could be confident, would come.

In his programme notes for the game Docherty had written, "So here we are playing our last match at Old Trafford before Wembley. I am sure you will join me in wishing the lads the best of luck. Already they have done marvellously to reach the Cup final, and to cap that with the trophy itself would be absolutely wonderful." So, it seemed to some extent, United hadn't even really considered the title a realistic ambition. Yet even after the Stoke setback they were only four points behind leaders Liverpool with a game in hand. In years to come this would be seen as the best chance for most of these players to win a league title with United and the Stoke game has taken on extra significance and not only for the result.

Peter Shilton was not only one of the best goalkeepers in the world, he was also high on the wish-list of Tommy Docherty. In his autobiography Docherty made the stunning claim that a goalkeeper such as Shilton could have saved his team thirty goals a season. That seems a huge exaggeration, it's true; but it's no stretch of the imagination to speculate about the finer margins. You don't even need to consider whether or not he was an upgrade on Stepney or if he wouldn't have made the mistakes that Roche had in those high-profile games; just his presence in the Manchester United goal instead of the Stoke City goal might have meant the Championship trophy would be heading to Manchester in 1976. Instead it was end up at Anfield as Liverpool beat Wolves on the Monday after the cup final to pip QPR to the title. Docherty had always had an interest in Shilton but a firm offer wouldn't be made until late in 1976, even if he had let club officials know of his interest beforehand. It should be said that in an interview for this book Docherty claimed that Shilton was one of the first players he wanted to bring to the club back in 1973.

If they were always outsiders in the league title race, they were firm favourites for the FA Cup Final. "I think when we played Southampton everybody said we are playing so well in the league, it's a formality," Gordon Hill says. "The worst thing that could ever be said is 'formality' in this game."

What Southampton had in their favour was experience. Maybe it was the occasion, their age or the big pitch, but Manchester United couldn't get going. "When we got to Wembley we were obviously everyone's favourite to beat Southampton," Sammy McIlroy recalls. "Losing that FA Cup final was an absolute tragedy because the team that Doc had built against what they called an old experienced side, there's only one winner… but experience won the day for Southampton. That's the quickest game I've ever played in, the FA Cup final just flew by and we didn't perform."

Alex Stepney felt that the manager's approach, in trying to joke with the younger players, meant they weren't prepared for the seriousness of the occasion. "Tommy liked to lark about with the young kids and have a laugh and joke. You see that on the pitch at Wembley and I actually spoke to most of them, I said, 'C'mon forget all of this, let's play like we've done all season', because we had played well all season. It didn't work out and that's what Wembley could do to you, a lot of players go there and freeze and unfortunately… we hit the bar, I think, but apart from that we played alright, but we didn't kill it off as we'd been doing all season. Okay, there were questions whether it was it offside or not, I know Bobby Stokes, as far as I'm concerned, he mis-hit it and that beat me because if he had hit it right, I'd have got it."

Martin Edwards feels that the criticism the players put on themselves was a little harsh. "If you actually analyse the 1976 Cup Final, the first twenty minutes we were all over Southampton, we should have scored, McIlroy hit the woodwork, we should have scored in that period, and we didn't," says Edwards. "I thought over the 90 minutes we were probably the better side and of course, with 10 minutes to go, they got their run-away goal. I was directly in line so I know that Stokes was a yard offside when he got the ball, there was no question about it. If we'd had VAR it wouldn't have stood but nevertheless the through ball went, he was offside, he took it through, beat Alex Stepney with a shot to the corner and the game was over with 10 minutes to go, we hadn't got time to come back."

Yet Tommy Docherty made a bold claim to the thousands of fans who welcomed United's bus to Albert Square the day after the Cup Final, by promising them that Manchester United would be back with the FA Cup the following year. He'd said as much already to his players and to journalists. "In fairness that was tongue in cheek, that's what I was hoping rather than what I was visualising could happen but then obviously I was proved right again," Docherty laughs now.

The players were still a little surprised to hear their manager be so public with the proclamation. "He had told I don't know how many thousands that were in Albert Square we would be back next season, we will be back at Wembley and this time we will win it," Lou Macari says. "As players we thought he was mad and we all thought he was putting a lot of pressure on us to go back to Wembley... because to get to Wembley, you've got to have the luck of the draw, you've got to have luck in the game and then on the day at Wembley you've got to overcome whoever it is that's there, trying as hard as you're trying, to win the FA Cup. We all thought 'He's lost the plot here!'"

"I'll always remember coming back to the town hall on that open top bus without an FA Cup again feeling a wee bit embarrassed but the crowds were absolutely unbelievable," remembers Sammy McIlroy. "The supporters were unbelievable and Tommy Docherty got on at the town hall, praised the fans and told the fans 'we will be back at Wembley and win the cup and bring it back to you magnificent fans.'"

In fact, the dream of returning to Wembley would override all other ambitions for 1977.

THE THRILLING FIELDS

IN THE WAKE OF 1976'S NEAR MISS, levels of expectancy had risen. Manchester United were expected to challenge on all fronts and, following their qualification for the UEFA Cup, there was a keen anticipation as to how the team's style would work in continental competition. Tommy Docherty had led his tyros to a third placed finish in Division One, a more than respectable outcome, although it could be fair to say there was something of a Wembley hangover at the start of the 1967/77 season.

By mid-November things weren't looking quite as positive as they had six months before. United were in 15th position, nine points off leaders Liverpool. This time Docherty's signings had proved disappointing - Chris McGrath and Alan Foggon were recruited to provide some squad depth and back up his brilliant wingers but, with all due respect, neither were able to cut it at the club, and neither were near the level of Steve Coppell and Gordon Hill. Veteran defender Colin Waldron was brought in as back up centre-half, but when he replaced the injured Martin Buchan for almost the whole of October and November goals started to fly past Alex Stepney at an alarming rate. After a 4-0 defeat at West Brom in October, Waldron was replaced in the middle by Stewart Houston with young Arthur Albiston coming in at left-back.

The idea behind Docherty's signings seemed sound enough; it was going to be a long, demanding season. The manager believed that the reason for his side's failure to land a trophy in 1976 was nothing to do with talent; rather, their small squad and tiredness. And so his transfer dealings were clearly an exercise in acquiring capable replacements rather than upgrades; this was a tricky pursuit. Just one year before Docherty had acquired Gordon Hill for £70,000 and, considering the most recent transfer record was in February 1974 for £350,000, it wasn't a stretch to say 'Merlin' — and Steve Coppell, for that matter — were now worth around that amount. The United boss hoped lightning would strike again and again as McGrath and Foggon were brought in for a combined fee of under £100,000 but their form merely proved how Coppell and Hill were exceptions to the rule.

None of this is to say United's start to the 1976/77 season was disastrous. Far from it. They were drawn to face European giants Ajax in the first round of the UEFA Cup; the Dutch side may not have been quite the European Cup winning team of 1971-73, but that level of success gave an indication as to the quality of their team. Ajax won the first leg at home, but United put in a pulsating performance — the sort of all-energy display their domestic opponents had been used to facing — to turn around the one-goal deficit and win the tie 2-1 on aggregate.

The draw didn't get any easier, United would face Juventus in the second round. The 'Old Lady' had been Serie A champions in 1972, 1973, and 1975; they would also go to win the League that season too. Their side was littered with famous names; Dino Zoff, Claudio Gentile, Antonello Cuccureddu and Roberto Bettega to name just four. Docherty urged his players to keep calm and play their own style of football despite what was sure to be extreme provocation and physicality. When one remembers United's struggles to keep a lid on their tempers against AC Milan and Estudiantes under someone known for calmness like Sir Matt Busby, you can appreciate the size of the task for the firebrand Docherty.

Yet they did all that was asked and more during the first leg at Old Trafford; after surviving a turbulent opening quarter when the Italians could have scored several times, a Buchan-less United defence just about held firm. In the 32nd minute Old Trafford erupted when a cross found Gordon Hill at the far post. Most people would have taken a touch but Hill wasn't most people; his first time volley caught Zoff off guard and flew in at the near post.

The response was unpredictable; United expected a fight-back but Juventus retreated. Docherty might have been caught off guard by the visitor's inclination to protect a 1-0 defeat. His young players were unable to break through a second time. Colin Waldron, who was an unused substitute, said that after the game the Juve players were seen 'going down the tunnel jumping up and down throwing their arms in the air' in celebration at the narrow defeat. Juventus manager Giovanni Trappatoni admitted part of his game plan for Hill had failed. "Sometimes there were three or four of my men on him but he got through," Trappatoni said, "a very clever player indeed."

Before the return leg Hill had excelled again, scoring his first hat-trick for United in a 7-2 win over Newcastle in the League Cup that Docherty described as probably the best victory in his entire career.

The following week, however, Juventus took United apart in Turin. They were a goal up at half-time; going through the tunnel into the changing rooms, some of the United players claim the hosts were even less veiled in their physical assaults than they had been on the pitch. Gordon Hill claimed that Sammy McIlroy ended up with a punch to the face; Tommy Cavanagh had to force the United dressing room door shut to pull the players apart. Juventus went on to score twice more to knock Docherty's team out. It was a rough education, the Italians were one of the best teams in Europe, a point proved by them winning the UEFA Cup at the end of the season.

It was hoped that United would benefit from that experience. However, how that would transpire was not exactly a master-stroke from Docherty. A few days after the Juventus game a violent storm in the Midlands blew the roof off of one of Stoke City's stands. In urgent need of funds, Stoke manager Tony Waddington remembered Docherty once telling him to get in touch if he ever fancied selling striker Jimmy Greenhoff. It had been a flippant remark. Greenhoff — Brian's brother, of course — had been at Stoke since 1969 and was approaching his testimonial. In those days the revenue earned from a testimonial would be given to the player, normally at the end of his career, to serve as a buffer to help him make the transition into retirement. It was a lucrative proposition and not one a player would give up lightly.

For Waddington, though, the needs of the club came first, and after discussing it with the player he contacted Docherty to ask him if he would be interested in signing Greenhoff for £120,000. He was 30, but largely acknowledged of being the best uncapped English player in that era. A deal was agreed and completed without much difficulty. Greenhoff was keen, if sad, to move, and the move was even presented to the press as the forward making a financial sacrifice.

Whilst negotiating, Docherty tried to twist Waddington's arm for another of his stars. The United boss had just dropped Stepney once again but Paddy Roche had conceded three at home to Sunderland, leaving Docherty more convinced than ever, after a run of thirteen goals conceded in just five games, that he needed an upgrade in goal. He asked Stoke to name their price for Peter Shilton. They suggested £275,000. Docherty thought it was reasonable considering the benefit he felt Shilton — who he rated the best in the world — would bring to his side. The United board deliberated on it. When pushed, they finally acquiesced. When it came to negotiating terms, however, Shilton's wage request was £50 higher than the highest paid United player and the directors refused to sanction the deal. Alex Stepney, with more lives than a cat, considering how many times his legendary career had been threatened, was back in the side for the following game and would remain first choice.

Docherty would always claim that Shilton was the 'one that got away' and while his contention of his standing as the best goalkeeper in the game would be backed up by his subsequent career at Nottingham Forest, on this occasion Docherty would specifically claim that Sir Matt Busby had vetoed the deal. It was the first real indication that all wasn't right, with some speculating that Busby was unhappy with the way that Willie Morgan and particularly Pat Crerand had left United. In Eamon Dunphy's biography of Busby, it is suggested that he wanted Crerand to eventually get the manager's job at United. Docherty, sensing this, went into self-preservation mode and tried 'every stroke in the book' to ease Crerand out. This included the dressing room humiliation, accusations that Crerand had been drinking heavily and even telling his assistant that the team coach was leaving at a different time so that he'd miss it. There is also the suggestion, from some who wish to remain unnamed, that Docherty's closeness with chairman Louis Edwards was not totally unconnected to Busby's own deteriorating relationship with Edwards.

Events at the end of the season would bring matters to a head, with the scandalous news coming as a shock to most but not all. Depending on the account, it seems as if some at the club had a suspicion that Tommy Docherty's tenure may come to an abrupt end. The manager's contract was due to expire in the summer of 1978 and there were board members unhappy at Docherty declaring that he was one of the finest managers in the world in 1976. The Scot had defended himself, telling the *Express*, "I say I'm the best manager because I want my players to believe they are the best in the world. They wouldn't if I was going around saying I was rubbish."

Still, the remarks did not endear him to most of those responsible for extending his contract, although they did not seem to upset Louis Edwards too much, who responded to the suggestion that Derby County wanted to hire Docherty by offering his man a new four-year deal and made his feelings even clearer when he told press, "If I have my way he will be with us for the next forty years." Docherty was pleased with the news, but insisted that he wanted to win something before signing but with a title challenge out of the question and the club out of Europe and the League Cup before Christmas, all Docherty's eggs were in the FA Cup basket. Narrow 1-0 wins against Walsall and QPR at home followed by a 2-1 replay win over Southampton followed by victory by the same score in the home quarter-final against Aston Villa left United with a mouth-watering semi-final against Leeds United at Hillsborough.

Meanwhile all continued to not be well behind the scenes. After making his final appearance for the club against Derby County, Gerry Daly was the subject of an offer of £175,000 from the Rams. Docherty, perhaps feeling the need to balance the books, sanctioned the deal. Again, the accounts of the transfer differ; for Docherty it was straightforward while Daly claims he didn't want to leave but was told he would never play for the club again. The Eire midfielder later claimed Busby had implored him to reject the move saying, "There's something going on. We can't tell you what it's all about."

Yet on the surface all seemed sweetness and light as once more an FA Cup run had a galvanising effect on United's league performances. The club went unbeaten from January 3rd to April 2nd as Jimmy Greenhoff formed a promising partnership alongside Stuart Pearson, United climbing to fifth in the table by April 9th - a gap to leaders Liverpool that had seemed insurmountable in deep midwinter was now down to just 7 points in spring and United had three games in hand and a trip to Anfield to come.

Yet with so much of the season now seemingly focussed on United's return to Wembley and the genuine prospect of the manager fulfilling his promise of a return to the Twin Towers, league form took a sudden downturn with defeats at Sunderland and QPR and a disappointing home draw with Leicester. By the time Docherty's young pups ran out at Hillsborough they were 9 points adrift of the summit with only a game in hand. It was Wembley or bust!

Their semi-final opponents this time were Leeds United; and, just as 1976 was Hill's seminal moment, 1977 saw Steve Coppell take the spotlight with an outstanding goal in front of another raucous, three-quarters Red, crowd. United won 2-1 to set up a date with treble-chasing Liverpool on May 21st.

Having cantered to the First Division and qualified for the European Cup Final, the men from Anfield were chasing history. The last team to get this close to the treble had been the Busby Babes of 1956/57. The League and FA Cup double had only been achieved twice in the twentieth century and now they had gone a step further by qualifying for a final in Rome against Borussia Mönchengladbach. United finished sixth, ten points behind the Champions having crawled to the season's close losing five of their last ten league games – winning only two.

They would be underdogs on Saturday 21st May 1977.

TREBLE BUSTERS

YOU COULD PUT THE club's two seasons back in the top division side-by-side and make the argument that United had regressed. However, Docherty's side were still very young and on a learning curve towards a true, collective, maturity. The team which would line up against Liverpool in the final had a younger average age than the United team that would face the same opponents in the same competition 19 years later. The composition was eerily similar; for experienced bookends Stepney and Greenhoff, read Peter Schmeichel and Eric Cantona.

And there was a very real thought that an FA Cup victory in 1977 could provide the spur for the club to kick on and challenge for the title the following year. United's progression since their return to the big time had shown in their success in cup competitions. Back then the FA Cup was the be all and end all. Today, more than one generation has grown up baffled by their forefather's obsession with the tradition of the competition from early autumn non-league qualifiers, via midwinter giant-killings to a final played on the lush green grass of Wembley when it always seemed to be sunny. For decades it was the football trophy to win – ahead of any European competition or league title. And it was definitely that way in 1977.

That Manchester United team of young twenty somethings would have spent their formative years knowing the FA Cup Final was the football event of the year. "Fans wanted to win the FA Cup more than they wanted to win the league," remembers Cliff Butler. "There was something about the FA Cup, it felt more important. It was the day of the entire season; all the country watched it, it was like the Grand National, everybody stopped to watch the Cup Final and to be there was a privilege and something to be proud of." To reinforce the point, television coverage of the game (on both ITV and BBC mind you) would usually start in early morning right the way through until late afternoon.

United hadn't won a trophy since 1968 or, to put it another way, since Sir Matt Busby, so this was a genuine litmus test. Tommy Docherty, whose prediction of a return to Wembley had been proven correct, was feeling less bullish about actually winning on the day. "It's a strange feeling actually," Docherty says. "I'm a great believer of 'If your name is on the FA Cup you will win it' but I thought then is this our year? Can we do it this year… surely we can't lose again?"

In contrast to the Southampton game 12 months earlier, United were underdogs, a position the club has traditionally enjoyed on the big occasion. On the day their performance was spirited and their defenders in particular were outstanding. Captain Martin Buchan led by example but Brian Greenhoff was named man of the match. The big Wembley pitch used to be like quicksand for even the most talented wingers and so it proved again for United, who had to find ways other than Coppell and Hill to win the game. The goals did come but through a more conventional route, their strikers. After an even, goalless first half, Stuart Pearson struck with a nice low shot at the near post before Jimmy Case equalised with a 25 yard thunderbolt almost straight from the kick off. Parity did not last for long as Lou Macari's shot was deflected in to the Liverpool goal by Jimmy Greenhoff. There was some controversy over who should claim the goal but history has recorded it as Greenhoff's goal. All of the goals came in a manic five minutes at the start of the second half. Docherty's side showed a great indication of their growing experience to see the game out and deny their rivals a chance of being the first English team to win the treble of League, FA Cup and European Cup. The result of the 1977 FA Cup would assume even greater importance in the ongoing rivalry between England's biggest clubs after United's treble triumph of 1999.

For Alex Stepney, the FA Cup was the domestic trophy which had previously eluded him. "Tommy Doc did say, and fair dos to him, after that '76 final 'we'll be back next year' and we were," the goalkeeper says. "We beat Liverpool, but then again we were the underdogs and the goal that won it, I don't think we'll ever see one like that again… I mean Lou had a shot that was probably going into the stands at Wembley behind the goal and it hit Jimmy and spun around Ray Clemence."

Goalscorer Stuart Pearson is quick to point out it was a team effort. "I actually thought it was one of the best Cup Finals I've seen for years," he says. "I know me and Jimmy got the credit for everything, but there were some fantastic performances, the back four were different class, Alex Stepney never made a mistake, Lou Macari was immense… I've seen the game a couple of times since, he was just immense, he was up and down, he was in and out, he was nicking balls off people… Sammy was different class as well, the two wingers did their job, me and Jimmy were lucky enough to score the goals but it was a definite team effort. Obviously the manager played his part as well because he kept us all relaxed, we went away for a few days beforehand, and in the dressing room before it was 'Come on sit down lads, let's go out and enjoy it, play the way we normally do, Pancho you're picking him up, you're picking him up,' that was it. We went out with no worries at all, just went out to play."

It was a moment of great vindication, too, for Sammy McIlroy, the player who had come into the team being heralded as the next George Best while the real thing hadn't even hit his projected prime. "It was a major trophy, the FA Cup was a major trophy, every footballer dreams of playing in a cup final," he says. "To come back in '77, again, we hadn't won the FA Cup since 1963 under Sir Matt Busby, so it was time for Manchester United to win it, especially in jubilee year as well and against Liverpool… the rivalry then was getting more intense, we stopped them doing the treble and that was a great confidence boost."

Just to emphasise the point about the importance of the trophy, Martin Edwards is a firm believer that it was a massive moment in United's history. "It was huge, because if you think about it we hadn't won anything since winning the European Cup in '68, we had gone a barren 9 years without winning a trophy," says Edwards. "To United supporters it was even bigger… it was the first trophy for a number of years and it stopped Liverpool doing the double, or, as it turned out, the treble."

Paddy Barclay, who went on record earlier as saying United's flying return to the top flight hadn't been a complete shock, is happy to accede that their return to this pinnacle was perhaps a little ahead of schedule. "It was a considered a slight surprise because Manchester United, even in 1977, were considered a work in progress. The DNA of Manchester United was there in that match because, yeah, Liverpool were accustomed to winning games, big games... in fact they were about to become almost boringly successful, but Manchester United proved that they've got their own DNA, that they'd recovered that Busby swagger, or a bit of the swagger that was to be rediscovered under the Ferguson era, they've got that, we are Manchester United, they came of age in that cup final, definitely that was the signal, we are not a young, fresh faced bunch of lads entertaining you, we are here to win trophies."

That much is confirmed by the attitude of players like Gordon Hill, "I think it was a pinnacle at that stage, but it was (also) the start of getting to another pinnacle," he says.

Yet in the weeks following United's triumph newspaper speculation was not about who the club might bring in to bolster their playing squad to make a serious challenge for the First Division but about an alleged affair Tommy Docherty had been having with Mary Brown, wife of the club's physiotherapist, Laurie. Having failed to get in touch with his father, Docherty called Martin Edwards and forewarned him that the affair was about to become a tabloid sensation. Martin reassured Docherty in his father's absence, and indeed, this did appear to be the initial stand that Louis would take. "I know that father's first reaction, because Tommy Doc had actually rang me to tell me what was coming out in the newspapers, and I spoke to father and his first reaction was one of protection really, because we'd just won the cup, he got us back in the First Division the year before... Father had a good relationship with Tommy Doc and I think that if there was any way of saving the situation then I think he was looking for it."

Reassured, Docherty laid low, while Louis Edwards dismissed

the notion that he would sack his manager as 'nonsense' to the press. Docherty claimed to have held a cryptic conversation with Matt Busby who allegedly said, "You bloody fool, Tom, why didn't you let me know all about this? I could have spoken to people." Docherty also says that he received a letter from his predecessor, Frank O'Farrell, that said, "You will have found out by now, as I did to my cost, that the 'Knight' is not covered in shining armour as he makes out to the many who do not know him so well. He must be suffering torment at not being able to get rid of you as it is rumoured he has been trying to do. Long may you continue to torment him."

If it is true that Busby was the vetoing voice on the transfer of Peter Shilton then that remains the only indication of genuine dissatisfaction or interference since the confrontation O'Farrell says he had with Busby at the start of the 1972/73 season.

In Eamon Dunphy's seminal "A Strange Kind Of Glory" the author describes Docherty thus, "Within the context of professional soccer, Tommy Docherty was an imaginary villain." He suggests that the incident at Chelsea — where he had sent home players which effectively cost him his job - had warned him as to the unscrupulous side of the game and so he had simply decided to play the game himself. It is suggested that the United manager's growing relationship with Louis Edwards owed much to Docherty's acknowledgement of the work Edwards had done, particularly considering the majority of the praise went to Busby.

Yet there is no indication anywhere that supports the (alleged) claim by O'Farrell that Busby was unhappy about Docherty bringing success to United. Instead it is suggested that Busby had grown unhappy about the executive's refusal to allow his son Sandy onto the board. Bill Young, a director, is alleged to have objected on the grounds that Sandy was friends with Pat Crerand, which upset Busby deeply.

The Morgan incident, the Crerand incident and a split in the board — as well as Docherty's own hesitation, for various reasons — are all cited as reasons why a new contract was never formally agreed. In fact, only Derby County's interest had pushed Edwards into a public and verbal declaration that there would indeed be an offer.

After the board had an opportunity to meet to discuss the controversy, Docherty was summoned to a meeting at Louis Edwards' home, where the chairman, his son, Matt Busby, vice-chairman Alan Gibson, Denzil Haroun, Bill Young and club secretary Les Olive were present.

"The problem started once it all came out; players and staff started to approach the board with certain stories," Martin Edwards explains. "I think Laurie Brown being the physio was no different to a player in a way, he was part of the back room staff and one or two of the players didn't like what had happened. They said it was happening during working hours, and all the rest of it, and they came forward to support the physio. So that put us in a very difficult position because even though he is the manager, how do you support the manager when you've got players who are not happy with the situation or what's happened, and the manager having an affair with the physio's wife? It made it very difficult. I think it's probably fair to say that Matt took a very moral view on it as well. He was still an important board member at the time, I think in the end we just felt it was just too difficult to protect that position, and that, you know, if we had supported Tommy then we would maybe have trouble with one or two players, so I think the feeling was that it was inevitable that he had to go."

Louis Edwards reluctantly asked Docherty for his resignation. When Docherty asked on what grounds, he was told he had broken 'the moral code' of the club. It wasn't just the fact he'd had an affair; it had been with the wife of a club employee and it was alleged that Docherty had manipulated Laurie Brown's schedule so he could arrange meetings with Mary. Docherty insisted it wasn't simply an affair as he and Mary planned to marry once their divorces came through. It is worth noting that their marriage has lasted over 30 years.

It was also put to Docherty that he had been selling Cup final tickets. The manager was left dumbfounded by this as he thought it was no secret that he'd been doing it on behalf of other board members. He was bullish on this point but the board were also unhappy that he had sold the story of his affair to the *Sunday People* inviting more controversy in their eyes. They were additionally concerned about the consequential problem of how to deal with Laurie Brown's job if Docherty remained. "If you won't resign, we'll have to sack you," Louis Edwards told the manager. That evening the club released a statement confirming their manager had been dismissed for a 'breach of the terms of his contract'.

Despite the rumblings of speculation, the news of Docherty's sacking seemed to come as a genuine shock to the players. "It was rumoured but the players didn't know anything about it, but then the news broke," remembers Stuart Pearson. "On Monday I was in the ticket office and I saw TD and he said I've just had a chat with the Chairman and he said 'I'm okay, I'm fine, everything's fine,' and I said 'oh great'. Tuesday it broke that he'd been sacked. So I think every man and his dog was gutted, especially for him because, I mean he was the leader, he was the one that brought the players in and he was the one that was going to get us the league back, he was the main man and we all loved him to bits... we were gutted when he got the sack."

Being the summer break, many of the players were away. "I couldn't believe it when I picked the paper up and the headlines were telling me that Docherty had been sacked," Sammy McIlroy says. "I was shell shocked because nobody at the club, especially the players at the club, had any inkling about was going on there, no-one knew at all so we were all very shocked... we were looking for the boss to maybe bring people in, improve us to challenge Liverpool for that title, which everyone wanted, we'd won the cup, we hadn't won the league you know since '67... it was time Manchester United challenged Liverpool and we had that confidence then, we've maybe a couple of more people added to the squad we could push Liverpool for the title then this bombshell happened and it knocked everyone for six."

Gordon Hill says he heard about it from Sammy McIlroy. "We went away for a week, Sammy McIlroy informed me on the beach in Ibiza," he says. "We didn't go together, we just managed to grab a holiday off the shelf and he said 'The Doc's been fired, he's been seeing Mary Brown for two years' and I said, 'get out of here, we would have known,' well, we didn't know.''

Lou Macari was also stunned. "I've got to be honest with you, Tommy Doc's sacking was a massive shock to me, not just because we had won the Cup at Wembley," he says. "He had a good relationship with the Chairman. I'd say they were close friends apart from being Chairman and Manager, they were close friends and I think when you see that sort of friendship day in day out at Old Trafford, the last thing you're ever thinking about is that the manager is getting the sack. I went on holiday, can't remember exactly when he did get the sack but it was certainly a shock for me. You just kept your mouth shut at the time and I didn't pass any opinion about whether it was justified, what you thought about it because that wasn't your job as a player, your job as a player was to play football, leave that side of it to the people that ran Manchester United. It was disappointing, it was a shock, you quickly realise you've got to keep going and get on with working for the next manager that comes in."

Alex Stepney, found out on holiday too, "I was in Majorca and a guy came up to me and said had I heard the news. You had to wait until you got home really to assess the situation, but it was a surprise... were the board looking for an excuse? I don't know... They could have been waiting for something to happen. What went on behind closed doors, we wouldn't know about."

Looking back, Martin Edwards says it was one of the most difficult decisions of his tenure at the club, "There are plenty of difficult decisions along the way, he ranks pretty highly, yeah. That's all you can say really."

For Docherty it was the beginning of the end. He would never be as successful or high profile again. "I just felt that it was something... you should lose your job for failure, for lack of ability but not for what happened," he says. "I feel they were the losers at the end of the day because we just started something that was going to take us ahead. You do what you think is right at the time and I was just amazed at what I lost my job for, it was nothing to do with football at all."

However Docherty was also an employee of the club and it made it a difficult decision not just for those within the club but those outside moralising. And, when they did, the potential achievements of the team in future often became a secondary consideration.

"I think no matter who the manager was at the time, under the same circumstances I'm sure the club would have made the same decision," Cliff Butler says. "I think it was sad in a way because he was getting there, he put together a really exciting team, we'd just won the FA Cup which was almost the seal of approval and then this happened… it was tragic in a way because he knew what the fans wanted, he knew about Manchester United and I think he was definitely on the right track before that happened."

The sentiment is echoed by Paddy Barclay. "The Docherty regime was set fair to go on and restore the loss of the Busby era," he claims. "Everything had gone right, Matt had finally replaced himself and United were playing well, the crowds were soaring, what could possibly go wrong? But Tommy Docherty fell in love with the wife of Laurie Brown, the club's physiotherapist and one of his own closest aides. Laurie Brown was very much part of the inner circle of the Docherty regime, they were always together and the club then had a dilemma, they had to choose between the right thing to do and what was right for Manchester United and they chose the right thing to do. They couldn't sack Laurie Brown for his misfortune in losing his wife, so they sacked Docherty."

For United fans the events of the summer of 1977 would always be a case of 'what if?' Albeit in a less tragic way than 1958, the loss of Tommy Docherty hit a whole new generation of fans hard, to the extent that his name was still being sung at home games in the 80s whenever the club suffered a downturn in form – the style and panache of Docherty's 1974–77 team remained fresh in the memory for years.

AFTERMATH

IN APRIL 2018 TOMMY DOCHERTY celebrated his 90th birthday with a dinner with most of the FA Cup Final team from 1977, save for the late Brian Greenhoff, and Steve Coppell and Gordon Hill who lived overseas in India and the United States respectively. Coppell made a telephone call to Docherty at the restaurant where the dinner was held, the Scot joking that he hoped he wasn't picking up the cost of the call. The event had been arranged by Tommy's wife Mary, the former Mrs Brown, the couple still together over 40 years on from the affair that led to his dismissal.

It seems unlikely that a successful football manager would be sacked for an extra-marital affair with the wife of a fellow employee today. Some of the players even believe there would be 'uproar' if something like that happened after a manager had won a trophy. The dinner, over forty years after their biggest collective triumph, shows that a large number of the players still hold an affection for Docherty.

As well as it being their pinnacle together, for most of the players representing Manchester United that day in 1977, it was as good as it would get for the rest of their careers. So, in the manager's estimation, how far could that team have gone?

"Over and above taking them down, which was never a pleasant thing to do, it's very difficult to say; probably you get a bit greedy, we got back up into the First Division again and then went to two Cup Finals and won one of them. At a club like United, I suppose you're expected to win a lot more than that but we did our best... I just felt that when I left United we were on a great run, we were going to go big time. And then I got the sack."

For the players whose career had a similar trajectory to Docherty's, the feeling was the same. "I think that we were cut down in our prime," Gordon Hill reflects, "we were just mounting a long term attack. Number one, we had age on our side; number two, we had flamboyancy in the way that we played that the players knew what we were doing, the players knew each other and the longevity of it would have lasted quite some time… Football has a strange way of kicking you in the teeth, it can give you the most blessed glory you've ever had and it can give you misery and I felt all of it."

Hill has been regarded as the symbolic free spirit of that era but the whole team was packed with talent and skill. Alex Stepney and Jimmy Greenhoff aside, the rest had their best years ahead of them. Stuart Pearson feels that if Docherty had added a goalkeeper, as he had wished, there was better to come, "If you go through the team, whoever the keeper is you've got Jimmy Nicholl at right back; Martin Buchan, the captain, he was only 25 at the time; you had Brian Greenhoff, you had Arthur Albiston, who had just got in the team; Sammy and Lou were pretty young and then you had Hilly, Stevie Coppell, me and Jimmy, and Jimmy was probably the oldest. It's just a shame he didn't come three or four years earlier."

When you look at the success of Nottingham Forest and Aston Villa in the years which followed Docherty's sacking then you have to think it's a logical argument to suggest that United could have been competing, as they were tipped to, with Liverpool at the very least. Given that it was accepted at the time that it was harder to win the League than the European Cup, perhaps Docherty's team may have triumphed in place of Liverpool, Forest and Villa in the forthcoming seasons. Certainly they were ahead of two of those teams in May 1977 and gaining ground on the other.

"The Manchester United team that Docherty was forced to part company with would have had limitless potential," Paddy Barclay suggests, "especially as Docherty was decent in the transfer market and would probably have bought well to prolong the life of that team… he'd already proved that he could be ruthless in getting rid of people who were weakening the team because of age or whatever else, so I think with Manchester United under Docherty the potential is limitless. Yes it's true that people don't talk about the Docherty team in the same way they talk about Ferguson's teams, or Busby's teams or even Atkinson's teams but believe you me, there was no reason why that couldn't have been one of the greatest teams in the history of Manchester United. But I still think Manchester United had a moral decision to make, and they made the right one."

"The sky was the limit," Cliff Butler says ruefully, "he was good at bringing players in, he knew which ones he wanted and he knew the way he wanted to play the game and it was exciting, that's what the fans wanted, they were a really exciting team and I think he would have kept improving it, he could have been a real success. It's a human failing but it was tragic that he got the sack for that. I think a lot of people have probably forgotten this little era of the club, it's an age thing as well. I remember it really well and enjoyed every minute of it but what's happened since we've had Sir Alex winning countless trophies, I think people tend to almost erase that little era but I certainly don't. I think it was one of the best eras the club has had, it would have been really interesting to see where Tommy Docherty had taken us. I think he was really on the road to success with Manchester United."

★

As usual with United managers, the personality of Dave Sexton, Docherty's successor, was a complete contrast. A quiet thinker on the game not given to grandstanding to the press, Sexton was renowned as an outstanding coach who had succeeded Docherty once before at Chelsea to great effect, winning an FA Cup and a Cup Winners' Cup at Stamford Bridge. He had also managed QPR during the greatest period in their history, finishing a close second to Liverpool in 1975/76 with a wonderful free-flowing team featuring the likes of Stan Bowles, Gerry Francis and Don Masson.

Tommy Docherty was hired by Derby County in September 1977 but lasted just two seasons at the Baseball Ground. At the time he joked he'd had more clubs than golfer Jack Nicklaus; he also remarked that after leaving United the only way was down, and so it proved for the Scot who was never able to rekindle his old magic. His stock was not damaged so much by his spell at Derby but by an ill-fated decision to return to former club QPR. Rangers were in the Second Division but were owned by controversial chairman Jim Gregory. He and Docherty had a stormy relationship and the Scot was sacked twice in this spell at Loftus Road, being reinstated after nine days. His reputation never recovered.

Of the 1977 FA Cup Final team; Alex Stepney was finally ousted as number one by Sexton as he brought in South African youngster Gary Bailey. Several members of the United team in the eighties would contend that they would have done better with a different goalkeeper, as talented as Bailey was. Right-back Jimmy Nicholl had a fine career at United, playing almost two hundred league games at Old Trafford and almost four hundred more elsewhere, including two spells at Glasgow Rangers where he won two league titles.

Arthur Albiston, then a rookie left-back, was selected on FA Cup final day 1977 due to an injury to Stewart Houston. He played as first choice in that position until 1986, amassing 485 appearances in all competitions until his exit in 1988, including another four Wembley cup final appearances and two more FA Cup winner's medals.

Captain Martin Buchan made 456 appearances for the club before leaving for Oldham in 1983. Brian Greenhoff, his partner in the centre of defence, was one of the high-profile casualties of Sexton's reign. As a ball-playing centre-half he was deemed too adventurous by Sexton and was moved to full-back before being replaced by Gordon McQueen and transferred to Leeds United. Brian passed away in May 2013. His career peaked with his man of the match performance at Wembley in 1977; he was one of those who had far more to give.

Sammy McIlroy remains one of the club's favourite sons. Under Docherty's guidance he blossomed into a fantastic player in his own right. He survived the Sexton reign but was sold by Ron Atkinson soon after the signing of Bryan Robson. McIlroy went to play for Stoke City and Manchester City, but most famously went on to represent Northern Ireland at the 1982 and 1986 World Cups — the latter as captain. He went on to be a successful manager, notably at Macclesfield Town where his seven year spell earned him the right to manage his country for three years.

Stuart Pearson was sold by Sexton in 1979. He was the only player to taste genuine success elsewhere, winning the FA Cup with unfancied West Ham in 1980. Jimmy Greenhoff became a cult hero at United and remained at the club until December 1980, by which time was 34, before moving to Crewe.

Lou Macari played for United until 1984 when he moved to Swindon Town to become player-manager. The 1977 FA Cup was his last winner's medal. Steve Coppell's career was cut short when he suffered an injury at the 1982 World Cup. He was forced to retire in 1983 at the age of 28. He enjoyed a successful career as a manager, most notably with Crystal Palace with whom he lost the 1990 FA Cup final to give Alex Ferguson his first trophy at United. Like his fellow winger, Gordon Hill was the other notable victim of Sexton's conservative management and was sold less than a year after the '77 Cup Final, despite being United's top scorer. The sale was met with protests from the Old Trafford support. He was signed by Docherty at Derby but soon after suffered a knee ligament injury. Despite attempts to get back, the injury ended his top flight career in England. Hill embarked on a career in North America starring in the indoor game after demise of the NASL. He has mostly coached unisex youth football in the United States since retiring.

Cliff Butler describes the break-up of the team as 'tragic'. That can certainly apply when looking at the abrupt end of the careers of the two most thrilling exponents in Docherty's team.

Despite his later reputation among United fans, Dave Sexton had managed entertaining teams. His reputation was undoubtedly enhanced by his work at Queens Park Rangers, and whilst nobody could say he didn't earn it in his own right, he was perhaps helped in that regard by the groundwork laid by his predecessor Gordon Jago. It may well have been that theory that the United board were banking on as they sort a successor to The Doc. But

Sexton attempted to add instruction to the team which effectively removed the liberation Docherty had sought. Nevertheless, after a disappointing 1977/78 campaign, he took the club to the 1979 FA Cup final only to lose to a last minute Arsenal goal and the following season led them to a runners-up spot behind perennial champions Liverpool, losing the league by just two points. It would be the closest the club came to the title until they won it again in 1993.

Yet despite these near misses Sexton's football paled in comparison to Docherty's. A dearth of goals and falling attendances meant that even a seven-game winning streak at the end of the 1980/81 season wasn't enough to prevent his dismissal. So United, true to form, plumped for someone in the Docherty mould; West Brom boss Ron Atkinson was bold, brash, quotable and liked his teams to play expansive football. And that they did, winning two FA Cups along the way and consistently staying in the top four in the league. Ultimately, reliance on a few individuals proved to be Atkinson's Achilles Heel. Quite simply, without Bryan Robson they were half the team and he was never able to find an adequate back up for the United and England captain.

Atkinson's successor, Sir Alex Ferguson, proved to be the man to end United fans' interminable wait for real success. The fundamental overhaul he undertook and the trophies which followed means it would be a disservice to say Ferguson benefited from the situation he inherited at the club. Yet the accepted tale that he walked into a complete shambles is also a little wide of the mark. However that was exactly the scenario that Tommy Docherty had walked into 15 years before; a club on the brink of relegation and a roster of fading stars refusing to budge who had the ear of their former manager who had a place on the board.

What Docherty restored to the club was the heritage Busby had carefully constructed since 1945, which was in real danger of being lost just four and a half years after the triumph of 1968. Busby favoured wingers and attacking football and Docherty worked out how to make the system successful with a modern defensive shape, and also found midfielders with the qualities required to make the entire team successful.

As divisive a character as Docherty is, there is one thing even his biggest critics can't deny. "You've got to say he did well," Pat Crerand admits. "In actual fact, the job he did — because he didn't get the sack for his football management, he got the sack for his off-field activities — whether I like him or not he did a great job for Manchester United. I am a Manchester United fan, I want the club to be successful."

Willie Morgan, who was taken to court by Docherty for that alleged slander incident, concurs. "He's Jekyll and Hyde, the nice side is that he's great company; there are great stories, he's great to be around, great to go out and have a drink with. The dark side is that he has a big dagger that he keeps sticking in people's backs. I keep coming back to the thing about footballers, certainly from my era, working class lads, right, and they'll tell you to your face, there's not a problem for telling someone up front but he wouldn't do it, he'd rather stab you in the back. For all that. I think he could have been the best Scottish manager of all time. He was a great Scottish manager, I loved playing under him at Scotland and you know, in spite of him taking me to the Old Bailey and trying to ruin me and all that, I still say he was great and we would have been fantastic in small doses. But on a daily basis, and then getting into the politics with the directors, he just gets a bit busy for his own benefit... it's sad because from a purely football viewpoint he was a great manager... he knew his team, he knew what he wanted, he knew how he wanted to play and he got a great blend... wherever you are, Thomas, good luck to you... don't run into me though!"

"Limitless" was the term used by Paddy Barclay to assess the potential of Docherty's all-attacking, cavalier Manchester United team. It is a lofty description for a team which is often overlooked. Were they good enough to win the First Division? Could Docherty really have been the only man aside from Sir Matt Busby and Sir Alex Ferguson to bring the European Cup to Old Trafford? We'll never know.

But judging by the observations of many, it's not out of the question. Considering the shape of the club and the squad he inherited, the return to prominence and the speed of it was almost as staggering as the speed and scale of the decline before 1974.

Of course the answer to the title of this book is that, of course, even former European Champions Manchester United were not too good to go down. The answer to the subsequent questions about relegation being a good thing can only be given based on the evidence we have. There was a benefit to confidence, morale and unity which came from winning matches, which was easier to do in the Second Division. That doesn't mean it couldn't have happened in the First Division, because it already seemed the club had turned a corner before they were relegated.

Relegation was a consequence of several years of multiple problems that had built up and had been largely ignored. These were the problems Docherty inherited. That he solved them one by one and stood on the brink of a glorious new era for the club after less than 5 years in charge is one of the most remarkable stories in the club's history. As controversial and divisive as he was, he was the right man for the job; the right man to solve the problems, and the right man to restore the identity and the glory.

The success of his ongoing legacy at Manchester United is, perhaps, the only understated thing about Tommy Docherty.

INDEX

APPENDIX

MANCHESTER UNITED 1968-77 IN STATISTICS

1968/69

Sat Aug 10	Div. 1	Everton	Home	W	2-1
Wed Aug 14	Div. 1	West Bromwich Albion	Away	L	1-3
Sat Aug 17	Div. 1	Manchester City	Away	D	0-0
Wed Aug 21	Div. 1	Coventry City	Home	W	1-0
Sat Aug 24	Div. 1	Chelsea	Home	L	0-4
Wed Aug 28	Div. 1	Tottenham Hotspur	Home	W	3-1
Sat Aug 31	Div. 1	Sheffield Wednesday	Away	L	4-5
Sat Sep 7	Div. 1	West Ham United	Home	D	1-1
Sat Sep 14	Div. 1	Burnley	Away	L	0-1
Wed Sep 18	EC 1 - 1 Leg	Waterford	Away	W	3-1
Sat Sep 21	Div. 1	Newcastle United	Home	W	3-1
Wed Sep 25	World Club Final 1 Leg	Estudiantes	Away	L	0-1
Wed Oct 2	EC 1 - 2 Leg	Waterford	Home	W	7-1 (10-2 aggregate)
Sat Oct 5	Div. 1	Arsenal	Home	D	0-0
Wed Oct 9	Div. 1	Tottenham Hotspur	Away	D	2-2
Sat Oct 12	Div. 1	Liverpool	Away	L	0-2
Wed Oct 16	World Club Final 2 Leg	Estudiantes	Home	D	1-1 (1-2 aggregate)
Sat Oct 19	Div. 1	Southampton	Home	L	1-2
Sat Oct 26	Div. 1	Queens Park Rangers	Away	W	3-2
Sat Nov 2	Div. 1	Leeds United	Home	D	0-0
Sat Nov 9	Div. 1	Sunderland	Away	D	1-1
Wed Nov 13	EC 2 - 1 Leg	Anderlecht	Home	W	3-0
Sat Nov 16	Div. 1	Ipswich Town	Home	D	0-0
Sat Nov 23	Div. 1	Stoke City	Away	D	0-0
Wed Nov 27	EC 2 - 2 Leg	Anderlecht	Away	L	1-3 (4-3 aggregate)
Sat Nov 30	Div. 1	Wolverhampton W.	Home	W	2-0
Sat Dec 7	Div. 1	Leicester City	Away	L	1-2
Sat Dec 14	Div. 1	Liverpool	Home	W	1-0
Sat Dec 21	Div. 1	Southampton	Away	L	0-2
Thu Dec 26	Div. 1	Arsenal	Away	L	0-3
Sat Jan 4	FAC 3	Exeter City	Away	W	3-1
Sat Jan 11	Div. 1	Leeds United	Away	L	1-2
Sat Jan 18	Div. 1	Sunderland	Home	W	4-1
Sat Jan 25	FAC 4	Watford	Home	D	1-1
Sat Feb 1	Div. 1	Ipswich Town	Away	L	0-1
Mon Feb 3	FAC 4 replay	Watford	Away	W	2-0
Tue Feb 11	FAC 5	Birmingham City	Away	D	2-2
Sat Feb 15	Div. 1	Wolverhampton Wanderers	Away	D	2-2
Mon Feb 24	FAC 5 replay	Birmingham City	Home	W	6-2
Wed Feb 26	EC 3 - 1 Leg	Rapid Vienna	Home	W	3-0

Sat Mar 1	FAC 6	Everton	Home	L	0-1
Wed Mar 5	EC 3 - 2 Leg	Rapid Vienna	Away	D	0-0 (3-0 aggregate)
Sat Mar 8	Div. 1	Manchester City	Home	L	0-1
Mon Mar 10	Div. 1	Everton	Away	D	0-0
Sat Mar 15	Div. 1	Chelsea	Away	L	2-3
Wed Mar 19	Div. 1	Queens Park Rangers	Home	W	8-1
Sat Mar 22	Div. 1	Sheffield Wednesday	Home	W	1-0
Mon Mar 24	Div. 1	Stoke City	Home	D	1-1
Sat Mar 29	Div. 1	West Ham United	Away	D	0-0
Mon Mar 31	Div. 1	Nottingham Forest	Away	W	1-0
Wed Apr 2	Div. 1	West Bromwich Albion	Home	W	2-1
Sat Apr 5	Div. 1	Nottingham Forest	Home	W	3-1
Tue Apr 8	Div. 1	Coventry City	Away	L	1-2
Sat Apr 12	Div. 1	Newcastle United	Away	L	0-2
Sat Apr 19	Div. 1	Burnley	Home	W	2-0
Wed Apr 23	EC SF - 1L	AC Milan	Away	L	0-2
Thu May 15	EC SF - 2L	AC Milan	Home	W	1-0 (1-2 aggregate)
Sat May 17	Div. 1	Leicester City	Home	W	3-2

FOOTBALL LEAGUE DIVISION ONE

P	W	D	L	F	A	PTS	POSN
42	15	12	15	57	53	42	11TH

Appearances (Sub): Stiles 56; Best 55; Stepney 51; Crerand 49; Charlton 48; Dunne 47; Law 45; Kidd 41 (1); Morgan 40; Fitzpartick 38 (2); Sadler 33 (4); James 29; Burns 19 (3); Foulkes 17 (3); Brennan 17; Sartori 15 (2); Kopel 9 (1); Rimmer 7 (1); Ryan; Gowling 2

Scorers: Law 30; Best 22; Morgan 9; Charlton 7; Fitzpatrick, Kidd 4; Crerand, Stiles 2; Ryan, Burns, Sartori 1; Own goals 4

1969/70

Sat Aug 9	Div. 1	Crystal Palace	Away	Drew	2-2
Wed Aug 13	Div. 1	Everton	Home	Lost	0-2
Sat Aug 16	Div. 1	Southampton	Home	Lost	1-4
Tue Aug 19	Div. 1	Everton	Away	Lost	0-3
Sat Aug 23	Div. 1	Wolverhampton Wanderers	Away	Drew	0-0
Wed Aug 27	Div. 1	Newcastle United	Home	Drew	0-0
Sat Aug 30	Div. 1	Sunderland	Home	Won	3-1
Wed Sep 3	LC 2	Middlesbrough	Home	Won	1-0
Sat Sep 6	Div. 1	Leeds United	Away	Drew	2-2
Sat Sep 13	Div. 1	Liverpool	Home	Won	1-0
Wed Sep 17	Div. 1	Sheffield Wednesday	Away	Won	3-1
Sat Sep 20	Div. 1	Arsenal	Away	Drew	2-2
Tue Sep 23	LC 3	Wrexham	Home	Won	2-0
Sat Sep 27	Div. 1	West Ham United	Home	Won	5-2
Sat Oct 4	Div. 1	Derby County	Away	Lost	0-2
Wed Oct 8	Div. 1	Southampton	Away	Won	3-0
Sat Oct 11	Div. 1	Ipswich Town	Home	Won	2-1
Wed Oct 15	LC 4	Burnley	Away	Drew	0-0
Sat Oct 18	Div. 1	Nottingham Forest	Home	Drew	1-1
Mon Oct 20	LC 4 replay	Burnley	Home	Won	1-0
Sat Oct 25	Div. 1	West Bromwich Albion	Away	Lost	1-2
Sat Nov 1	Div. 1	Stoke City	Home	Drew	1-1
Sat Nov 8	Div. 1	Coventry City	Away	Won	2-1
Wed Nov 12	LC 5	Derby County	Away	Drew	0-0
Sat Nov 15	Div. 1	Manchester City	Away	Lost	0-4
Wed Nov 19	LC 5 replay	Derby County	Home	Won	1-0
Sat Nov 22	Div. 1	Tottenham Hotspur	Home	Won	3-1
Sat Nov 29	Div. 1	Burnley	Away	Drew	1-1
Wed Dec 3	LC Semi - 1 Leg	Manchester City	Away	Lost	1-2
Sat Dec 6	Div. 1	Chelsea	Home	Lost	0-2
Sat Dec 13	Div. 1	Liverpool	Away	Won	4-1
Wed Dec 17	LC Semi - 2 Leg	Manchester City	Home	Drew	2-2 (3-4 aggregate)
Fri Dec 26	Div. 1	Wolverhampton W.	Home	Drew	0-0
Sat Dec 27	Div. 1	Sunderland	Away	Drew	1-1
Sat Jan 3	FAC 3	Ipswich Town	Away	Won	1-0
Sat Jan 10	Div. 1	Arsenal	Home	Won	2-1
Sat Jan 17	Div. 1	West Ham United	Away	Drew	0-0
Sat Jan 24	FAC 4	Manchester City	Home	Won	3-0
Mon Jan 26	Div. 1	Leeds United	Home	Drew	2-2

Sat Jan 31	Div. 1	Derby County	Home	Won	1-0
Sat Feb 7	FAC 5	Northampton Town	Away	Won	8-2
Tue Feb 10	Div. 1	Ipswich Town	Away	Won	1-0
Sat Feb 14	Div. 1	Crystal Palace	Home	Drew	1-1
Sat Feb 21	FAC 6	Middlesbrough	Away	Drew	1-1
Wed Feb 25	FAC 6 replay	Middlesbrough	Home	Won	2-1
Sat Feb 28	Div. 1	Stoke City	Away	Drew	2-2
Sat Mar 14	FAC Semi	Leeds United	Neutral*	Drew	0-0
Tue Mar 17	Div. 1	Burnley	Home	Drew	3-3
Sat Mar 21	Div. 1	Chelsea	Away	Lost	1-2
Mon Mar 23	FAC Semi replay	Leeds United	Neutral*	Drew	0-0
Thu Mar 26	FAC Semi 2nd rep	Leeds United	Neutral*	Lost	0-1
Sat Mar 28	Div. 1	Manchester City	Home	Lost	1-2
Mon Mar 30	Div. 1	Coventry City	Home	Drew	1-1
Tue Mar 31	Div. 1	Nottingham Forest	Away	Won	2-1
Sat Apr 4	Div. 1	Newcastle United	Away	Lost	1-5
Wed Apr 8	Div. 1	West Bromwich Albion	Home	Won	7-0
Fri Apr 10	FAC 3rd/4th	Watford	Neutral**	Won	2-0
Mon Apr 13	Div. 1	Tottenham Hotspur	Away	Lost	1-2
Wed Apr 15	Div. 1	Sheffield Wednesday	Home	Drew	2-2

FOOTBALL LEAGUE DIVISION ONE

P	W	D	L	F	A	PTS	POSN
42	14	17	11	66	61	45	8TH

Appearances (Sub): Charlton, Sadler 57; Stepney 54; Best 53; Morgan 49; Kidd 48 (1); Dunne, Ure 48; Burns 39 (3); Crerand 28 (2); Edwards 27 (1); Fitzpatrick 26; Sartori 21 (6); Law 13 (3); Stiles 13; Brennan 10 (1); Gowling 6 (2); Givens 5 (4); Rimmer 5; Foulkes, James 3; Ryan 0 (1).

Scorers: Best 23; Kidd 20; Charlton 14; Morgan 9; Burns, Fitzapatrick, Gowling, Law, Sadler, Sartori 3; Aston, Crerand, Givens, Ure, Edwards 1; own goals 2

1970/71

Sat Aug 1	Watney Cup 1*	Reading	Away	Won	3-2
Wed Aug 5	Watney Cup SF*	Hull City	Away	Won	1-1 (4-3 pens*)
Sat Aug 8	Watney Cup Final*	Derby County	Away	Lost	1-4
Sat Aug 15	Division 1	Leeds United	Home	Lost	0-1
Wed Aug 19	Division 1	Chelsea	Home	Drew	0-0
Sat Aug 22	Division 1	Arsenal	Away	Lost	0-4
Tue Aug 25	Division 1	Burnley	Away	Won	2-0
Sat Aug 29	Division 1	West Ham United	Home	Drew	1-1
Wed Sep 2	Division 1	Everton	Home	Won	2-0
Sat Sep 5	Division 1	Liverpool	Away	Drew	1-1
Wed Sep 9	LC 2	Aldershot	Away	Won	3-1
Sat Sep 12	Division 1	Coventry City	Home	Won	2-0
Sat Sep 19	Division 1	Ipswich Town	Away	Lost	0-4
Sat Sep 26	Division 1	Blackpool	Home	Drew	1-1
Sat Oct 3	Division 1	Wolverhampton Wanderers	Away	Lost	2-3
Wed Oct 7	LC 3	Portsmouth	Home	Won	1-0
Sat Oct 10	Division 1	Crystal Palace	Home	Lost	0-1
Sat Oct 17	Division 1	Leeds United	Away	Drew	2-2
Sat Oct 24	Division 1	West Bromwich Albion	Home	Won	2-1
Wed Oct 28	LC 4	Chelsea	Home	Won	2-1
Sat Oct 31	Division 1	Newcastle United	Away	Lost	0-1
Sat Nov 7	Division 1	Stoke City	Home	Drew	2-2
Sat Nov 14	Division 1	Nottingham Forest	Away	Won	2-1
Wed Nov 18	LC 5	Crystal Palace	Home	Won	4-2
Sat Nov 21	Division 1	Southampton	Away	Lost	0-1
Sat Nov 28	Division 1	Huddersfield Town	Home	Drew	1-1
Sat Dec 5	Division 1	Tottenham Hotspur	Away	Drew	2-2
Sat Dec 12	Division 1	Manchester City	Home	Lost	1-4
Wed Dec 16	LC Semi - 1 Leg	Aston Villa	Home	Drew	1-1
Sat Dec 19	Division 1	Arsenal	Home	Lost	1-3
Wed Dec 23	LC Semi - 2 Leg	Aston Villa	Away	Lost	1-2 (2-3 agg)
Sat Dec 26	Division 1	Derby County	Away	Drew	4-4
Sat Jan 2	FAC 3	Middlesbrough	Home	Drew	0-0
Tue Jan 5	FAC 3 replay	Middlesbrough	Away	Lost	1-2
Sat Jan 9	Division 1	Chelsea	Away	Won	2-1
Sat Jan 16	Division 1	Burnley	Home	Drew	1-1
Sat Jan 30	Division 1	Huddersfield Town	Away	Won	2-1
Sat Feb 6	Division 1	Tottenham Hotspur	Home	Won	2-1
Sat Feb 20	Division 1	Southampton	Home	Won	5-1

Tue Feb 23	Division 1	Everton	Away	Lost	0-1
Sat Feb 27	Division 1	Newcastle United	Home	Won	1-0
Sat Mar 6	Division 1	West Bromwich Albion	Away	Lost	3-4
Sat Mar 13	Division 1	Nottingham Forest	Home	Won	2-0
Sat Mar 20	Division 1	Stoke City	Away	Won	2-1
Sat Apr 3	Division 1	West Ham United	Away	Lost	1-2
Sat Apr 10	Division 1	Derby County	Home	Lost	1-2
Mon Apr 12	Division 1	Wolverhampton Wanderers	Home	Won	1-0
Tue Apr 13	Division 1	Coventry City	Away	Lost	1-2
Sat Apr 17	Division 1	Crystal Palace	Away	Won	5-3
Mon Apr 19	Division 1	Liverpool	Home	Lost	0-2
Sat Apr 24	Division 1	Ipswich Town	Home	Won	3-2
Sat May 1	Division 1	Blackpool	Away	Drew	1-1
Wed May 5	Division 1	Manchester City	Away	Won	4-3

FOOTBALL LEAGUE DIVISION ONE

P	W	D	L	F	A	PTS	POSN
42	16	11	15	65	66	43	8TH

Appearances (Sub): Charlton 50; Best 48; Fitzpatrick 43; Dunne 42; Sadler 39; Law 34; Edwards 32 (1); Kidd 32 (1); Morgan 29; Rimmer 28; Crerand 27; Aston 22 (2); Stepney 22 Stiles 19; Gowling 18 (4); Burns 17 (5); Ure 17; James 16 (1); Watson 10; Sartori 3 (5); Donald, O'Neil 1; Young 0 (1)

Scorers: Best 21; Law 16; Kidd 13; Gowling, Charlton 8; Aston, Morgan, Fitzpatrick 3; Sartori 2, Sadler 1

1971/72

Sat Jul 31	Watney Cup 1*	Halifax Town	Away	Lost	1-2
Sat Aug 14	Div. 1	Derby County	Away	Drew	2-2
Wed Aug 18	Div. 1	Chelsea	Away	Won	3-2
Fri Aug 20	Div. 1	Arsenal	Home**	Won	3-1
Mon Aug 23	Div. 1	West Bromwich Albion	Home**	Won	3-1
Sat Aug 28	Div. 1	Wolverhampton Wanderers	Away	Drew	1-1
Tue Aug 31	Div. 1	Everton	Away	Lost	0-1
Sat Sep 4	Div. 1	Ipswich Town	Home	Won	1-0
Tue Sep 7	LC 2	Ipswich Town	Away	Won	3-1
Sat Sep 11	Div. 1	Crystal Palace	Away	Won	3-1
Sat Sep 18	Div. 1	West Ham United	Home	Won	4-2
Sat Sep 25	Div. 1	Liverpool	Away	Drew	2-2
Sat Oct 2	Div. 1	Sheffield United	Home	Won	2-0
Wed Oct 6	LC 3	Burnley	Home	Drew	1-1
Sat Oct 9	Div. 1	Huddersfield Town	Away	Won	3-0
Sat Oct 16	Div. 1	Derby County	Home	Won	1-0
Mon Oct 18	LC 3 replay	Burnley	Away	Won	1-0
Sat Oct 23	Div. 1	Newcastle United	Away	Won	1-0
Wed Oct 27	LC 4	Stoke City	Home	Drew	1-1
Sat Oct 30	Div. 1	Leeds United	Home	Lost	0-1
Sat Nov 6	Div. 1	Manchester City	Away	Drew	3-3
Mon Nov 8	LC 4 replay	Stoke City	Away	Drew	0-0
Sat Nov 13	Div. 1	Tottenham Hotspur	Home	Won	3-1
Mon Nov 15	LC 4 2nd replay	Stoke City	Away	Lost	1-2
Sat Nov 20	Div. 1	Leicester City	Home	Won	3-2
Sat Nov 27	Div. 1	Southampton	Away	Won	5-2
Sat Dec 4	Div. 1	Nottingham Forest	Home	Won	3-2
Sat Dec 11	Div. 1	Stoke City	Away	Drew	1-1
Sat Dec 18	Div. 1	Ipswich Town	Away	Drew	0-0
Mon Dec 27	Div. 1	Coventry City	Home	Drew	2-2
Sat Jan 1	Div. 1	West Ham United	Away	Lost	0-3
Sat Jan 8	Div. 1	Wolverhampton W.	Home	Lost	1-3
Sat Jan 15	FAC 3	Southampton	Away	Drew	1-1
Wed Jan 19	FAC 3 replay	Southampton	Home	Won	4-1
Sat Jan 22	Div. 1	Chelsea	Home	Lost	0-1
Sat Jan 29	Div. 1	West Bromwich Albion	Away	Lost	1-2
Sat Feb 5	FAC 4	Preston North End	Away	Won	2-0
Sat Feb 12	Div. 1	Newcastle United	Home	Lost	0-2
Sat Feb 19	Div. 1	Leeds United	Away	Lost	1-5

Sat Feb 26	FAC 5	Middlesbrough	Home	Drew	0-0
Tue Feb 29	FAC 5 replay	Middlesbrough	Away	Won	3-0
Sat Mar 4	Div. 1	Tottenham Hotspur	Away	Lost	0-2
Wed Mar 8	Div. 1	Everton	Home	Drew	0-0
Sat Mar 11	Div. 1	Huddersfield Town	Home	Won	2-0
Sat Mar 18	FAC 6	Stoke City	Home	Drew	1-1
Wed Mar 22	FAC 6 replay	Stoke City	Away	Lost	1-2
Sat Mar 25	Div. 1	Crystal Palace	Home	Won	4-0
Sat Apr 1	Div. 1	Coventry City	Away	Won	3-2
Mon Apr 3	Div. 1	Liverpool	Home	Lost	0-3
Tue Apr 4	Div. 1	Sheffield United	Away	Drew	1-1
Sat Apr 8	Div. 1	Leicester City	Away	Lost	0-2
Wed Apr 12	Div. 1	Manchester City	Home	Lost	1-3
Sat Apr 15	Div. 1	Southampton	Home	Won	3-2
Sat Apr 22	Div. 1	Nottingham Forest	Away	Drew	0-0
Tue Apr 25	Div. 1	Arsenal	Away	Lost	0-3
Sat Apr 29	Div. 1	Stoke City	Home	Won	3-0

FOOTBALL LEAGUE DIVISION ONE

P	W	D	L	F	A	PTS	POSN
42	19	10	13	69	61	48	8TH

Appearances (sub): Best, Charlton 53; Stepney 52; O'Neil 50; Sadler 49; James, Morgan 48; Gowling 47 (3); Kidd 43; Law 41 (1); Dunne 41; Burns 23 (2) Buchan 15; McIlroy 11 (10); Storey-More 11; Edwards 6; Young 5 (2); Aston 4 (10); Connaughton 3; Sartori 1 (2); Fitzpatrick 1

Scorers: Best 26; Law 13; Charlton 12; Kidd 10; Gowling 9; Storey-Moore 5; McIlroy 4; Morgan 2; Buchan, Burns, James, Aston 1.

1972/73

Sat Aug 12	Division 1	Ipswich Town	Home	Lost	1-2
Tue Aug 15	Division 1	Liverpool	Away	Lost	0-2
Sat Aug 19	Division 1	Everton	Away	Lost	0-2
Wed Aug 23	Division 1	Leicester City	Home	Drew	1-1
Sat Aug 26	Division 1	Arsenal	Home	Drew	0-0
Wed Aug 30	Division 1	Chelsea	Home	Drew	0-0
Sat Sep 2	Division 1	West Ham United	Away	Drew	2-2
Wed Sep 6	LC 2	Oxford United	Away	Drew	2-2
Sat Sep 9	Division 1	Coventry City	Home	Lost	0-1
Tue Sep 12	LC 2 replay	Oxford United	Home	Won	3-1
Sat Sep 16	Division 1	Wolverhampton Wanderers	Away	Lost	0-2
Sat Sep 23	Division 1	Derby County	Home	Won	3-0
Sat Sep 30	Division 1	Sheffield United	Away	Lost	0-1
Tue Oct 3	LC 3	Bristol Rovers	Away	Drew	1-1
Sat Oct 7	Division 1	West Bromwich Albion	Away	Drew	2-2
Wed Oct 11	LC 3 replay	Bristol Rovers	Home	Lost	1-2
Sat Oct 14	Division 1	Birmingham City	Home	Won	1-0
Sat Oct 21	Division 1	Newcastle United	Away	Lost	1-2
Sat Oct 28	Division 1	Tottenham Hotspur	Home	Lost	1-4
Sat Nov 4	Division 1	Leicester City	Away	Drew	2-2
Sat Nov 11	Division 1	Liverpool	Home	Won	2-0
Sat Nov 18	Division 1	Manchester City	Away	Lost	0-3
Sat Nov 25	Division 1	Southampton	Home	Won	2-1
Sat Dec 2	Division 1	Norwich City	Away	Won	2-0
Sat Dec 9	Division 1	Stoke City	Home	Lost	0-2
Sat Dec 16	Division 1	Crystal Palace	Away	Lost	0-5
Sat Dec 23	Division 1	Leeds United	Home	Drew	1-1
Tue Dec 26	Division 1	Derby County	Away	Lost	1-3
Sat Jan 6	Division 1	Arsenal	Away	Lost	1-3
Sat Jan 13	FAC 3	Wolverhampton Wanderers	Away	Lost	0-1
Sat Jan 20	Division 1	West Ham United	Home	Drew	2-2
Wed Jan 24	Division 1	Everton	Home	Drew	0-0
Sat Jan 27	Division 1	Coventry City	Away	Drew	1-1
Sat Feb 10	Division 1	Wolverhampton W.	Home	Won	2-1
Sat Feb 17	Division 1	Ipswich Town	Away	Lost	1-4
Sat Mar 3	Division 1	West Bromwich Albion	Home	Won	2-1
Sat Mar 10	Division 1	Birmingham City	Away	Lost	1-3
Sat Mar 17	Division 1	Newcastle United	Home	Won	2-1
Sat Mar 24	Division 1	Tottenham Hotspur	Away	Drew	1-1
Sat Mar 31	Division 1	Southampton	Away	Won	2-0

Sat Apr 7	Division 1	Norwich City	Home	Won	1-0
Wed Apr 11	Division 1	Crystal Palace	Home	Won	2-0
Sat Apr 14	Division 1	Stoke City	Away	Drew	2-2
Wed Apr 18	Division 1	Leeds United	Away	Won	1-0
Sat Apr 21	Division 1	Manchester City	Home	Drew	0-0
Mon Apr 23	Division 1	Sheffield United	Home	Lost	1-2
Sat Apr 28	Division 1	Chelsea	Away	Lost	0-1

FOOTBALL LEAGUE DIVISION ONE

P	W	D	L	F	A	PTS	POSN
42	12	13	17	44	60	37	18TH

Appearances (Sub): Buchan 47; Morgan 44; Stepney 43; Charlton 39 (2); Young 32 (2); Storey-Moore 30; Dunne 27 (1); James 26; Best 23; Sadler 22; Kidd 20; Graham 19; MacDougall 18; O'Neil 17; Davies 16 (1); Macari 16; Holton 15; Martin 14 (2); Forsyth 9; Fitzpatrick 6; Donald 5; McIlroy 4 (9); Rimmer, Watson 4; Anderson 2 (5); Edwards 1; Fletcher 0 (2)

Scorers: Charlton 7; Storey-Moore 6; Best 6; Macari 5; MacDougall 5; Davies, Kidd, Morgan 4; Holton 3; Martin, Law 2; Anderson, Graham, McIlroy 1.

1973/74

Sat Aug 25	Division 1	Arsenal	Away	Lost	0-3
Wed Aug 29	Division 1	Stoke City	Home	Won	1-0
Sat Sep 1	Division 1	Queens Park Rangers	Home	Won	2-1
Wed Sep 5	Division 1	Leicester City	Away	Lost	0-1
Sat Sep 8	Division 1	Ipswich Town	Away	Lost	1-2
Wed Sep 12	Division 1	Leicester City	Home	Lost	1-2
Sat Sep 15	Division 1	West Ham United	Home	Won	3-1
Sat Sep 22	Division 1	Leeds United	Away	Drew	0-0
Sat Sep 29	Division 1	Liverpool	Home	Drew	0-0
Sat Oct 6	Division 1	Wolverhampton Wanderers	Away	Lost	1-2
Mon Oct 8	LC 2	Middlesbrough	Home	Lost	0-1
Sat Oct 13	Division 1	Derby County	Home	Lost	0-1
Sat Oct 20	Division 1	Birmingham City	Home	Won	1-0
Sat Oct 27	Division 1	Burnley	Away	Drew	0-0
Sat Nov 3	Division 1	Chelsea	Home	Drew	2-2
Sat Nov 10	Division 1	Tottenham Hotspur	Away	Lost	1-2
Sat Nov 17	Division 1	Newcastle United	Away	Lost	2-3
Sat Nov 24	Division 1	Norwich City	Home	Drew	0-0
Sat Dec 8	Division 1	Southampton	Home	Drew	0-0
Sat Dec 15	Division 1	Coventry City	Home	Lost	2-3
Sat Dec 22	Division 1	Liverpool	Away	Lost	0-2
Wed Dec 26	Division 1	Sheffield United	Home	Lost	1-2
Sat Dec 29	Division 1	Ipswich Town	Home	Won	2-0
Tue Jan 1	Division 1	Queens Park Rangers	Away	Lost	0-3
Sat Jan 5	FAC 3	Plymouth Argyle	Home	Won	1-0
Sat Jan 12	Division 1	West Ham United	Away	Lost	1-2
Sat Jan 19	Division 1	Arsenal	Home	Drew	1-1
Sat Jan 26	FAC 4	Ipswich Town	Home	Lost	0-1
Sat Feb 2	Division 1	Coventry City	Away	Lost	0-1
Sat Feb 9	Division 1	Leeds United	Home	Lost	0-2
Sat Feb 16	Division 1	Derby County	Away	Drew	2-2
Sat Feb 23	Division 1	Wolverhampton W.	Home	Drew	0-0
Sat Mar 2	Division 1	Sheffield United	Away	Won	1-0
Wed Mar 13	Division 1	Manchester City	Away	Drew	0-0
Sat Mar 16	Division 1	Birmingham City	Away	Lost	0-1
Sat Mar 23	Division 1	Tottenham Hotspur	Home	Lost	0-1
Sat Mar 30	Division 1	Chelsea	Away	Won	3-1
Wed Apr 3	Division 1	Burnley	Home	Drew	3-3
Sat Apr 6	Division 1	Norwich City	Away	Won	2-0
Sat Apr 13	Division 1	Newcastle United	Home	Won	1-0

Mon Apr 15	Division 1	Everton	Home	Won	3-0
Sat Apr 20	Division 1	Southampton	Away	Drew	1-1
Tue Apr 23	Division 1	Everton	Away	Lost	0-1
Sat Apr 27	Division 1	Manchester City	Home	Lost	0-1*
Mon Apr 29	Division 1	Stoke City	Away	Lost	0-1

FOOTBALL LEAGUE DIVISION ONE

P	W	D	L	F	A	PTS	POSN
42	10	12	22	38	48	32	21ST

Appearances: Buchan M, Stepney 45; Morgan 44; Greenhoff 39: Macari 37 (1); Holton 37; Young 32; Mcllroy 25 (6); Graham 25 (1) ; Kidd 23 (1); James 23; Forsyth 20 (1); Daly 15 (2); Martin 14 (4); Best 12; Anderson 11 (1); McCalliog 11; Griffiths 7; Fletcher 2 (3); Bielby 2 (2); Sadler 2 (1); Sideottom, Sotery-Moore 2; Buchan, G 0 (4)

Scorers: Mcllroy, macari 6; McCalliog 4; Greenhoff 3; Best, Holton, Houston, James, Kidd, Morgan, Stepney 2; Anderson, Daly, Forsyth, Graham, Storey-Moore, Young 1

1974/75

Sat Aug 17	Division 2	Orient	Away	Won	2-0
Sat Aug 24	Division 2	Millwall	Home	Won	4-0
Wed Aug 28	Division 2	Portsmouth	Home	Won	2-1
Sat Aug 31	Division 2	Cardiff City	Away	Won	1-0
Sat Sep 7	Division 2	Nottingham Forest	Home	Drew	2-2
Wed Sep 11	LC 2	Charlton Athletic	Home	Won	5-1
Sat Sep 14	Division 2	West Bromwich Albion	Away	Drew	1-1
Mon Sep 16	Division 2	Millwall	Away	Won	1-0
Sat Sep 21	Division 2	Bristol Rovers	Home	Won	2-0
Wed Sep 25	Division 2	Bolton Wanderers	Home	Won	3-0
Sat Sep 28	Division 2	Norwich City	Away	Lost	0-2
Sat Oct 5	Division 2	Fulham	Away	Won	2-1
Wed Oct 9	LC 3	Manchester City	Home	Won	1-0
Sat Oct 12	Division 2	Notts County	Home	Won	1-0
Tue Oct 15	Division 2	Portsmouth	Away	Drew	0-0
Sat Oct 19	Division 2	Blackpool	Away	Won	3-0
Sat Oct 26	Division 2	Southampton	Home	Won	1-0
Sat Nov 2	Division 2	Oxford United	Home	Won	4-0
Sat Nov 9	Division 2	Bristol City	Away	Lost	0-1
Wed Nov 13	LC 4	Burnley	Home	Won	3-2
Sat Nov 16	Division 2	Aston Villa	Home	Won	2-1
Sat Nov 23	Division 2	Hull City	Away	Lost	0-2
Sat Nov 30	Division 2	Sunderland	Home	Won	3-2
Wed Dec 4	LC 5	Middlesbrough	Away	Drew	0-0
Sat Dec 7	Division 2	Sheffield Wednesday	Away	Drew	4-4
Sat Dec 14	Division 2	Orient	Home	Drew	0-0
Wed Dec 18	LC 5 replay	Middlesbrough	Home	Won	3-0
Sat Dec 21	Division 2	York City	Away	Won	1-0
Thu Dec 26	Division 2	West Bromwich Albion	Home	Won	2-1
Sat Dec 28	Division 2	Oldham Athletic	Away	Lost	0-1
Sat Jan 4	FAC 3	Walsall	Home	Drew	0-0
Tue Jan 7	FAC 3 replay	Walsall	Away	Lost	2-3
Sat Jan 11	Division 2	Sheffield Wednesday	Home	Won	2-0
Wed Jan 15	LC Semi - 1 Leg	Norwich City	Home	Drew	2-2
Sat Jan 18	Division 2	Sunderland	Away	Drew	0-0
Wed Jan 22	LC Semi - 2 Leg	Norwich City	Away	Lost	0-1 (2-3 aggregate)
Sat Feb 1	Division 2	Bristol City	Home	Lost	0-1
Sat Feb 8	Division 2	Oxford United	Away	Lost	0-1
Sat Feb 15	Division 2	Hull City	Home	Won	2-0

Sat Feb 22	Division 2	Aston Villa	Away	Lost	0-2
Sat Mar 1	Division 2	Cardiff City	Home	Won	4-0
Sat Mar 8	Division 2	Bolton Wanderers	Away	Won	1-0
Sat Mar 15	Division 2	Norwich City	Home	Drew	1-1
Sat Mar 22	Division 2	Nottingham Forest	Away	Won	1-0
Fri Mar 28	Division 2	Bristol Rovers	Away	Drew	1-1
Sat Mar 29	Division 2	York City	Home	Won	2-1
Mon Mar 31	Division 2	Oldham Athletic	Home	Won	3-2
Sat Apr 5	Division 2	Southampton	Away	Won	1-0
Sat Apr 12	Division 2	Fulham	Home	Won	1-0
Sat Apr 19	Division 2	Notts County	Away	Drew	2-2
Sat Apr 26	Division 2	Blackpool	Home	Won	4-0

FOOTBALL LEAGUE DIVISION TWO

P	W	D	L	F	A	PTS	POSN
42	26	9	7	66	30	61	1ST

Appearances: McIlroy 50 (1); Buchan 50; Stepney 49; Houston 48; Greenhoff 47 (2); Daly 45 (1); Forsyth 45; Macari 44 (3); Pearson 39 (3); McCalliog 26 (1); Holton 17; Sidebottom 16; James 15; Young 10 (12); Coppell 9 (1); Albiston 3; Baldwin, Roche 2; Davies 0 (10); McCreery 0 (2); Grahm, Nicholl 0 (1).

Scorers: Pearson, Macari 18; Daly 13; McIlroy 10; Houston 7; Greenhoff, Morgan 4; McCalliog 3; Coppell, Forsyth 1; own goals 3

1975/76

Sat Aug 16	Division 1	Wolverhampton Wanderers	Away	Won	2-0
Tue Aug 19	Division 1	Birmingham City	Away	Won	2-0
Sat Aug 23	Division 1	Sheffield United	Home	Won	5-1
Wed Aug 27	Division 1	Coventry City	Home	Drew	1-1
Sat Aug 30	Division 1	Stoke City	Away	Won	1-0
Sat Sep 6	Division 1	Tottenham Hotspur	Home	Won	3-2
Wed Sep 10	LC 2	Brentford	Home	Won	2-1
Sat Sep 13	Division 1	Queens Park Rangers	Away	Lost	0-1
Sat Sep 20	Division 1	Ipswich Town	Home	Won	1-0
Wed Sep 24	Division 1	Derby County	Away	Lost	1-2
Sat Sep 27	Division 1	Manchester City	Away	Drew	2-2
Sat Oct 4	Division 1	Leicester City	Home	Drew	0-0
Wed Oct 8	LC 3	Aston Villa	Away	Won	2-1
Sat Oct 11	Division 1	Leeds United	Away	Won	2-1
Sat Oct 18	Division 1	Arsenal	Home	Won	3-1
Sat Oct 25	Division 1	West Ham United	Away	Lost	1-2
Sat Nov 1	Division 1	Norwich City	Home	Won	1-0
Sat Nov 8	Division 1	Liverpool	Away	Lost	1-3
Wed Nov 12	LC 4	Manchester City	Away	Lost	0-4
Sat Nov 15	Division 1	Aston Villa	Home	Won	2-0
Sat Nov 22	Division 1	Arsenal	Away	Lost	1-3
Sat Nov 29	Division 1	Newcastle United	Home	Won	1-0
Sat Dec 6	Division 1	Middlesbrough	Away	Drew	0-0
Sat Dec 13	Division 1	Sheffield United	Away	Won	4-1
Sat Dec 20	Division 1	Wolverhampton W.	Home	Won	1-0
Tue Dec 23	Division 1	Everton	Away	Drew	1-1
Sat Dec 27	Division 1	Burnley	Home	Won	2-1
Sat Jan 3	FAC 3	Oxford United	Home	Won	2-1
Sat Jan 10	Division 1	Queens Park Rangers	Home	Won	2-1
Sat Jan 17	Division 1	Tottenham Hotspur	Away	Drew	1-1
Sat Jan 24	FAC 4	Peterborough United	Home	Won	3-1
Sat Jan 31	Division 1	Birmingham City	Home	Won	3-1
Sat Feb 7	Division 1	Coventry City	Away	Drew	1-1
Sat Feb 14	FAC 5	Leicester City	Away	Won	2-1
Wed Feb 18	Division 1	Liverpool	Home	Drew	0-0
Sat Feb 21	Division 1	Aston Villa	Away	Lost	1-2
Wed Feb 25	Division 1	Derby County	Home	Drew	1-1
Sat Feb 28	Division 1	West Ham United	Home	Won	4-0
Sat Mar 6	FAC 6	Wolverhampton W.	Home	Drew	1-1
Tue Mar 9	FAC 6 replay	Wolverhampton Wanderers	Away	Won	3-2

Sat Mar 13	Division 1	Leeds United	Home	Won	3-2
Wed Mar 17	Division 1	Norwich City	Away	Drew	1-1
Sat Mar 20	Division 1	Newcastle United	Away	Won	4-3
Sat Mar 27	Division 1	Middlesbrough	Home	Won	3-0
Sat Apr 3	FAC Semi	Derby County	Hillsbor-ough	Won	2-0
Sat Apr 10	Division 1	Ipswich Town	Away	Lost	0-3
Sat Apr 17	Division 1	Everton	Home	Won	2-1
Mon Apr 19	Division 1	Burnley	Away	Won	1-0
Wed Apr 21	Division 1	Stoke City	Home	Lost	0-1
Sat Apr 24	Division 1	Leicester City	Away	Lost	1-2
Sat May 1	FAC Final	Southampton	Wembley	Lost	0-1
Tue May 4	Division 1	Manchester City	Home	Won	2-0

FOOTBALL LEAGUE DIVISION ONE

P	W	D	L	F	A	PTS	POSN
42	23	10	9	68	42	56	3RD

Appearances: Buchan, Houston 52; Daly, McIlroy 51; Greenhoff 50; Coppell, Pearson 49; Stepney 47; Macari 45; Forsyth 35; Hill 33; Jackson 19 (1); Nicholl 18 (7); McCreery 13 (19); Roche 5; Albiston 2 91); Coyne 1 (1); Grimshaw 0 (2); Kelly, Young 0 (1)

Scorers: Macari 15; Pearson 14; McIlroy 13; Daly 11, Hill 10; Coppell 5; McCreery 4; Forsyth 3; Houston 2; Coyne, Greenhoff 1; own goals 6

1976/77

Sat Aug 21	Division 1	Birmingham City	Home	Drew	2-2
Tue Aug 24	Division 1	Coventry City	Away	Won	2-0
Sat Aug 28	Division 1	Derby County	Away	Drew	0-0
Wed Sep 1	LC 2	Tranmere Rovers	Home	Won	5-0
Sat Sep 4	Division 1	Tottenham Hotspur	Home	Lost	2-3
Sat Sep 11	Division 1	Newcastle United	Away	Drew	2-2
Wed Sep 15	UEFA 1 - 1 Leg	Ajax	Away	Lost	0-1
Sat Sep18	Division 1	Middlesbrough	Home	Won	2-0
Wed Sep 22	LC 3	Sunderland	Home	Drew	2-2
Sat Sep 25	Division 1	Manchester City	Away	Won	3-1
Wed Sep 29	UEFA 1 - 2 Leg	Ajax	Home	Won	2-0 (2-1 aggregate)
Sat Oct 2	Division 1	Leeds United	Away	Won	2-0
Mon Oct 4	LC 3 replay	Sunderland	Away	Drew	2-2
Wed Oct 6	LC 2nd replay	Sunderland	Home	Won	1-0
Sat Oct `16	Division 1	West Bromwich Albion	Away	Lost	0-4
Wed Oct 20	UEFA 2 - 1Leg	Juventus	Home	Won	1-0
Sat Oct 23	Division 1	Norwich City	Home	Drew	2-2
Wed Oct 27	LC 4	Newcastle United	Home	Won	7-2
Sat Oct 30	Division 1	Ipswich Town	Home	Lost	0-1
Wed Nov 3	UEFA 2 - 2 Leg	Juventus	Away	Lost	0-3 (1-3 aggregate)
Sat Nov 6	Division 1	Aston Villa	Away	Lost	2-3
Wed Nov 10	Division 1	Sunderland	Home	Drew	3-3
Sat Nov 20	Division 1	Leicester City	Away	Drew	1-1
Sat Nov 27	Division 1	West Ham United	Home	Lost	0-2
Wed Dec 1	LC 5	Everton	Home	Lost	0-3
Sat Dec 18	Division 1	Arsenal	Away	Lost	1-3
Mon Dec 27	Division 1	Everton	Home	Won	4-0
Sat Jan 1	Division 1	Aston Villa	Home	Won	2-0
Mon Jan 3	Division 1	Ipswich Town	Away	Lost	1-2
Sat Jan 8	FAC 3	Walsall	Home	Won	1-0
Sat Jan 15	Division 1	Coventry City	Home	Won	2-0
Wed Jan 19	Division 1	Bristol City	Home	Won	2-1
Sat Jan 22	Division 1	Birmingham City	Away	Won	3-2
Sat Jan 29	FAC 4	Queens Park Rangers	Home	Won	1-0
Sat Feb 5	Division 1	Derby County	Home	Won	3-1
Sat Feb 12	Division 1	Tottenham Hotspur	Away	Won	3-1
Wed Feb 16	Division 1	Liverpool	Home	Drew	0-0
Sat Feb 19	Division 1	Newcastle United	Home	Won	3-1
Sat Feb 26	FAC 5	Southampton	Away	Drew	2-2

Sat Mar 5	Division 1	Manchester City	Home	Won	3-1
Tue Mar 8	FAC 5 replay	Southampton	Home	Won	2-1
Sat Mar 12	Division 1	Leeds United	Home	Won	1-0
Sat Mar 19	FAC 6	Aston Villa	Home	Won	2-1
Wed Mar 23	Division 1	West Bromwich Albion	Home	Drew	2-2
Sat Apr 2	Division 1	Norwich City	Away	Lost	1-2
Tue Apr 5	Division 1	Everton	Away	Won	2-1
Sat Apr 9	Division 1	Stoke City	Home	Won	3-0
Mon Apr 11	Division 1	Sunderland	Away	Lost	1-2
Sat Apr 16	Division 1	Leicester City	Home	Drew	1-1
Tue Apr 19	Division 1	Queens Park Rangers	Away	Lost	0-4
Sat Apr 23	FAC Semi	Leeds United	Hillsborough	Won	2-1
Tue Apr 26	Division 1	Middlesbrough	Away	Lost	0-3
Sat Apr 30	Division 1	Queens Park Rangers	Home	Won	1-0
Tue May 3	Division 1	Liverpool	Away	Lost	0-1
Sat May 7	Division 1	Bristol City	Away	Drew	1-1
Wed May 11	Division 1	Stoke City	Away	Drew	3-3
Sat May 14	Division 1	Arsenal	Home	Won	3-2
Mon May 16	Division 1	West Ham United	Away	Lost	2-4
Sat May 21	FAC Final	Liverpool	Wembley	Won	2-1

FOOTBALL LEAGUE DIVISION ONE

P	W	D	L	F	A	PTS	POSN
42	18	12	13	71	62	47	6TH

Appearances: Greenhoff B, Stepney 57; McIlroy 56 (1); Coppell 56; Hill 55 (1); Nicholl 55; Macari, Pearson 53; Houstopn 51; Buchan 46; Greenhoff J 34; Daly 26 (2); Albiston 19 (6); McCreery 13 (24); Forsyth 4 (1); Waldron 4; Paterson 3 (2); Jackson 3; McGrath 2 (5); Roche 2; Foggon 0 (3); Clark 0 (1).

Scorers: Hill 22; Pearson 19; Macari 14; Greenhoff J 12; Coppell 8; Daly 7; Greenhoff B, Houston 5; McIlroy 3; McCreery 2; Nicholl 1; own goals 5